To Vic
I Hope You
Like My Book

Unfortunately
Boo Orr
Diont

Kelly
+ The boys

POWER PLAY

POWER PLAY:

The Memoirs of
Hockey Czar
Alan Eagleson

with

SCOTT YOUNG

M&S

Canadian Cataloguing in Publication Data
  Eagleson, R. Alan (Robert Alan), 1933-
    Power play : the memoirs of hockey czar
  Alan Eagleson

  Includes index.
  ISBN 0-7710-9095-1

  1. Eagleson, R. Alan (Robert Alan), 1933-
  2. Hockey - Canada - Biography.   3. Lawyers -
  Canada - Biography.   I. Young, Scott, 1918-
  II. Title.

  GV848.5.E23A3 1991   796.962′092   C91-094363-X

McClelland & Stewart Inc.
The Canadian Publishers
481 University Avenue
Toronto, Ontario
M5G 2E9

Printed and bound in Canada

CONTENTS

DEDICATION

To "Team Fifty" of the 1972 Canada-U.S.S.R series;
to "Team Sixteen" who voted for me in 1989;
and to Nancy, Allen, and Jill, who are always there
when it counts.

CHAPTER ONE

AN OPPRESSION
OF HOCKEY PLAYERS

"You know, Al, if those guys were horses they
would call the Humane Society."

– *Bobby Orr, then eighteen, reacting to the
Springfield stuff.*

In light of later developments it may seem ironic that here
I am starting a book about my life (so far) with something
other than how the National Hockey League Players Association was born, or the Canada Cup, or the eight-game
1972 series with the Soviets, or a treatise on my life and
times with Bobby Orr. However, elements of all those topics
are involved. In fact, they dovetail. In the autumn and early
winter of 1966, I was thirty-three, married (the best contract
I ever signed), father of two, a back-bench member of the
Conservative-led Ontario legislature, and member of a busy
law firm, and I was involved for the first time in conflict
with the National Hockey League.

At the time, Orr was a rookie with the NHL's Boston
Bruins. One of his friends at the time was Carl Brewer,
a former all-star with Toronto Maple Leafs who had decided
to play that season with Father David Bauer's Canadian
national team. Fighting to have Brewer released from his
pro contract so he could join the Nationals was taking a
lot of my time. Orr also had considered for a while that
summer going the same route, joining the Nationals. Before
the season started he opted instead for Boston at a precedent-
setting salary I had negotiated for him ($40,000-plus a year
for a rookie having caused widespread gloom among club
owners).

All that was the background when around the middle
of December that year I received a phone call that went
something like this:

"Hi. My name is Bill White and I used to play with
the Toronto Marlies at the same time as Carl Brewer and
now I'm with Springfield Indians. Brewer gave me your
number. We've got a problem. We are on strike. Could you
come down and see us?"

I'd read about the strike in the papers the day before.
Hockey legend Eddie Shore, the hard-nosed Boston Bruin
star of the twenties and thirties, by then a robust sixty-four,
owned and operated the Springfield team in the American
Hockey League. Everybody in hockey had heard the horror

stories of what it was like to play for Shore, but the players' strike brought a very serious situation into the open for the first time. I knew none of the Springfield players. Also, nobody in Springfield knew anything about me except what they had read or heard. One item was my fight to have Brewer released in time to play for Canada in the 1967 world championships. Another was my battle with Hap Emms of Boston before the Orr signing. I had a law practice and my Lakeshore seat in the Ontario legislature to look after, so I can't say I was exactly itching for something to do – but some of what Bill White said convinced me that I was going to Springfield right away.

I'd never been there. I bought an economy-class ticket from Mohawk Airlines that landed me at the Bradley International Airport in Hartford. I get off the airplane, about the second or third last one off. I look around and at first I can't see anybody there to meet me. Then I saw a couple of guys wearing hockey jackets from Galt or Sudbury or somewhere, and I went up to them.

"Are you from the Springfield Indians?" I asked.

"Oh, yeah," one said. "I'm Gerry Foley and this is Brian Kilrea."

"Well, I'm Alan Eagleson."

"Oh," they both said.

It turned out they'd been expecting somebody a lot older. They thought they'd bought some big-shot lawyer and here this snotty-nosed young guy (that was me), steps off the plane.

So I met with them that night and listened to how life was with the Springfield Indians.

Foley was a veteran of fourteen pro seasons, four in the NHL and close to ten more in the minors. White later played nine seasons in the NHL, but at that time he had never been out of the minors. That pretty well represented the spread in experience I found throughout the rest of the team. But rookie or veteran, they had legitimate complaints – in spades.

We had a meeting the next morning in a room in this little Mickey Mouse motel, the Agawam Inn. There are twenty-eight guys in the room. I literally couldn't fully believe the stories, but they were in earnest. Eventually I said, "Here's the deal. I want you to write out exactly the things that have happened to you that you've told me about and we're going to meet again tomorrow morning." The next morning I took their stories and put them on one page each and then told them, "Look, we're going to get a local lawyer and get sworn affidavits on these stories, you have to swear that they are true. I'm not going to take the risk that any of you are bull-shitting me."

So I got affidavits. Then I said that to deal with the situation, first I'd meet with the president of the AHL, Jack Butterfield.

Well, they chorused, there was no use talking to him, he was general manager of the Springfield club as well as being league president. "And also he's Shore's nephew," one said thoughtfully, gilding the lily a little.

I called him anyway. The players turned out to be right.

Butterfield said, "I can't help you, I can't do anything for you."

"What about the league?" I asked.

"They won't do anything for you. Get those players back playing."

In short, that first approach indicated to me that nobody in authority, the league or the club, wanted to do anything. (The coach, Harry Pidhirny, no doubt *did* want to do something, because a couple of weeks later he quit and was replaced by Ted Shore, Eddie's son. This didn't improve the situation at all because his father was around all the time calling the shots, as he always had.)

However, by that time other people in hockey were watching the whole thing avidly. The story was beginning to spread. Bob Pennington from the *Toronto Telegram* came to Springfield and wrote a piece or two. Other reporters couldn't resist the sheer incredibility of what the players were saying. A local columnist, Sam Pompeii of the *Springfield Daily News*, was great. He gave me story after story backing up what the players had said, telling me, "just so you know this is not the first time these things have happened."

Armed with both the affidavits and the official rejection, I told the players, "I'm going to need some time. First, you have to get back on the ice. I'm going to tell Shore and Butterfield that you're going back under protest. But at least you'll be going back. You can't screw up the fans if you want to keep them on your side. We are going to give the management a month while I work on it. It's now December 17 and by January 17 I will have this thing solved or there will be another strike."

I guess to back up the concern I and others felt about what had been happening in Springfield, I should tell some of the stories.

Some were fairly mild – like Shore making his players lie on their backs and pump their feet in the air for twenty minutes. But that was nothing. Jacques Caron was one of the goalies. Later played for Los Angeles, St. Louis, and Vancouver. Apparently Shore didn't think Caron stood up enough against people trying to score. Caron has a long neck as it is, but he said Shore's philosophy on how to make him a better stand-up goalie was to put one end of a belt around his neck and the other end around the crossbar, in which circumstances a guy would learn to be a stand-up goalie if he didn't hang himself first.

Then there was the ridiculous story about a young French-speaking player who had stomach aches that Eddie diagnosed as cancer. What he did was give this player several ounces of castor oil every day for three days and make him shit into a pail. At the end of the day Eddie would poke around in the pail.

After the third day's inspection he exclaimed, "Okay, we got it! There's the cancer bug!"

What is a kid around twenty or so who speaks about twenty words of English going to do against Eddie Shore, the all-time hockey great?

Then there was Wayne Mosdell. His father, NHL veteran Ken Mosdell, had played sixteen years in the league. Wayne was tall, more than six feet, and had been having some back trouble. His story was that one day he walked into the dressing room and Shore, sitting there all hunched up, looked at him and said, "Hey, Mr. Mosdell," – he used to call everybody mister – "stretch out here on your stomach." Then he set two benches apart, ordered Mosdell to put his shoulders and head on one and his thighs and feet on the other, and jumped on him with his knees in the middle of Mosdell's back.

"There," he said, "you'll walk better now."

At that point Mosdell couldn't walk at all.

Roger Cote was a tough player in junior and everywhere else. He always had a toothpick in his mouth. After one game when Shore felt he hadn't played well, he said, "All right, Mr. Cote, three laps around the field."

Cote was still in his hockey outfit, which he started to remove.

"With your equipment!" Shore said.

Roger bent to take his skates off.

"In your skates!" Shore said. Then Eddie Shore followed Cote three laps around the running track at the Northeastern Coliseum in his car, a big Cadillac with the licence plate reading, Mr. Hockey. When Cote slowed down Shore would give him a blast on the horn.

The players sold tickets, sold popcorn, cleaned the ice. Once Eddie traded for somebody whose contract included a $500 bonus if he scored thirty goals. When he reached Springfield the guy had fifteen goals. He scored fourteen in the next fourteen games. He never got off the bench for the rest of the year. Finished the season with twenty-nine goals, no bonus.

I remember Orr's reaction to the Springfield stuff. He said, "You know, Al, if those guys were horses they would call in the Humane Society, and yet there's nothing you can do for human beings."

My biggest frustration in the whole issue was Clarence Campbell, long-time president of the NHL. I had met him earlier over Carl Brewer's wish to retire from the Leafs so he could play with the national team.

To backtrack a bit, Brewer had been on a collision course with Punch Imlach, Leafs' coach and general manager, even during the years in the early 1960s when Brewer was a mainstay on defence while the Leafs won three Stanley Cups. In September, 1966, just after Orr signed with Boston, I asked the *Star*'s Jim Proudfoot, the *Telegram*'s George Gross, and some other key media people to lunch at the Albany Club in Toronto and announced that Brewer was returning to amateur hockey with the Nationals.

Of course, Imlach and Stafford Smythe of the Leafs said there was no bloody way that was going to happen.

I had laid the groundwork. I knew there was a good chance the case would wind up in court. What I would be asking was a court's declaratory judgement that after these many years as a Leafs' chattel, both in junior and in pro, Brewer's contract was over. Preparing the case, I didn't rely on my own expertise, but went to brilliant lawyers Joe Sedgwick and Arthur Pattillo to get advice. They gave it, in effect guided my hand. I had every possibility covered by two of the brightest legal minds in the country. They didn't charge me a cent.

Pattillo disliked Smythe anyway so he was happy to do what he could. He told me exactly what to do and how to handle it. "But I'm not going to write the letter," he said. "You have to do that."

I did everything he said. I wrote a letter to Campbell, set it all out, why we had to do this, why we had to do that, otherwise we were going to go to court on December 1 to seek a declaratory judgement, which, as they well knew, might go far beyond the Brewer case in attacking the NHL's standard player contract. The NHL never likes to go to court. Maybe nobody does.

On or about November 29, two days before the court date, I got a letter from Campbell, and he also announced publicly, that the Maple Leafs were releasing Brewer for the good of the country, and all that. To me, he wrote, "I want to assure you that your letter to me had nothing to do with our timing and our decision."

To launder a favourite remark of Sam Pollock's, in a pig's ear it didn't!

In that case, because it was a challenge to the whole NHL contract system, I could at least understand the difficulties he was under. So I knew he was terse and I knew he was difficult, but until the Springfield business I had always thought he was basically a fair person.

On December 28, 1966, I took the Springfield affidavits with me and met Campbell at the league office in Montreal. I was convinced that all I had to do was show these affidavits to the fair Mr. Campbell and he'd solve this in a hurry. My reasoning was that almost all the AHL teams had links with NHL teams and in that sense the lesser league was dependent on the NHL, which therefore had the power to blow the whistle on Mr. Shore.

How wrong I was. He looked at the affidavits, then said, "Mr. Eagleson, this is all very interesting but I can't do anything for you."

I said, "Just a minute – you're president of the NHL!"

He said, "But Springfield is an independent team."

I said, "Well, but all but two teams in the league are connected to NHL teams, and most players are owned by NHL clubs. Surely you can go to the NHL-connected clubs and say, hey, we've got to straighten this out."

"Can't do anything for you."

"Well," I said, "if you won't do it I just want you to know that I'm going to do it myself. I'll tell you exactly what I'm going to do. I've got these affidavits and I'm going to talk to other players in the American Hockey League and we're going to challenge the whole system and if we don't get some action we are going to have a strike."

He must have known even then that this was something he couldn't just brush off – one day that week another AHL club, Baltimore, had gone on a one-hour sitdown strike in sympathy.

The day I met with Campbell the Boston Bruins were in Montreal for an NHL game. I'd met most of the Boston players through Bobby Orr. One of them was Eddie Johnston. Whether he called me or whether we met in the hotel lobby I don't remember, but anyway he was looking for me and said, "Al, can you come up to my room after the practice?"

I go up and there's, I think, pretty well the whole team – Pit Martin, John Bucyk, Murray Oliver, and Gilles Marotte among the best of them in those days. It was Orr's first year. I tell them about some of the stuff I'd learned in Springfield, and Campbell's lack of concern. We chat for a little and then Eddie Johnston said, "What we want to talk about is forming a union."

I realized right away that there was more to this approach than just a reaction to the Springfield story. Nearly ten years earlier NHL players had tried to form an association, an idea fought bitterly by owners of the six clubs in the league at that time.

Some clubs had reacted by trading players who had been prominent in the attempt. Apart from resulting in the formation of a toothless owners-players council, that early try had died. The impetus behind it turned out still to be there, if dormant. After the Springfield story hit the papers I'd had a call from a lawyer in Detroit who said that Normie Ullman, then a Detroit star, had spoken to him about the same thing – that he'd heard about somebody trying to form a union for all professional sports.

The Boston players and I sat in the Montreal hotel room and batted the subject around. As far as I'm concerned, right there in that room was the very beginning of the formation of the National Hockey League Players Association. I can't say exactly that the owners were running for cover that early, but there were straws in the wind, including the Brewer case. Even letting Brewer go wasn't an outright release – the Leafs would keep his NHL rights (a commodity they later used in a trade with Detroit).

Yet to get back to Springfield, Shore had a pretty good hockey team that year, as it proved. When my deadline to settle the matter or strike came nearer and nearer, I felt a break was imminent so extended the deadline by four days to January 21. On January 20 there was an announcement from Springfield. Its timing was something like Campbell giving in at the last minute on Brewer. The announcement was that Eddie Shore, for reasons of ill health, could not continue with the Springfield Indians. The club would be offered for sale.

Game over. Except that by that time six new teams were to be admitted to the NHL to begin the 1967 season. I was then living in the Kingsway in Toronto. One night Larry Regan, who had been named general manager of Jack Kent Cooke's expansion team, the Los Angeles Kings, had dropped in to talk hockey business – particularly the possibility of Cooke buying the Springfield Indians.

I had told the L.A. people early on that they had to get Shore right out of the organization. Now he was out. Larry had left a message as to where he would be, so Cooke called him at my home. Larry talked to Cooke with a lot of "Yes, Mr. Cooke," "Mmmhmmm, Mr. Cooke," and eventually, "Yes, Mr. Cooke, I'm here with Alan Eagleson now. Yes, he will talk to you."

The conversation started with, "Hello, Alan. How are you? Larry has told me a lot of wonderful things about you and I'm just wondering, Alan, what about this Springfield club?"

"Well, Jack," I said, "here's what I think . . . "

Larry in the background is going, urgently, *"Call him mister!"*

I went on, "Here's what I would do, Jack. They want a million. Offer six hundred thousand. Make the deal because here's what you'll be getting – at least six or seven NHL players. Howie Menard can play in this league, Brian Smith and Brian Kilrea the same, George Wood in goal, Dave Amadio, Bill White. Dale Rolfe has the potential to be an all-star . . . " I mentioned eight or nine players. "You won't buy players any cheaper . . . but keep Eddie Shore out of the deal. I got him out of hockey. Don't let him back in!" Cooke promised (and later kept his word).

When I hung up the phone Larry said, "Holy Christ, Alan, am I going to catch hell about this!"

"What?" I said.

"Well, Jack likes to be called Mr. Cooke."

"Well, if he brings it up tell him if he calls me Mr. Eagleson I will call him Mr. Cooke."

Cooke did make the deal, at $750,000, along with fulsome (I'm sure well meant but also good public relations) praise for the great hockey background of Eddie Shore, and how it was a privilege and a pleasure to be following the great Eddie Shore as owner of the club that Shore had guided for so long. Many of the Springfield players did move right to the Los Angeles Kings when training camp opened that fall.

Half a year or more before that 1967 expansion had teams on the ice, I decided on the basis of what I'd talked to the Boston players about – the seeds of a new players' association – that I should talk to all the teams and players who eventually would be involved. In short, I would tour the hockey world, the Western League as it then was, the American League, and the six NHL teams. I didn't have time for the Central League right then, but I started in on the others in February, a few weeks after my Boston meeting.

From February through April I had meetings with all of the teams in the NHL, AHL, and WHL. Although the way they were sometimes jerked around by owners was one of the main issues, hockey players have a lot of respect for money. One of my talking points that impressed many players was simply that with expansion to twelve teams they were going to have to play seventy-four games, four more than the season they were in. I'm telling them that if they get any less than a 5 per cent raise in their next contracts, they'd actually be taking a cut – that a man making $15,000 should get at least $15,750 or he'd be getting less pay per game.

Another good talking point I used was the necessity for overhauling the standard player contract, which hadn't been changed substantially since 1940. In all those years, once a player had signed with a club or even one of its minor affiliates, down to kids in their early teens, he had to play for that club until sold or traded to another club, where the same rules would prevail. A player could be fired, traded, sent to the minors with a drop in pay, without the player having any input at all. I thought that was scandalous, a form of serfdom outlawed in any other profession. In other pro sports, football and baseball, changes were being made to allow players to play out their option and maybe go elsewhere. In hockey, even players who had gone along more or less without protest for most of their careers, feeling there was nothing they could do about it, knew that this total control by owners was wrong.

In keeping with the modest $125 (U.S.) membership fee we'd decided to charge, I travelled from hockey club to hockey club literally on a shoestring. The players would arrange a motel for me, or sometimes I would stay at a player's house, such as Billy Needham's in Cleveland, which was in the AHL then. So was Quebec. I remember sleeping in the Quebec airport one night – John D'Amico, eventually to be one of the best NHL on-ice officials, was there, too. When the plane was delayed because of snow, John and I just stretched out on benches and slept until the snow stopped and the flight was called.

The meetings were going well. In Chicago Bobby Hull introduced me to the players and said, "Al Eagleson's done more for the players in the last six weeks than anybody's done in twenty years."

In New York I remember when I was making my pitch I said, "Now, is there any player here who is in favour of a union?"

Boom Boom Geoffrion jumped right in. "Hey, just a minute, Mister Lawyer! Wrong question! Say this, 'Is there anybody here who is *not* in favour of *this* union?'" He was right. I've used that technique many times since. Every time I do, I think of Boom Boom Geoffrion.

Everything was happening so fast that it was amazing, yet it was still one of the best-kept secrets in sports. One sports columnist who caught on early to what was happening was Dick Beddoes, then with the *Globe and Mail*. Beddoes had told me that when I got to Montreal I should call Red Fisher of the *Montreal Star*.

So on that trip I called Red. I had coffee with him at the cafeteria in the *Star* building. He asked a few questions and did a nice article about what my aims were and what progress we had made. His last paragraph went something like this: "I asked Eagleson why he's in town. 'Oh, just looking around,' he said. But I happen to know that he had a meeting last night with the Montreal Canadiens about forming a player association."

Red has always reminded me of that. "I found out, you s.o.b.," he'd say. "You couldn't hide anything in this town from me." At that time he didn't know all the details, or didn't print them. Montreal was one of the important clubs, of course. Ralph Backstrom introduced me to the other players. I must admit that I wasn't so sure what Jean

Béliveau's attitude was likely to be. I said to him that because of his position in the Canadiens' organization, not only the team captain but also with a position in management, I could understand if he wished to stay out.

He said quietly, which is his way, "This union is good for players. I am a player, first."

Then and later, the media people I met whom I found I could trust completely never changed – Jim Taylor and Jim Kearney in Vancouver, George Gross, then of the *Telegram* and later with the *Toronto Sun*, Red Burnett, Jim Proudfoot, and Milt Dunnell of the *Toronto Star*, Beddoes, Red Fisher and Tim Burke in Montreal, Claude Bédard in Quebec. And there were others along the way. As well, some I never could share a confidence with without seeing it published the next day, half wrong. In time I would answer their questions, wouldn't lie to them, but I wouldn't *offer* any information.

Along in there somewhere, we got a constitution. Bobby Orr and I went to a meeting of representatives of pro sports player associations in New York, called by the Teamsters Union in hopes of forming an overall pro sports union. That was the first time I met Marvin Miller, head of the Major League Baseball Players Association, and got the matter of an NHLPA constitution settled. We decided against going with the Teamsters, but Marvin Miller led me by the hand. He showed me exactly what to do. The constitution of the NHLPA is word for word (except for the word hockey) with the constitution of the Major League Baseball Players Association.

Even when I pretty well had covered every club in the league, and we were about to go public to the owners and everyone else, the full ramifications were still either unknown or not fully believed. Then, just on the eve of the league's annual June meeting, Beddoes came out with a pretty complete story in *The Globe Magazine*. Among other things, he reported that I had not only nearly total support in the NHL (nine abstainers among about 120 players, he said) but also from all but eight of the 180 AHL players and all but twenty-eight of those who had toiled in the Western League. All had signed a pledge authorizing me to represent them in pursuing the union's formation.

The meetings that year in the Queen Elizabeth Hotel in Montreal included the draft in which the six new clubs would pick players from a list of those not protected by the six old clubs. This all was taking place along with various other league-connected meetings here and there throughout the hotel. Every corridor was full of hockey gossip, a lot of it about the players' chances of union recognition.

I remember one incident just before the owners-only sessions were to start. I'd been invited to see Charles Mulcahy, the Boston Bruins lawyer with whom I had negotiated Bobby Orr's contract. When I arrived Sam Pollock was there and we were introduced.

Then Mulcahy said, "Alan, tell Sam how many Montreal Canadiens have joined the players' association."

"Every one of them," I said. "Including Béliveau."

Sam just shook his head, and took off, with Mulcahy saying, "See you later, Sam."

When he'd gone I asked, "What was that all about?"

"I've just been talking to Sam about your association. He'd said he knew every player on his team and not one player would have gone to a meeting or would have signed anything."

By then it was well known among most owners how strong we were. Along in there somewhere, perhaps a day or two earlier, I'd gone to Clarence Campbell and told him, "Here's the situation, here's what I've done." I thought when I'd laid it all out to him he would agree to support immediate recognition. Again, I was so wrong about him and couldn't believe his reaction. He was so afraid of the owners that he just brushed me off. He obviously didn't really know what the attitudes were among many of the owners, but he soon found out.

On the day of the owners-only meetings, Emile Francis, then coaching the Rangers, handed me a note from Bill Jennings, head of the Rangers, with a room number on it, I think room 1711. I walked in, and in the room were Francis, Jennings, Bill Wirtz from Chicago, and Mulcahy from Boston. You'll note they were all Americans. No sign of Stafford Smythe of the Leafs or Sam Pollock from the Canadiens.

They asked me what I had. I said that of the 120 regular players who had finished the previous season, all but two were members of the association. The two were Johnny Bower and George Armstrong of Punch Imlach's Leafs. Bower told me, "Al, I'm with you but Punch gave me my chance to play in the NHL and I don't want to hurt him." Fair enough. When the owners present heard my reply to their "How many?" they basically said that they knew they were going to get some flak (presumably from some other owners) but would support recognition.

The next day the players and owners met in a joint session. Bob Pulford, as the association's first president, led in an imposing group of players – including Ed Johnston from Boston, Harry Howell and Bob Nevin from Rangers, Pierre Pilote from Chicago, J.C. Tremblay and Bobby Rousseau from Canadiens, Norm Ullman from Detroit.

What Pulford said, for openers, was as straight-ahead as the way he played the game. Facing along the long table at which the owners sat, he said: "I have been directed to tell you that we want Alan Eagleson to speak on our behalf. A players' association has been formed and he is our executive director. Talk it over among yourselves. If you agree to meet with Eagleson, fine. If you don't, our player-owner meetings won't last this year for five minutes."

It was obvious that the owners had been well briefed, with a minimum of arm-twisting, by Wirtz, Jennings, and

Mulcahy. They had forecast the outcome to me. Within a few minutes, the owners selected a seven-man committee with Mulcahy as chairman to discuss with me the association's aims. A few hours later Mulcahy and I were front and centre at a press conference telling the press that the National Hockey League had decided to recognize the association.

When the questions came I said, truthfully, that I'd anticipated a longer and perhaps tougher fight for recognition. Someone asked me if I considered it a triumph. My attitude was, why should I rub it in? I said that in the circumstances "triumph" was not a good word to use. I was thinking back to Springfield and Eddie Shore, the battle over Brewer, the day Ed Johnston had invited me to his room and he and the other Boston players had said that what they were thinking about was a union, the travelling from club to club, almost always in secrecy, to talk to players who anted up the membership fee and said, "Go to it."

Later in the evening, according to Beddoes, I did let my hair down a little and said, "This is the most gratifying day of my life."

I certainly knew that it was only a start. The agenda we had discussed in all those motel rooms and phone calls and team meetings might take years to accomplish in full, but we were on the way. Antediluvian procedures of dealing with players that the owners had taken as a more or less divine right soon were going to be history.

It wasn't all smooth sailing. We thought when we left Montreal in June that we had the owners' agreement that before training camp in September they would sign all seventy-two players who had been protected in the expansion draft. This would be an improvement on the age-old custom of opening camp and then negotiating contracts under all the other pressures of camp. When September came and the owners had made little or no attempt to sign the protected players, some of our members thought a show of strength would be a good idea, such as the entire seventy-two refusing to show up until signed. Of the Leafs, Pulford, Mike Walton, Brian Conacher, and Tim Horton did stay away briefly. If I had sent the word out for everybody to stay home, we would have been into our first big fight. That I didn't give that signal might have been surprising to some who thought I was just itching to flex muscles, but I must have been feeling extra bountiful that week early in September. Either that, or extra pressured. I was running for re-election to the Ontario legislature and lost despite a lot of campaigning by hockey players, and at least partly because of problems I'll explain in another, more political, chapter. Anyway, one-armed paperhangers were loafers compared to what I was trying to do that fall; working at my law practice, trying to win an election, trying to be the right kind of a husband and father at home, and in those days taking no one would believe how many phone calls. Every time a player had a beef, it was a case of "Call Al."

Also, I had no wish to disrupt the training camps by getting on my high horse and showing how tough the players' association could be. I told the press that, and also that if we were wrong – and no agreement regarding signings and training camps really *had* been reached – I would go on the assumption that this was an honest mistake. The owners had been reasonable on most points and I couldn't see any reason for them to be unreasonable on this one.

At the same time, our first president, Pulford, my old friend from playing lacrosse in the 1950s and whom I'd privately advised on his contract talks with the Toronto Maple Leafs since 1961, was also Leafs' player rep. When he did get to training camp, I got a call.

He said, "Gee, Al, two of our players have decided not to join, Armstrong and Bower." Armstrong was Leafs' captain, Bower, the goalie, a star in Leafs' successes in the 1960s. "If I can't deliver a hundred per cent of my club, I think it's best that I step down as president."

I said, "Pully, I think you're wrong but I hear what you're saying. Leave it with me."

I called Bobby Baun, who in June had been drafted by the expansion California Seals and was then at Seals' training camp. He said, sure, he'd be president.

However, at the same time and for the same reasons, Pulford decided someone else should be the player rep with the Leafs. Whereupon Mike Walton volunteered, with the airy statement, typical Walton, "I'll soon get things straightened out around here!" Anyone who remembers the long-running battle between Walton and Leafs' coach and general manager Punch Imlach will understand the extra pressures *that* was to bring about. Imlach was fighting me and the union at every turn, and, never mind the NHLPA, Mike, although a very talented player, was a constant thorn in Imlach's flesh.

Making Mike player rep was strictly a case of serious personality conflicts being given a large dose of quick-grow fertilizer. Mike would tease Imlach and Imlach would tease Walton and of course I and the NHLPA were caught in the middle. Mike would break the curfew by one minute just to see what Imlach would do. Then Imlach would impose some stupid rule about the NHLPA access to the players just to see what Mike would do.

One other hitch was not known publicly at the time, but it probably had something to do with Walton's go-go attitude to having the Leafs 100 per cent in the NHLPA. As reported in Imlach's 1969 book, *Hockey is a Battle*, around November 1, 1967, Leafs' star Frank Mahovlich had missed two days of practices. Imlach had covered for him with hockey writers by saying he'd injured his back, but he had a feeling something else was bothering Mahovlich. In *Hockey is a Battle* he explained:

> I had a talk with him privately and what he told me made me as mad as I'd ever been in my life. He said he was upset about the Players Association. They all knew that I didn't like the idea of anybody from outside having anything to do with my hockey club, but whether a player

joined I guess was his own business, his own decision. Being the easygoing team man that he was, it [the decision] must have been a hard one for Frank to make when most of his team-mates were members. But this day he told me that the Players Association was bothering him. He was the team's big man. The members on the Leafs felt it hurt them not to have him in. He said he had had letters asking him to pay his dues, and other guys on the team soliciting him, and it was bothering him very much.

Imlach felt that I was carrying on a vendetta against him, with Walton my latest emissary. He said once that Brewer never would have left Leafs if he hadn't had me around to help.

He said that I was always going around telling people that he interfered too much with the lives of the players. "And here," he wrote indignantly, "the players' association was bothering Frank in a way that I never would. One thing sure – if I bothered Frank or anybody else, any time, it was about hockey, not about his private life and whether or not he joined a union.

"When Frank left me that day I went into the dressing room. I was flaming mad. I said, if I ever find a son of a bitch in here soliciting for that union – look out, you're gone. I don't give a damn who it is because none of you is as good a hockey player as Mahovlich is. If that goddam thing there, the union, is going to put me out a good hockey player, there is no way I can be in favor of it. So now you know which sides we're on."

That night Leafs beat Canadiens 5–0, with Johnny Bower the first star and Frank second star. He had played a magnificent game – on the ice for four of Leafs five goals, scored one himself, and assisted on two others.

"And," Imlach wrote, "when his name was announced as second star, there were boos mixed in with the cheers.

So there is no doubt about it, that week he had two blows to his peace of mind.''

One being the boos and the other being the pressure on him inside the club about the players' association.

Leafs had a game to play in Detroit the next night. A sleeping car was set aside at Union Station all night so that players could sleep before the car was hitched to a Detroit-bound train the next morning. Mahovlich got on the train about midnight, with the others. His berth was across the aisle from Pulford's, and around four or five in the morning Pulford heard him say that he was going home, and to let Imlach know that he'd left because he wasn't feeling well.

From there he went straight to the home of a doctor and later was admitted to Toronto General Hospital. A diagnosis of deep depression and tension was announced that afternoon by Dr. Hugh Smythe, who estimated that he would be out of the lineup for about two weeks. It turned out to be four, and naturally Imlach at least partly blamed the association for Mahovlich's depression and tension, along with the boos that sometimes came even when he had played great hockey.

No doubt Imlach's own cast of mind about the association's impact on the Leafs had been determined by one other factor. He had planned to leave Mike Walton unprotected in the expansion draft the previous June but had been overruled by club president C. Stafford Smythe for reasons that might have been a family matter. Earlier that year Mike had married a niece of Stafford's. The decision to protect Walton over Imlach's objection naturally was exacerbated when Walton was not only still there, but now a dressing room adversary as player rep in the NHLPA.

We ran into some flak in Montreal, too. One day that winter I walked into the Montreal Forum when the Canadiens were practising. I had arranged to see the players after the practice. I sat down in the seats and looked across the rink and saw Sam Pollock. He later was to become one of my closest friends, certainly my closest ally in hockey, but at that time we were on opposite sides. He was management and I was with the players.

That day I'm sitting there. I saw Sam leave the ice area. The next thing I knew, two security guards came to me and one said, "Mr. Eagleson, we're sorry but this is a private practice, only for members of the Canadiens' organization, and we're going to have to make you leave." That was the best thing that could have happened to the NHLPA in our first season. The players simply couldn't believe that I, their leader, would be escorted out of the Montreal Forum.

There were other trouble spots. After Pulford had stepped down Bobby Baun, our newly installed president, also was California's player rep. Talk about leaving a Stanley Cup winner and landing in a hot frying pan. Frank Selke, Jr., had moved from Montreal at the time to be president of the Seals, with Bert Olmstead, one of the toughest men in hockey, as coach and general manager. None of the expansion teams had much, if any, recognized star quality at the time, most players being castoffs from the original six teams. If there was ever a man bound and determined to make silk purses out of sows' ears, it was Olmstead. A tall man, a ferocious checker, and a great playmaker (for many years he held the league record for most assists in a single season), he had played for Canadiens with Rocket Richard, Jean Béliveau, Doug Harvey, and other greats through Montreal's string of five Stanley Cup wins in the 1950s and another Stanley Cup with Toronto in 1962. In Montreal, for more than thirty years, his four goals and four assists in a single game was tied with Rocket Richard (five goals, three assists) for the club record of most scoring points in a game. So Olmstead was used to playing with and dealing with skilled, well-motivated players. He appeared as California coach just at the time when players were asserting their rights through the NHLPA, with Bobby Baun – an old teammate of Olmstead's with the Leafs – on the firing line as both NHLPA president and California player rep.

The stories that came out of California about that time weren't quite on a par with Eddie Shore and Springfield, but there were resemblances. At one time Olmstead had the conviction that the way to get his team playing better was to work eight-hour days. On Thanksgiving Day, the story goes, he had them practise in the morning, stay in the dressing room to eat lunch, practise again, and then go back to the dressing room to go over what hadn't been going right.

By Christmas there were so many beefs between the NHLPA and Olmstead that Baun called me and said, "This is driving me crazy. I've got to get out of the presidency, get the heat off a little anyway."

At the NHLPA meetings in January of 1968 he officially resigned and Norm Ullman of Detroit took over the presidency. Ullman was going to be one of the best presidents the association ever had, quiet, steady, great on the ice and off. He wasn't long for Detroit.

He took office just a few weeks before one of the bigger trades in hockey up to that time – Detroit sending Ullman, Paul Henderson, and Floyd Smith to the Leafs for Mahovlich, plus Gary Unger, Pete Stemkowski, and the rights to negotiate with Carl Brewer and try to bring him back into the NHL, where most hockey men believed he belonged.

In early negotiations, Detroit also had insisted on getting Walton, but Imlach said simply, "Not Walton." He might not have liked Walton much, if at all, but liking or disliking was rarely a factor with Imlach if the guy could play – and Walton led Leafs in scoring at the time. Detroit accepted Stemkowski instead.

While there was a large public outcry about Mahovlich being traded, it was immediately obvious that leaving Toronto would help Mahovlich. What not many people knew was that Imlach, recognizing that Toronto pressures, including his own, were part of what ailed Mahovlich, had tried earlier to trade him. One try was even-up for Jean Béliveau. Neither had come off. Some hockey people said that moving the two principals in the trade, Ullman and Mahovlich, meant that Detroit wanted to get rid of Ullman because he was a union man, while Mahovlich was not a strong union man. Anyone who thought that way was ignoring other facts. You simply can't imagine Imlach trading for the union president unless he thought he was getting the better of the deal.

At the time of the trade Leafs, even with Mahovlich, were a distant fifth, fourteen points behind Chicago, going nowhere. Anyone who knew Imlach knew that he would have traded for the devil himself if he'd thought it would lift the Leafs.

I had nothing to do with any of it, of course, but the trade worked out well both ways. I was there in the Gardens the first night Mahovlich came back in a Detroit uniform. He scored the first time he got the puck. Some of the best years of his career were with Detroit and then Montreal, while Ullman, Smith, and Henderson played well for Toronto, almost (but not quite) helping them catch Chicago and get into the playoffs that year.

Before we leave that part of the story, we have to get back briefly to Walton. In the spring of 1969 there was another blowup. Walton quit the club because he felt he wasn't appreciated. He was getting on the ice mainly in power plays, not as a regular centre, the position he thought he deserved. He missed a game in Montreal and there was a media furore all week. Imlach probably wouldn't believe this entirely, but I had some part in getting Mike back. I phoned several of the senior players and as a result was able to tell Mike that he *was* appreciated, they missed him, wanted him back and playing. Mike then called Imlach, arranged a talk with him, and they agreed he'd come back. A couple of nights later Mike scored the tying goal in a 1–1 game with Philadelphia and everything seemed to be back on the beam. In retrospect, taken over all, Mike's time as Leafs' player rep up to that time was probably as peaceful as far as union matters were concerned as any other.

As to Imlach, one part of his 1969 book that I appreciated was when he wrote that while he was certainly not on my side on a lot of things, I had done things for the players "that needed to be done."

In return I can say that despite my deeply held opposition to some of his methods, he was one of the great coaching motivators in the game, iron hard in what he believed and in getting mileage out of his players, as he proved in his first few years with Buffalo in the 1970s. In that sense, among present-day coaches I can only compare him to Mike Keenan in Chicago in demanding that players give everything they've got or go peddle their wares somewhere else.

I have one other little memory of Imlach. I sometimes wondered if he remembered it. This was long before the NHLPA came into being. A group of us, including Imlach and a lot of Leaf players, had a stag for Pulford in the Thistletown office of Blaney, Pasternak, Smela, Eagleson and Watson, my law firm. Down in the basement there we had sandwiches, beer, and a crap game. When the evening was over, Punch and I laughed – we were the two winners in the crap game. I was a winner in another way that night. I met a lot of Leafs I'd never met before, which stood me in good stead when we formed the NHLPA in 1967.

Somebody once said that when the players' association was being organized, the players and I were close enough to the same age and hell-raising inclinations that we were something like brothers, or hell-raising high school kids. There's something to that. I think of the old Mount Royal Hotel in Montreal where all the hockey teams used to stay, one of the best lobbies in the world for just sitting and watching the hockey world go by.

Naturally the NHLPA stayed there, too, in the start-up years. The association didn't have any money. They used to give us rooms for $5 a night. At the June meetings the young and single ones, a lot more likely to whistle at a girl than tip their hats, hardly needed TV – they spent many a pleasant afternoon just sitting by open windows watching the girls in their summer dresses. More settled and married guys like Bob Baun and Bob Pulford, Red Berenson, Eddie Johnston, Norm Ullman, Lou Angotti all have memories of those meetings, and so do I. One of mine involves Angotti.

A glance at the all-time NHL player index tells you something (but not all) about Lou Angotti: good enough to be in the NHL, with Rangers, Chicago, Philadelphia, Pittsburgh, St. Louis. What it doesn't tell you is that he was always popular but never a star. You had to be there to remember the way the Chicago crowd used to rise and roar LOOOOOOO when he came on the ice and started his imitation of a five-foot-eight human buzzsaw. His stats are okay, too, for a certain category of player – the kind who sometimes now are called role players: ten years in the league, 653 games, 103 goals, 186 assists, 228 penalty minutes (an average of eleven minors per year from a guy who never backed up). He played in sixty-five playoff games and had eight goals, eight assists, and seventeen minutes in penalties (meaning six minors and one fighting major).

Lou was an early NHLPA vice-president. We used to tease him. It seemed that every meeting we'd have with the owners in June, there'd be an interruption and someone would come in and say, "Louie, we just want you to know you've been traded."

Or, "Louie, sorry, you just went in the waiver draft."

He bounced between the minors and the Rangers in the early 1960s. Rangers sold him to Chicago in 1966. Chicago left him unprotected in the expansion draft of 1967.

Philadelphia picked him. He was the team's leading points scorer (12 goals, 37 assists) in Philadelphia's first year. Still, that June somebody came into the meeting and said, "Louie, we just want to let you know you are now with Pittsburgh." Then he was traded to Chicago before St. Louis got him. He bounced around like a billiard ball. We all liked him, and he was a good NHLPA vice-president.

I remember all those things, but the night I remember best with Louie was in Montreal. We had our meeting during the day and that night Eddie Johnston said, "My brother is throwing a party." It was my impression that a lot of Eddie's brother's friends carried guns. The party was in a seedy part of Montreal. We get out there and everybody's having a lot of laughs and a few drinks and about 2 a.m. Lou and I phoned a cab and then waited and waited for it to come, but none appeared. Apparently they didn't like the district.

Finally we're waiting there, watching, and hear something coming and it's a pizza delivery truck. The driver jumped out and ran into the building next door to deliver the pizza. Lou and I just looked at each other and didn't need to take a vote. We jumped into the truck, drove downtown to the hotel, hopped out, and got to our rooms. Then we started worrying about the poor guy figuring he'd lost his truck. We phoned the police to say that a pizza truck was parked outside of the hotel. Didn't bother giving our names.

The NHLPA was far from affluent in those days. Red Berenson was with St. Louis or Detroit then, a team rep, and was on the players' association executive. We were still getting cheap room rates at the Mount Royal, $5 or $10, and my big suite was only $20, but with no air conditioning, and it was a hot, hot June night so we were sitting with all the windows open wide.

Red and I had ordered room service and, too hungry for salad, we'd asked for hot sandwiches. They came on a heavy tray with a pan of hot water underneath to keep the food warm, and a big heavy silver cover. We'd been sitting on the sill by a wide open window so we put the room service tray between us, still covered by this big lid with a handle on it. Red turned or I turned and hit the lid and out it goes, sailing down all those floors through the dark toward the street. I was thinking, God, if that hits somebody it'll kill them. Then we hear the crash when it hits, followed by the bang, bang, bang as it bounces down the sloping street. While we watched, every light on that side of the hotel was going on, people sticking their heads out and yelling down to the police who had appeared, "What the hell's going on?"

Only Red and I knew. Maybe somebody from room service had a clue, but if so they weren't talking. Not about hockey people. Not at the Mount Royal.

I've mentioned that every time there was a beef on NHL teams around that time someone would say, "Phone Al." Most of the problems were small enough, easily fixed. But one in 1971 stands out in memory. Detroit Red Wings were in a low period that eventually saw them out of the playoffs for ten seasons out of eleven, and Ned Harkness had been hired as coach. His only experience was with the Cornell University Redmen. In Detroit he tried using the same techniques that had worked with college players, which was a disaster.

One day when Detroit was due to play in Buffalo I got a call from Bruce McGregor, the player rep. "Geez, Al," he said, "we've got a hell of a mess here. Could you meet us in Buffalo?"

I met them in a hotel room. They had a statement signed by all the players. Gordie Howe was the first one to speak. Apparently Harkness was using the closest thing you could imagine to Eddie Shore's old tough approaches. The team wouldn't take it any more.

I listened, took the statement, and got it to Bruce Norris, the Detroit owner. The matter was soon settled: Harkness was moved into a front office job. Doug Barkley took over as coach and did much better. That's a pretty good example of the kind of no-nonsense attitude the players had achieved not long after the formation of the players' union had shown them that they had some power, too, when they were being abused.

CHAPTER TWO

INVOLVEMENTS

"I'll tell you what dinner is like at our place. My mom will say something. My dad will disagree. I'll agree with one of them. Then we will have an argument with each other. Jill watches."

– *my son Allen.*

Not many years ago at a party I gave for then Ontario Premier Bill Davis, probably in the early 1980s, one of those present was my father. The mix of guests was mainly from parts of my life not connected with hockey – politics, law, business. At one point my dad said to me, "I feel pretty good, Alan. I've just been talking to that judge over there." He pointed to Judge Joseph Addison. "He introduced himself to me and said, 'You must be very proud of your son.'

"I said, 'I am, but I think I would have been prouder if he was still doing court work.' And the judge said, "Well, I'll tell you, Mr. Eagleson, for what it's worth, when I used to see your son a lot from about 1957 to 1961 or 1963, he was one of the best and the brightest in my court every day, day in and day out, he had an amazing ability to please everybody and get the job done.'"

Naturally, I liked to hear that, but I'm not repeating it here to blow my own horn (I can do that from time to time without apologizing to anybody) – I'm talking about my dad being pleased, as he was that day, not only telling me but later repeating it all to my mother. Parents are allowed to dote a little.

That incident did make me think back to some of the times Joe Addison had been talking about, years when I was still a law student, 1957 to 1959, learning all I could.

I'd go to court, magistrate's court, night court, juvenile court, any court, on some matter or other. When I was a student I was still single, but money was nonetheless hard to come by. Maybe a crown attorney would be overloaded and would say to lawyers and students there on other business, "We've got eight people here who are unrepresented. Who's got some time?" I would always put my hand up. I'd go and talk to somebody charged with whatever, hear the story, and then try to put the defence as well as I could, winning some, losing some, maybe getting a fine reduced, doing what I could.

Night court is a special kind of atmosphere – small cases involving things like traffic tickets. If there was any chance of making a dollar or two I'd deal with anybody. "Give me half the face value of the ticket," I'd say to some guy. "If I lose I pay the ticket and if I win I keep what you gave me." So if it was a $10 ticket the person would hand over $5 right then. If I won I'd make that $5. I didn't lose too many. If I did lose, I could usually plead the ticket down far enough that I could pay the fine with my original half and it wouldn't cost me anything. And the exposure was good. Often other people in court would hear me argue cases and say, "Do you want to do mine?" I got a lot of business that way. I still didn't know more about court work than anybody else there, but by the sheer number and variety of cases I worked on, I did a lot of learning. That went on, I guess, through 1957 to 1959, my last year of law school, and then again in 1960, my first year in practice.

At that time magistrates often were getting bogged down because of the extreme variety of cases they had to hear. In some courts they'd have a criminal case and then fifteen minutes later they'd have to switch to family law, and in another fifteen minutes they'd be doing a case involving a juvenile. I'd go down to the juvenile and family court on Jarvis Street. Nine times out of ten the people there had never been in a court before, didn't know how to act. A woman, all she wanted was to get her $20 a week or $40 a week that had been awarded her in a separation or divorce case, and that she couldn't collect, and sometimes the defaulter would be there, too, trying to explain his circumstances. It was almost like a debtors' court in some ways.

I shouldn't forget, either, one thing that always frustrated me in night court, juvenile court, other courts, and I don't know that it has changed much since, is that a lot of the court officers were retired policemen, many rude and obnoxious, particularly to an immigrant. A lot of immigrants tend to think that anyone in a uniform must be important. I would see that a woman was trying to say something that she had a right to say, and one of these men would yell, "Sit down!" That's not his right. These officers pushed their importance too much. If a judge wanted her to sit down, he could say so. It was demeaning for the people there and gave the court an atmosphere so much like a zoo that it had to give a bad impression to juvenile offenders getting their first taste of what a court was like.

Sometimes the judges didn't help much, either, weren't so great themselves in how they treated people in their court. And it's part of my nature – if I found something going on that was very provocative, or at least provoked me – I'd take the challenge. Some judges were good and some were tyrants. A leading figure in the latter category was Tupper Bigelow, very senior, often very crusty and obnoxious, and not only to me.

Tupper Bigelow would be going on and on in court. Once I remember rising and saying to him, "Your worship, I don't think this woman understands you, you are speaking too quickly."

He was sort of a sparely built man, baldish, often had his lunches at the Royal Canadian Military Institute, a few minutes' walk away on University Avenue, where he consorted with admirals and generals and the like, not the lower classes.

He fixed me with that eagle eye. "Are you her counsel?"

I replied with the phrase, "Amicus curiae,"meaning "friend of the court." It was supposed to give a lawyer some kind of conditional licence to speak when he wasn't being spoken to. I used that phrase so often it was like my middle name.

I said, "Your worship, I'm sitting here and I'll be honest with you, you're speaking so quickly that I'm missing part of it."

What would happen. Maybe he would slow down. But he'd get even with me one way or another, find out what case I was really there for, and make sure my case would be heard last.

I enjoyed myself. In those days and later, in bigger cases, bigger courts, I'd run into all the best criminal lawyers of the time, get to know them – Dave Humphrey, Hugh Locke, Harry Rose, Wally Rose, Arthur Martin, Arthur Maloney – great lawyers and, to my mind, great men. One of the frustrating things about what I've been doing in the last twenty-five years or so, with the players' association and elsewhere, is that I miss the lawyers I used to see every day, great counsel in all respects even though their main sphere might have been criminal law.

There was a mystique about them, for me. Arthur Martin was one of my favourites, Harry Rose another, right from student days.

"Al," Harry Rose might say, "come on and work on this case, there's $50 in it for you."

I would always check with my boss first: "I'm up here anyway, can I do it? I can make some money."

"Sure, go ahead." So I'd do all his leg work, even though I was working for another law firm.

That day when Joe Addison made my dad feel good by saying I'd been one of the best and brightest in his court, it took me back a long way past law school into things that we did as a family. I was born in St. Catharines on April 24, 1933, and not long after that we moved to Guelph. I was ten years old when, in the autumn of 1943, we moved from Guelph to New Toronto.

That was the beginning of the times I can remember best about my childhood, the times when my mother, my dad, my three sisters – the Eaglesons of New Toronto – were my whole world, a world I'd fight for, and sometimes had the bruises to prove it. We had a close family, my sisters and our parents, and we were very much home-oriented. Sunday was the night for everybody to be home for dinner and then for some Bible readings and hymn singing. We were never permitted to play sports on Sunday. I managed to sneak out a few times and play the odd game of lacrosse or baseball, but invariably my parents would find out. You always assume when you're young that you're getting away with something, but the older you get you realize that your parents were simply blinking an eye, turning a blind eye, to what you were doing.

My sisters Fran and Marg were a little older than I, my sister Carol a little younger, but we shared a lot of interests, one being swimming. My father had coached my sisters and me in swimming in Guelph and elsewhere, sort of as a hobby. In New Toronto we heard a lot about the Lakeshore Swim Club, met Gus Ryder, the swim club's guiding light, and soon were deep into serious competitive swimming.

On Wednesday nights we'd go to a place on New Toronto's 11th Street where volunteers with cars would take us to a pool. There we tried out for and then practised with the Lakeshore club's swimming team. Gus Ryder had a 1942 Oldsmobile, a lovely car. I tried to ride with him whenever I could. I loved the car ride as much as anything else in those days.

Gus and his wife had no children of their own. The swimmers were their family. Gus would have been about forty then, and for the next seven or eight years until I graduated from high school, at least one evening a week, sometimes two, plus Saturdays and Sundays, for at least part of the day I'd be in Gus Ryder's company.

This was good for me because in school I was a couple of years younger than most others in my class, and small to begin with, so for a lot of sports I just wasn't big enough. In swimming or running or lacrosse, I could keep pace with almost anybody. Over my years at Mimico High School I went from being a competitive swimmer with Gus, racing in age groups from under fourteen, under sixteen, and under eighteen, to having my instructor's badge with Red Cross, my examining badge, and various lifesaving awards. My sisters were better swimmers than I was, but the four of us and my mom and dad really tied in to the swimming club. It became our home away from home. Gus was way ahead of his time in seeing that kids had something interesting to do with their spare time. My mother spent those years fund-raising for Gus's dream, a home pool for the Lakeshore club. Meanwhile, I always did well at school so had a fair amount of spare time. All those things I parlayed into teaching swimming. In those days competitive swimming at our level practically ended at eighteen. It hasn't changed much, except in the colleges and universities.

Eventually, Gus put me in charge of transport, by car and bus, for the group. The kids would pay ten or fifteen or twenty cents each and for that they got picked up at their corners and later brought home. My job was to collect the money, make all the stops to pick up people along the Lakeshore, and then head up Park Lawn Road to Humberside Collegiate. Gus rented their pool on Monday and Wednesday nights, and on Saturdays he rented the pool at the West End Y. The odd time on Sundays we'd go to a small private indoor pool belonging to some people named Harris who helped support Gus's club.

His extension into working with handicapped, retarded, crippled, and blind children was especially important to me. West End Y had been particularly for race training, but then on Saturdays we switched to working with the handicapped at Oakwood Collegiate. That's where I first came face to face with cerebral palsy and other physical and mental conditions that limited the kind of activity most people can take for granted. Until then, to me, those handicaps were merely something that other people had. That work with the handicapped had a permanent influence on me, gave me a feeling of how good it was to be doing something for others, and eventually was a springboard years later into working with organizations like Big Brothers, specifically organized to help a lot of people who are not so fortunate.

(Come to think of it, maybe this experience in working with those less fortunate had something to do with me taking on the problems of the Springfield Indians many years later!)

I entered University College, University of Toronto, in 1951 when I was just past my eighteenth birthday, but I still kept my connection with Gus and swimming. I won't forget, either, one of my final coaching assignments from Gus.

He called and said to me, "Alan, how about you taking a couple of the kids and working with them?" One of the young girls he sent along to me was Marilyn Bell, a little peanut of a kid who two years later became famous for her 1954 swim across Lake Ontario, cheered by about a quarter of a million people, including me, at the Canadian National Exhibition when she staggered ashore and immediately took her place among the world's most famous marathon swimmers. When she first trained with me I was eighteen and she was about fourteen and I guess she had a bit of a crush on me. I tease her about it now when she visits Toronto.

Meanwhile, to go back a bit. I've mentioned my mother's fund-raising efforts. Gus's dream was to raise enough money to build the Lakeshore Swim Club's own pool. In the early fifties, lotteries were illegal under the Criminal Code but everybody and his brother was ignoring that with raffles, bingo, and other gambling-oriented ways of raising money. We decided that a good fund-raiser for the Lakeshore Swim Club would be to buy a 1952 Chevrolet and raffle it off. One of our club members painted a sign to go on the car. They gave me the car keys and said, "Now go out and sell tickets."

I'd park the car someplace busy, especially on Saturdays and holidays, and maybe two or three of us would sell tickets beside the car. We were selling hundreds of dollars worth a week. The tickets were a quarter each, or a book of five for a dollar. I had to turn in a dollar for every five tickets sold. If I sold five tickets singly at a quarter each, I could keep the fifth quarter myself. I tried hardest to sell single tickets, because I didn't make a nickel for selling a book of five. We did pretty well out of the raffle, managed to stay out of jail for breaking the anti-gambling law, and by the mid-1950s the pool was finally established.

Oddly enough, that was pretty well the end of the Eagleson family's active involvement with the Lakeshore Swim Club. For all those years we'd kept the pool fund right at the top of our priorities. It was as if getting there, raising the money, was most of the fun. Once that was done – with a lot of help from sports columnists and other media people who gave Gus's fund-raising ventures a plug whenever he needed one – we backed off from much involvement except on special occasions. Among the club's top swimmers were Cliff Lumsdon, Marilyn Bell, and others. My dad was the coach in Cliff's boat in some of the annual Lake Ontario swims that were a big feature of the Canadian National Exhibition.

University days were a dream come true for me. I had been small for my age – I grew to 5-foot-10 and 170 pounds and suddenly felt invincible. I had more fun on and off the athletic fields in those days than I have had at any other time of my life. I graduated in 1954 with my B.A. degree. The yearbook for that graduating class at University College tells succinctly enough what I'd been doing apart from studying. I was playing coach for the University College first lacrosse team and coach of the second team, was on the swim team, the water polo team, and the junior basketball team. And had some proud moments. At the annual University College Physical and Health Education athletic banquet I was awarded the University College Centennial Trophy as the lacrosse player "showing to the most advantage the qualities of ability, leadership and sportsmanship." The presentation was made by a man who became a friend and important lawyer, Eddie Goodman. I was also assistant athletic director and played lacrosse not only in school but in the Ontario Lacrosse Association with Woodbridge Dodgers.

I have a couple of Woodbridge clippings here that I saved for the same reason that a lot of other things are in this book – some are not necessarily important in the big scheme of things, but they are what lucky lives are made of.

One of those clippings reads that Woodbridge beat Owen Sound 16–6, and "Al Eagleson paced the winners with five goals." The other reads that we beat Scarborough 11–7, and "Al Eagleson and Bob Pulford, with three goals each, paced the winners." I just now noticed the similarity of phraseology in the two clippings: *"paced the winners."* From Minor Atoms to the NHL, it's a feeling hard to beat, pacing the winners. We had some great nicknames on that team. Three other scorers in the 11–7 game were "Dud" Kearney, "Punchy" Proverbs, and "Ozark" Fox.

After University College I spent three years at the University of Toronto law school, receiving a Bachelor of Laws degree in June, 1957. The yearbook for my graduating year seems to indicate that, among other things, I still never turned down a job. I managed the intercollegiate senior basketball Varsity Blues, headed the lacrosse committee, coached the UC-PHE interfaculty champion lacrosse team, was playing coach of the law school's lacrosse team, and coached Varsity girls lacrosse. I also played water polo and volleyball and was sports editor of the University College newspaper, *The Gargoyle*. No wonder I stayed in good shape.

One thing that the yearbook doesn't tell is that I had wangled a job as usher at intercollegiate football games. I still have the armband that I kept and used for years after leaving university. I'd get in on the strength of the armband, then drop it over the wall at a pre-arranged spot so it could be used again – actually, make that again and again and again, because we'd use it until all my buddies were in the stadium, too.

Everybody landing inside, courtesy of the armband, knew the rendezvous, the aisle on the 55-yardline. It became our private box.

It was at one of those university football games in London, Ontario, that I met Nancy Elizabeth Fisk, who was to become my wife. I'd noticed her especially because she was not only pretty but also was wearing a fur hat from Royal Military College at Kingston.

I guess I couldn't have given a lot of thought to how I was going to meet her and make a good impression. I came up from behind at halftime, grabbed that great hat, then ran. She chased me. She was not only good-looking but fast on her feet. Anyway, she caught me. I asked her for a date and we went to church together the next morning. We've been dating ever since.

From the start, she knew the side of me that wasn't exactly suave and gentlemanly. Some time after the incident of the hat, we watched an intercollegiate basketball game at Hart House and stayed for the dance afterwards. A big guy, probably a little loaded, challenged me to a fight on the dance floor. I tried to back off. He taunted me with how he'd heard I was a tough guy in lacrosse and so on, so what's the matter, am I scared or something?

I said, "Hey, run along! Leave us alone. I'm here with my girl friend, everybody's having fun, why fight?"

So I'm trying to talk him out of it. He had something to prove, I guess, damned if I know what. He came at me, wide open. I hit him about as good a punch as I had in me, right on the nose, and down he went. That was it, a one-punch fight, except that a little later I happened to go to a washroom and there he was, washing the blood off and groaning – boy, could he groan.

He didn't look up, so didn't know it was me. "What happened?" I asked innocently. "Get in a fight?"

He still didn't look at me. "Oh, some son-of-a-bitch kicked me in the face when I was on the ground."

I grabbed him and spun him around and showed him my fist. "That's what kicked you in the face, you jerk!"

Meaning that even out with Nancy, both of us full of peace and good will, I couldn't always stay out of trouble.

At that time my sisters had moved out of competitive swimming and on to other parts of their lives as well, two as teachers and one as a legal secretary. My own last active involvement with swimming came about in a strange way. In June, 1957, I was twenty-four, getting ready to article as a law student. I was living at home. That summer Dad, still very active in high-level coaching, was training a Winnipeg girl, Vivian King. She was a Canadian champion several times over, had won one of the Lake Ontario swims, and was entered in the much-publicized Atlantic City swim.

Mom and Dad went to Atlantic City with Vivian. One day not long before the swim a friend and I decided to hitchhike there to see them and take in the sights. It took one day with our thumbs to get there. I didn't know how to get in touch with Dad, but I knew the name of the man running the swim, Jim Toomey. I looked him up in the phone book, told him my name, and said my dad was down here somewhere. "Do you know where I could find him?"

"Sure do. Come over to our place."

They bunked us in at their home for the night. All the talk was about swimming. At one point in that relaxed evening Jim Toomey said, "We've got a swimmer here who hasn't got a coach." Something had happened to her coach, I don't remember what, but anyway he asked me if I'd be interested in coaching her.

I said sure, why not?

The next day I meet this beautiful eighteen-year-old, Greta Patterson. Turned out she liked to swim in the nude. Between coaching and watching, it was a very memorable time. Her father was there, a dentist. They lived in Batavia, New York, and asked us if we'd stop in to see them on our way back to Toronto.

So when we were hitchhiking home we stopped there and spent a couple of days with them. Greta had swum Lake Erie and now decided she'd like to swim Lake Ontario. We talked about it and I said that when I got home I'd make a couple of phone calls. I called both the *Telegram* and the *Star*. I think the *Star* was more or less sponsoring its own Lake Ontario swimmer at the time, so it was the

Tely – Ian Patterson was on the *Tely* sports staff then – that said sure, they'd sponsor Greta.

Having graduated, I was about to start articling with J.D.W. Cumberland, QC, in New Toronto. I'd already told Greta, maybe proved to her at Atlantic City, that I was not really a pro at coaching so it was my dad who went in the boat with her for the Lake Ontario swim. She swam and swam almost the whole way until, as often happens, you get three miles from shore and it is the longest three miles in your life. Eventually my dad told her, "You're not getting anywhere and it's getting cold." At that point she packed it in.

That was pretty well my last close contact with swimming, except that for many years Gus and I saw one another, or talked on the phone, every few days. I'll never forget the influence he had on my life – happy times, good to remember. He died in May of 1991 when this book was being written. He is sorely missed.

Before we leave the New Toronto home scene of the late 1940s and early 1950s, I should mention something else about my mother and father. Being Irish we often had recent immigrants from Ireland staying with us. They'd land in, needing to get established, and sometimes would stay for two or three weeks or even months. Many would be people who came from my parents' own home area, Ballymena in Northern Ireland. It was like a network of relatives and friends from home, and there were plenty of both. My mother was a McNabney, with eleven brothers and sisters. Two of the brothers, Bob and Sam, were outstanding soccer players for Ulster United. When I visited Ballymena myself in the 1960s, a sentimental visit, I heard a lot about the McNabney family – that whenever there was a problem, the McNabneys would be first to come around and help. All I knew in my own experience was that my parents always seemed to be able to find a job for anyone from that part of Ireland. If they couldn't land them in work anywhere else, they always seemed to be able to find a job at Eaton's department store or mail order department. When my mother died in 1989, only the fourth of the twelve McNabney young ones to die, I had so many memories of her and what she had done in her life, so often for others.

Not many people know that in her unofficial position in welcoming the Irish, my mother helped the famous singing group, the Irish Rovers, come to Canada. This would be between 1950 and 1955, my teens and early twenties. It started when Bob Miller arrived from Ireland and boarded with us for six months or more until he was settled and brought over his wife, Elsie, and their kids, Sandra, Wilbert, and George. The Millers and Eaglesons were very close, and the Miller family eventually became well known as the Irish Rovers.

I think the Rovers might have made their first public appearances in Canada at a church concert run by my mother to raise money for Gus Ryder's pool. Wee Bob Miller and his Wee Sons, Bob and Wilbert, were on the squeeze boxes and George on the spoons, all of them singing.

One time many years later, maybe in the late 1970s, I was in Vancouver appearing on Jack Webster's phone-in show. The phone rings and a caller said, "Hello, Alan, I bet you don't know who this is."

I said, "I bet it's Elsie Miller." And it was – it was easy to pick off a Ballymena accent.

The past never goes away, praise be to God (as the Irish sometimes say). Just a year or so ago, watching TV, out of the blue I happen to think that I hadn't seen or heard the Irish Rovers for a while. Thinking that, I flipped the dial and there was a closeup of Bob Miller, then about seventy-five. Behind him, the Rovers were singing. When the song was over, his son Wilbert said, "I'm especially happy to have my dad, wee Bob Miller, here with us tonight."

I was hit then, as so often happens, with many, many memories of our place in New Toronto and what life was

like then. Dad had a 1935 Reo and on weekends the six
of us often would drive to Orillia and pitch a tent. Talk
about togetherness – six in a tent on a rainy day.

My dad was a union steward at Goodyear Tire, sometimes
on strike. When he was on the picket line I'd sometimes
take him something to eat. He had respect for his job as
well as for his fellow union members, and he never backed
down from anything. I learned that from him at an early
age, sometimes getting into trouble because of it. Once in
a high school basketball game a guy kept tripping me.

Finally I said, "Don't do that again."

"What are you going to do about it?"

What I did on the next play was go down the court and in
for a layup, but instead of shooting I drove the basketball into
his face. How to win friends. He never bothered me again.

Nancy and I started our married life in 1960 not well off,
to put it mildly. I made $2,000 in my first year in the practice
of law. As a high school teacher Nancy made twice as much.
She had to work the first four years of our marriage so
that we could survive financially. Our first home was really
my parents' home. Dad had taken a job coaching swimming
in Fergus, Ontario. For a while their place was going to
be rented or empty. They offered it to us and we decided
we'd take it. This was not one of the great decisions of
our lives. When Mother came to town on a visit I used
to laugh (but only to myself) – it was like a field marshal
conducting an inspection. We soon looked for a home of
our own and found an apartment in the same general area
that we were used to, well west of downtown. Our first
small cottage was on Lake Couchiching near Orillia. We
had a small boat. We played tennis, swam, and fished
whenever possible as a family.

Even when Bobby Orr and Mike Walton practically
became star boarders, they came to our place, not us to

theirs. Then or later, I never went on vacations with "the boys" or indeed outside of my family. Remembering my own childhood, and Nancy remembering hers, we kept the same kind of family involvement at our house after our children were born, Allen in 1961 and Jill in 1964. As you might imagine, family involvement at the Eagleson house does not necessarily mean perfect peace. I remember Allen once telling someone, "I'll tell you what dinner is like at our place. My mom will say something. My dad will disagree. I'll agree with one of them. Then we will have an argument with each other. Jill watches and listens. That's dinner at our house."

And it's true that Jill, being the youngest, often did just sit and watch. She would come up with some great lines, though. I remember one night when she said that she'd decided to go into law, as Allen had. I was pleased, but flabbergasted.

"Gee," I said, "that'll be fun, we'll have a family firm, 'Eagleson and Son and Daughter.'"

Jill said, "No. It'll be 'Eagleson, Father and Brother.'"

Both have been good at sports. Allen was quite a good hockey player, but we retired him when we found his practices on Saturdays and Sundays would interfere drastically when we could be up north together skiing as a family. Which brings us to a place where I will have to exercise all of my famous restraint to avoid boasting a little.

After Allen retired from hockey at league level, he did play the game at Upper Canada College and later played intramural hockey at Dalhousie University and intercollegiate when he was at Duke. Also, he was a member of the ski and tennis teams at McGill. Jill was a member of the ski team at Concordia, ski and tennis teams at Queen's, and the tennis team at U of T. Her Toronto Varsity team took the intercollegiate championship when she and her partner won the deciding match.

Both are tennis instructors and ski instructors. For several summers Allen taught tennis at outstanding tennis camps in North America and Europe. Both are bilingual and both taught at a French tennis camp in the south of France during summers in university years.

In law, Jill is a litigator with the Holden Day Wilson firm in Toronto. Allen was a lawyer with McMillan Binch in Toronto and then travelled to Scotland to take his master's degree in international law at the University of Edinburgh.

He must have done pretty well there: after completing his degree he was invited to stay on as professor of international law, teaching the master's course. He completed that work and now is thinking of practising in New York state to broaden his international law horizons. In 1991 he learned international law of a special kind – the way I practise it, acting as my assistant in the 1991 Canada Cup.

Not long before this book was written Jill got big front-page coverage for some work she was doing challenging the by-laws of Barrie, Ontario. When I saw the newspaper article I wrote to her and said if she kept that up, from now on I'll be known as Jill Eagleson's dad.

CHAPTER THREE

EARLY DAYS WITH ORR

"Come on up. Doug Orr wants to talk to you
about his son."

–a phone call from Bing Blanchard in MacTier.

In 1953 when I was still at university I took a job as a recreation director in MacTier, Ontario. As one entered MacTier on the highway a sign read: "MacTier, population 1,000, The Little Town with The Big Arena." In those days it was a busy Canadian Pacific Railway town. I boarded with the Woodroffe family. I didn't own a car so walked or hitched a ride wherever I went.

I had coached swimming and played lacrosse and fastball in the Lakeshore area, but when I think of MacTier I think of their fastball team, the MacTier Flyers. The manager, Aubrey Allsopp, the town grocer, asked me to join up. I played shortstop and second base reasonably well but was as well known, even locally famous, for base-running and base-stealing as for any other part of my game. We played in a league that included Parry Sound, Gravenhurst, South River, Trout Creek, and other small towns.

One of the guys I played some games against was Doug Orr from Parry Sound. We weren't bosom friends or anything like that. However, by the time I was elected to the Ontario legislature as the member for Lakeshore in 1963 I also had quite a few high-profile friends in hockey: Bobby Baun, Billy Harris, Carl Brewer, and Bob Pulford. Part of politics is to help other members any time you can. In the summer of 1964 the Parry Sound member, Alistair Johnson, asked me if I'd come up there to a sports banquet, present a trophy to the minor baseball league championship team, and bring somebody along who might draw a crowd to the banquet.

I took Carl Brewer, who'd been named NHL first-team all-star in 1963 and was good at drawing crowds. That's the first time either of us met Bobby Orr – who was captain of the baseball team I was giving the trophy to. He'd be sixteen then. We talked a little, certainly nothing I can really relate to what eventually happened that made Orr-Eagleson or Eagleson-Orr a pretty well-known handle in hockey.

His father, Doug Orr, came up and reminded me of our baseball battles at MacTier. He told me Bobby had been doing pretty well for the Oshawa team in the Metro Junior A league and before that had been hot stuff in local minor hockey. We talked some about how he'd got to Oshawa, a Boston farm club. That part was simple to understand: Boston also sponsored the Parry Sound Minor Hockey Association.

You might wonder why an NHL team would sponsor an entire minor hockey association.

Answer: In return they got first rights to all players, in this case including the one they really wanted, Bobby Orr.

That is also how Toronto Maple Leafs got Frank Mahovlich – by sponsoring the entire Schumacher Minor Hockey Association – and that's how many young stars wound up signing with a particular NHL club. A kid might yearn to play for the Leafs but if Rangers got their local sponsorship in first, good-bye Leafs.

But that wasn't a huge issue with me at the time. It was just a fact of life. Bobby had been scouted by the Leafs, among others, but before Leafs or any other team did anything Boston scout Wren Blair saw this smallish kid with a crewcut playing one night in Gananoque. He was so impressed that Boston told him to make sure Boston got him. To make sure of this one player, Blair got Bruins to lay on a blanket sponsorship of Parry Sound minor hockey. Such a sponsorship didn't usually cost much, anyway – a few dozen sticks, sweaters, rolls of tape, a little coaching help and, in this case, a $1,000 donation from Boston to Parry Sound's minor hockey program. That sponsorship meant that no other NHL club could even approach any player from that minor hockey association without the sponsoring club's permission. From the moment the sponsorship went on record, Bobby was bound for Boston if he proved to be good enough, which, to put it mildly, turned out to be the case.

His first move up was to the junior Oshawa Generals, by way of Bowmanville, which is where the Generals played their home games in 1962-63 while the Oshawa rink, destroyed by fire, was being rebuilt. For much of Bobby's first season of junior, he lived at home in Parry Sound and commuted to Bowmanville.

Of course, it didn't mean much at the time that the boy we were talking about, horsing around with the others at the banquet, was Boston property to do with as they saw fit. That was hockey, then.

The only restriction was that under the NHL's agreement with the Canadian Amateur Hockey Association, Boston couldn't turn him pro until he was eighteen. Don't think they didn't wish they could. Right then Boston was in the middle of eight straight years of missing the Stanley Cup playoffs. In six of those years they finished last. Without wishing to rub it in, in case some of those guys are grandfathers now and have been telling tall tales about the night they beat Leafs 11–0 (which actually happened around that time), those Bruins were sometimes awful to watch. One Saturday night during Orr's second year at Oshawa, Baldy Cotton, Boston's chief scout, gloomily eyeing the Boston defence as it waved ineffectually at Maple Leaf forwards whizzing by, told a seatmate, "We got a fifteen-year-old kid in Oshawa who's better than any of those guys."

Anyway, Doug Orr had at least intimated on that night of the banquet in Parry Sound that maybe I could sort of keep an eye on Bobby in case he needed advice.

I didn't think much more about it at the time. The trophy was presented, Brewer signed autographs, and that was that – until a year or so later, August of 1965, I was at our cottage in Orillia and got a call from Bing Blanchard not all that far away in MacTier, saying, "Come on up. Doug Orr wants to talk to you about his son."

"His son?" I asked. "Who is his son?"

"Well, he's the best junior hockey player in Canada."

Then I did ask around and found out. Bobby had been running rings around the Metro Junior A league, getting thirty goals to set a scoring record for OHA Junior A defencemen. (Jacques Laperriere had held it at twenty-nine; I found out all these things by reading sports pages later.) I go up and meet with Bob and his dad in Bing's backyard and we talked about how Bobby was doing in Oshawa.

They said, well, here's what we're getting–something around $40 a week or less, plus room and board.

At that time I sure wasn't in it for the money. Still, I hear the stories about scoring records and all-star teams and so on. Burning up the league was no exaggeration. I had a good feeling for Bing and Doug Orr and the boy so I said okay, I'd go and talk to Wren Blair–who ran the Oshawa junior team and whose Whitby Dunlops had electrified Canada by winning the world championship a few years before.

Talking to Wren wasn't easy. He said flatly, "I'm not paying any more money."

That was a challenge. I never like to lose in something I set out to do. I thought it over and then went and talked to Jim Bishop, who ran one of the best lacrosse teams in the country, the Oshawa Green Gaels. I set it up with Jim that if Blair wouldn't give Bobby more money, Bobby would go and play lacrosse with the Green Gaels.

Well, of course, that filled the Oshawa area papers with a little fun, and to make a long story short I got Wren to agree to pay Bobby more money, maybe $50 or $60 a week, I think. By then I was interested. Bobby went back to the Generals that season and led them into the eastern Canadian championship and the Memorial Cup playoff against the Edmonton Oil Kings.

In one of the early Memorial Cup games, that was the spring of 1966, Bobby hurt his knee. Hap Emms was general manager of Boston at the time and had his mouth watering at the idea that the following season Bobby would play with Boston.

He ordered Bobby not to play the rest of that Memorial Cup series on that hurt knee.

That caused my first meeting of any consequence with Hap Emms. It happened to be in Maple Leaf Gardens. Bobby wanted to play. Emms was adamant. "If he plays again, and his knee gets hurt more, his career might be over. I own Bobby's rights and he's not playing."

Wren Blair put the matter quite directly to Emms, as in, "Up yours, Hap. He's playing."

I went to Bobby and had a long talk with him, putting to him the honest reasons for Emms's attitude.

He just said, "Mr. Eagleson, I'm playing."

I knew then that he was a stubborn little so-and-so. You have to take into account that for four years Bobby and Wren Blair and the whole Oshawa community had been aiming at the Memorial Cup, and were revved up in a way you can hardly imagine unless you've been involved in junior hockey.

So he played, and they lost the Memorial Cup to Edmonton, and one way or another I knew that I was now in a contest with Hap Emms on Bobby's behalf.

That summer of 1966 Father Dave Bauer's Canadian national team was doing everything it could to get strong players to represent Canada the following year at the world championships. Carl Brewer was one who wanted to do it, which would have to mean getting his amateur standing back.

Every weekend at our little cottage at Lake Couchiching, a place about the size of a couple of rooms in the average house, there were Bobby, Carl Brewer, Father Bauer, my wife Nancy and I, and our two kids, Allen, then five, and Jill, just a baby. I think Marc Tardif and Réjean Houle dropped by once–they were both good juniors at the time and Bobby had played against them. We talked and talked–and believe me, Father Bauer could talk–about Bobby and other good young players spending a year with the national team and how we can do this and we can do that.

Bobby was thinking about it, but all along I knew his real aim was to go to Boston, and somewhere in there we had made it definite that I would negotiate for him. I also knew that it wouldn't hurt those negotiations if Emms thought there was any way Bobby would go to the national team. We went through the whole hockey-talk summer that way – I don't know how Nancy stood it – until I announced publicly that I had been retained by Bobby Orr to conduct negotiations with Boston, and Hap Emms announced in Boston that he wasn't going to talk to any blankety-blank lawyer.

I always figured Hap Emms was my first real press agent. Suddenly all the Boston sports columnists and other U.S. hockey writers wanted to know who the hell was this lawyer that Emms wouldn't talk to. Out of that came a story in *Sports Illustrated* headed something like, "The High Price of Canadian Orr," and Leo Monahan of Boston, I met him for the first time, came up and did a big article in the Boston papers saying what Bobby had done and here's who Eagleson is and here's Eagleson's background. It was a good story on me and a good one on Bobby.

I still heard nothing from Hap Emms. Then one day Nancy and I and our two kids were out in our little boat, a fourteen-footer, going up the locks when this big cruiser comes along.

A lot of Hap Emms's early fame in hockey came from his Barrie Flyers, and I think at the time he still lived there or had a summer home there. I look up and there's Hap on his cruiser, staring over at me.

"Eagleson!" he yelled. "Alan Eagleson!"

We'd met a couple of times besides the business about Orr's knee and the Memorial Cup. As scary an old bugger as he was, I still got along with him all right. So we steer over alongside his cruiser and I got aboard with Nancy and the kids. Mrs. Emms gave them Cokes and cookies while Hap and I talked. As I recall it the first thing he said to me was, "What are we gonna do? We gotta get this thing done."

That was about the 15th of August. It probably wouldn't have made any difference in what eventually happened if we'd been living a thousand miles apart, but one of the things that made it easier was that because of his long-time connection with the area and because our cottage was right nearby and because Orr spent a lot of time at our place that summer, it wasn't hard to set up meetings. We had two or three more, usually on his cruiser. Also, one of Hap's former Barrie junior players was Red Favero. I had met him various times at a motor camp my parents used to stay in sometimes near Orillia; Red dated a girl at the camp. So I knew him, and Hap knew him, and Red was still around Barrie working as a photographer. Anyway, when we finally got close to an agreement, it was on the Sunday of the Labour Day weekend, with the NHL training camps about to open. In a sense, that also put extra heat on Hap because after Boston's string of finishing last six times and next to last twice, he sure as hell didn't want to open camp with the greatest young hockey player in the world not there and all the Boston papers giving him shit for being such a tightwad and maybe blowing the chance of a lifetime. It would have been something like waiting weeks for the Second Coming and then nothing happens.

Orr drove down to Barrie that day with his dad. Red Favero was on Hap's cruiser and had his camera with him. We had the final talks, dotting the i's and crossing the t's, and Hap called for Red Favero to come into the cabin. Very often something really big happens practically in private and has to be reconstructed to make it look spontaneous for photos. This time it was strictly on the up and up. Red didn't have to yell, "Smile!" at Orr and his dad and me. The picture he got was carried on the wire services and published in a lot of papers across Canada and the U.S. the next day. The sum usually mentioned was $50,000 a year, or $40,000 a year, either sum for a rookie unprecedented in the NHL as well as in many other sports. Not many players in the NHL at that time, even veteran stars such as Gordie Howe ($35,000) and Bobby Hull ($40,000), were making that much.

Of course, nobody could be truly sure about whether Bobby could live up to all the expectations. Lots of teenage phenoms don't. I won't list them, but every few years there's another name to add to the list of rookies praised to the skies who in the end didn't quite produce as advertised. The level of Jean Béliveau, Rocket Richard, Gordie Howe, Bobby Hull, Gilbert Perreault, Marcel Dionne, Guy Lafleur, and Wayne Gretzky or Mario Lemieux is so rarefied that just being mentioned in the same breath is an honour. Few players ever have established their right to be in that company as quickly as Orr did. In his first season he was named rookie of the year and voted to the NHL's second all-star defence. He was first-team all-star in his second year and for seven consecutive years after that. He also won the Norris Trophy in his second year, as the league's best defenceman, to go with his many other league and playoff awards and records.

All those years after he signed on Hap Emms's boat and embarked on his unprecedented and virtually unchallenged success, I have come to categorize as my happy years with Bobby Orr. I don't know how many magazine covers or weekend supplements over the next ten years used us together in cover photos, cartoons, or paintings. The idea that we were virtually an entity, inseparable, wasn't just malarkey, a case of me barging along on his coattails. One early incident might do something to illustrate how close we were.

In 1967, Canada's 100th birthday as a country, all across the land, cities and towns and villages celebrated the centennial. MacTier, where Bobby's father and I had first met playing softball, scheduled an exhibition softball game. It was to be Eagleson, Orr, and friends against a team organized by an area radio station. Actually, Bobby didn't play for most of the game but was there on the bench. In the last inning we were down 7–6 and he finally went to bat. He got a hit, a triple, and now there he is on third base with the tying run, with me at bat.

I took a pitch, and when the catcher tossed the ball back to the pitcher Orr took off trying to steal home. The throw-in had him by several feet, but instead of trying to slide he kept going full bore and ran into the catcher, knocking him loose from the ball before he could make a tag.

The other team's first baseman didn't like that at all. He ran in and threw a punch at Orr. It was all pretty crazy, in retrospect, but I dropped my bat and my glasses and punched the first baseman. Pretty soon, several players were into it against me and Orr, until Doug Orr ran in and broke it up. We apologized and that was that. Years later Orr was still uneasy about the memory, but I wasn't. It had happened, but getting into that fight was maybe closer to my way of doing things than it was to Orr's. I'd had fights even on tennis courts, but especially when I was playing lacrosse.

I remember one time after a fight in a lacrosse game I appeared in court defending a client charged with assault or something. I had two black eyes and a few cuts and scrapes here and there. I was a mess. The judge took a look at me and said, "Are you defending this man, or are you the one he assaulted?"

As the years went by, I usually managed to control my temper to the point of not engaging in fisticuffs, but I found other, more legal ways to get even.

Still, that fight in the exhibition softball game wasn't out of character in the way Orr and I stood up for each other. Rather than put it in my own words, here is what one writer, John Gault, wrote in *Toronto Life* magazine about the bond between us. At the time Orr's original money deal with Boston had grown over the years to a five-year million-dollar contract.

There has developed over the years an incredibly close relationship between Orr and Eagleson, a deep and abiding respect and yes, love. I've talked to each about the other, and concluded that there is a mutual awe. And Eagleson, let's face it, is in awe of hardly anybody.

That, I think, was a fair and accurate estimate of the years when I was not only dealing with his hockey negotiations but working out endorsement and other contracts with major companies such as General Motors and Standard Brands, always on the lookout for anything large or small that would keep Orr's millionaire status growing into what it became, helping to make him rich beyond anybody else in the game. At the same time he was in and out of our house in almost the same way that we'd spent so much time together before he even turned pro. He was like an older brother to our kids. Those were such good years of mutual respect and admiration that I never suspected they would ever end, at least not the way they did. But now we'll go back a bit.

CHAPTER FOUR

POLITICS

If there'd ever been an award for the best candidate for cabinet that never made it, I would have been a shoo-in.

I got into politics more or less through the back door. Until
my twenties, I wasn't a member of any political party, but
for years I'd been leaning to the Tories rather than to the
Liberals, who by 1957 – when an election was called – had
been in power federally for twenty-two years, so long a reign
that I, then twenty-four, had never known any other
governing party. There were a lot of voters in the same boat.
To these, when Diefenbaker won the Tory leadership in
1956 after spending sixteen years as a gadfly Tory backbencher in the House of Commons, he was a beautiful ride-
'em-cowboy contrast to old-line stuffed-shirt Liberals who'd
been in power so long they treated it as their divine right.
He went into the 1957 general election mainly on an anti-
arrogance ticket – the Liberals, especially Trade Minister
C.D. Howe, giving him all that kind of ammunition a mortal
man could handle. And I was yelling and groaning by turns
by the TV set on that election night in the spring of 1957
when John Diefenbaker's Progressive Conservatives finally won.

The Liberals weren't quite sunk with all hands that year;
enough voters were doing so from memory that Dief's great
upset produced only a minority government. The man he
beat, Prime Minister Louis St. Laurent, then was replaced
as Liberal leader by Lester B. Pearson – against whom in
1958 Diefenbaker won a landslide majority.

Four years later, by the time of the next election, the
party was in trouble, partly because, apart from fairly rare
shakeup years like Diefenbaker's 1958 (and later, Brian
Mulroney's 1984 and 1988), the solid Liberal vote is tra-
ditionally higher than its Tory counterpart. Also, in 1962,
for those voters who paid attention to more titillating issues,
some of Dief's cabinet ministers had been compromised by
their association with a German woman named Gerda
Munsinger. If there is such a thing as a mature bimbo, Gerda
was it. So one way or another the Tories were in trouble.

During the 1962 campaign, I went to a luncheon meeting
in Thistletown, near Toronto. John Hamilton was the main
speaker, my sitting member in York West, a lawyer I knew

only by reputation as a top transport authority. He and I talked at some length at that meeting. I liked him and his ideas so I agreed to work for him during the campaign, when he was in tough against the very high-profile Toronto Maple Leafs star, Red Kelly.

Kelly won, but we did well in the subdivisions I canvassed. I worked everybody to death and told them that was the only way an election could be won. In the overall national result, Diefenbaker was returned, but with a minority government that was shaky because the New Democrats, by and large, were supporting the Liberals. Everybody knew that another election would come soon. It came in 1963.

For that one, John Hamilton decided he wasn't going to run again. Somebody called me and asked if I'd be interested in seeking the nomination. We talked about it at length and eventually I decided I'd have a try.

First I had to win the nomination meeting. I found that to be great fun. I learned early how to pack a house for a nomination meeting. There were about six candidates and I won on the first ballot.

That meant I was running against the sitting member, Red Kelly. Of course, I knew Red through other Leafs who were my friends. Red and his wife Andra have been my friends since. I did pretty well at the public meetings. The hockey season was still on and Red didn't get to very many of the meetings. In an election campaign, the candidates are thrust against one another. I had to attack Red. You don't lose an opportunity to score for your side, but with Red and me, it was something like two lawyers fighting all day in court, but staying friends. There was never any malice between us, although questions often came up about Red's being involved with hockey – could he handle both hockey and the House of Commons and do justice to both? The papers often brought up the fact that the hockey team was split in this election – Bob Pulford, Bob Baun, and Carl Brewer out working for Eagleson and then going out on game nights to play on the same team as Kelly. Some of the Leaf players, including the three mentioned above, were in a small investment group I'd put together, along with some non-athletes, a couple of years earlier. We were friends. Some people made a big issue of that, but it was really minor, not the kind of issue that wins elections, and it didn't win that one.

Our riding at the time was the second biggest in Canada (behind Scarborough), and as I tell everybody, I got more votes than all but four other candidates in Canada, but still lost: my 26,000 votes against Red's 41,000. By then I'd got my feet wet in two elections, one as a worker and one as a candidate, and had lost them both. I thought, well, that's my political career. I had enjoyed it, had a lot of fun, learned a lot, and got to know John Diefenbaker and his wife, Olive. To be sure, he was very partial to anyone who ran for his party. What with the election and the side issues, he and I talked a lot of politics, and I guess I got the bug.

Within a month after my defeat it began to look as if a provincial election would soon be called. A fellow lawyer, Dalton Bales, called me and said, "I'm in charge of organizing Metro for this election. I'm going to run in Don Mills, and we've been thinking you could be the one to win in Lakeshore."

I thought about it and did some checking. If I took the nomination, I'd be up against Murray Cotterill, well known as an important union man with the United Steelworkers. He was running for the New Democrats. With Anaconda Brass and other big companies, New Toronto was seen as a union town, giving him an edge. The unanimous opinion seemed to be that Murray would walk away with it. I thought, what the hell, I have nothing to lose. Besides that, everybody knew that my dad was a union man, a steward at Goodyear, and that I was a local boy. So what if I was a Tory in a union constituency? I ran on the basis that I knew the area a hell of a lot better than Murray Cotterill. He was a very good organizer but that time, anyway, organizing didn't wash in the Lakeshore. I won the election. Out of an old riding that had been cut up through redistribution, Len Braithwaite won the north end for the Liberals, Les Rowntree won the middle for the Tories, and I won the Lakeshore. That was just a few months past my thirtieth birthday.

I took the legislature job very seriously but also had fun. Because of the size of our majority, the government side of the House didn't have enough seats to hold us all, so a number of us new Tory members – subsequent cabinet ministers Tom Wells, Darcy McKeough, and others – sat in a group across the House. We were young, feisty, and irreverent, specializing in shouted interjections and one-liners that enlivened the House but weren't always in accordance with the rules. I think it was the Liberal for Downsview, Vern Singer, who dubbed us the Chicago Gang.

The fun of my four years in the House, until I was beaten by Pat Lawlor of the NDP in the next election in 1967, came in different guise. There were some real characters in that legislature for the Chicago Gang to work on. Tory Ellis Morningstar of Welland, sometimes called Mighty Morningstar because of his immense size, often would fall asleep. We'd send a note telling him to wake up, and signing the speaker's initials. Among my opponents, also, there were people I enjoyed. Liberal Elmer Sopha from Sudbury could make spellbinding speeches that, when reproduced by Hansard, lost about 90 per cent of their lustre, that 90 per cent representing Elmer's rhetorical style. Liberal Eddie Sargent, a lovely guy from Owen Sound, sometimes would blow a referee's whistle if things weren't going as he thought they should. I remember one time in the House when somebody, maybe it was Eddie himself, said something to the effect that Eddie Sargent had spoken oftener in the House than anybody else, and I called from deep in the Chicago Gang, "Yes, and has said less."

Then there was the longest-winded member of all, Joe Gould, the Liberal for Toronto Bracondale. In the spring of 1964, Joe was among the candidates for his party's leadership. No doubt seeing a chance to let the public and members of his own party become more aware of what he saw as his true worth, Joe began speaking in the budget debate on February 28, 1964. Twice in the next few days he talked out the time allotted for the debate. Finally, eleven days after firing his opening guns, he went on for another four hours in his last kick at the cat. Part way through his last speech, I noted the thickness of his remaining notes and started a twenty-five-cent pool on his finishing time. Twenty-six members chipped in. The joint winners – each guess being just four minutes out – split the pot, getting $3.25 each. Not a great profit, but it helped give the speech an exciting ending – at least for us gamblers in the Chicago Gang.

In fact, the Chicago Gang got on the nerves of some more established Tory members almost as much as on the opposition Liberals and New Democrats. The fun side was in the heckling. I do like remembering that side, the notoriety we had, but at the same time I never lost sight of the fact that I wanted to make a serious impact. That was what was mainly on my mind when I made my maiden speech.

At the time, still spending many of my days in court, I had just encountered a situation that I hated. A baby only a few days old was at the heart of it. Adoptions in Ontario at that time mainly were arranged, and regulated, by Children's Aid societies, some Protestant, others Catholic. In almost every case, Children's Aid people made sure that religious backgrounds matched – a child of Roman Catholic parentage could only be adopted by Roman Catholics, with the same restriction imposed on Protestants.

As I said in my maiden speech to the legislature, a few weeks after I'd been elected, the facts were that more Protestant parents had applied to adopt children than there were Protestant children available for adoption. At the same time there were fewer Roman Catholic parents wanting to adopt than there were children available of the same faith.

This had come to a head because of a public outcry when a district court judge decided that the child of an unmarried Catholic mother could be adopted by Protestant parents.

Much of the outcry came from Catholics, spearheaded by the Catholic Children's Aid Society. No legislation at that time ruled on the matter, one way or another. In my maiden speech I argued that the religious controversy over inter-faith adoptions caused people to lose sight of the major issue.

"A child is not a chattel that can be stored until a certain day (when adoptive parents of the same faith are available)," I said. "A child is a living thing, a joy, a sorrow, a smile, a frown. . . . The main object should be to make happy homes, where at present we are left sometimes with lonesome adults and lonely children. Do we simply say that this is the end of the question, or do we go a few steps further? Do we say these children are to be forever denied a home and parents? Or shall we ultimately decide that these same children will be given the opportunities we were given?"

The headline reporting this speech put it succinctly: IGNORE RELIGION IN ADOPTIONS, NEW MPP PLEADS. The story mentioned that I was a new member, making my first speech in the House, and then quoted me at length, including the above, in what I thought then and still think of as an important issue, actually much broader in scope than any Catholic-Protestant split on the matter.

The reaction I got in the House was good, as it was in the press. Besides that, I received eighty-five messages in favour of what I was proposing, and only one against. The first breakthrough in this initiative came a few weeks later, when the Metropolitan Toronto Children's Aid Society announced that it would permit Jews, agnostics, and atheists to adopt Protestant children. But at the same time there had been a fierce counterattack on me and my ideas by the Catholic Children's Aid Society, so I was thrust into the position of making that group my main target. The fact that I was a Protestant, a member of the United Church, was used against me, suggesting that a lot of what I'd said could be attributed to religious bias, which was hogwash. But it must be remembered that religious divisions in Ontario are older than the province itself.

In the end, it took more than a year before the issue I'd been fighting for was approached in a new version of the Child Welfare Act. Even that tiptoed carefully in and out of the bulrushes and still did not make a really definitive statement on the matter.

When the whole thing was being threshed out in committee (the standing committee on Health, Welfare and Education), Stephen Lewis, then an NDP backbencher, demanded that the Act address the controversy in plain language. If the government indeed had accepted the principle of inter-faith adoptions, as it seemed to be hinting, "it is time we said so and stopped beating around the bush."

Welfare Minister Louis Cecile, waffling, replied that the government position now was neither for nor against inter-faith adoptions. It gave no encouragement, made no objection. He contended that the matter should remain a matter for the courts.

I thought, to hell with that. It had always been something you could take to court, usually without avail. I didn't have to wrestle with myself much at all to decide that I should go against my own party's stand and side with Stephen Lewis of the New Democrats, as he was siding with me.

I proposed an amendment (this was March, 1965, fourteen months after I'd raised the matter) that would insert a line into the new Act stating that, "No order will be denied solely because of the religion or non-religion of the adopting parents." I referred to the case of Joey Lamb, then four years old, whom a judge had ordered could be adopted by a Protestant couple when Joey was only four days old, a decision that was still being argued hotly on religious grounds. "If this (judge's decision) is the law of the land," I said, "let's spell it out, not leave it up to judicial interpretation." Stephen Lewis supported my amendment, but Louis Cecile repeated that regulations for the new Act were being drafted and eventually the legislature could decide.

After my initial speech, it was obvious that I was still a loyal Tory, but not slavishly. I was involved in other high-profile conflicts with my own party. One was over legislation proposed by Attorney-General Fred Cass, a bill the media and the opposition immediately dubbed the Police State Bill because of one really bad section. The stated (and valid) aim in this bill was to revise a lot of out-of-date rules and procedures and to strengthen the law's hand in dealing with criminals. But somehow slipped into what was generally a good bill was a fatal hitch, Section 14, which provided that people who refused to answer police questions could be held incommunicado for seven days while the police presumably could continue to ask questions. There was no doubt, as furious editorials argued and the public protested by letters and demonstrations, that this would have been an infringement of civil liberties.

As a member of the committee that drafted Fred Cass's bill, I had been against Section 14 from the beginning. When the bill came up in the legislature, hot attacks on Section 14 immediately followed. Forty members participated, representing all parties. To his credit, Premier Robarts quickly agreed that the protests were valid. He promised that the offending section, and any other offence against civil rights, would be removed.

The Liberals jumped on the anti-government bandwagon with an amendment that would have meant complete withdrawal of the bill, the good as well as the bad. A much less Draconian amendment was introduced by Stephen Lewis to remove Section 14 but leave the many worthwhile sections of the bill intact. I preferred that solution and both spoke for it and supported it with my vote. I was happy that in this case the eventual vote in favour of the NDP amendment was unanimous, 96–0, with Tories, Liberals, and everyone else taking the opportunity to land on the side of the angels.

None of that, making a media villain out of Fred Cass, was legislative fun. A thoroughly decent man, in this case badly advised by his staff, he decided to resign from the cabinet.

The most serious battle I had with the party began in June, 1965, when Harry Worton (Liberal, Wellington South) tabled a resolution calling for Ontario to start talks with Ottawa to change Ontario's divorce laws. Since 1930, when Ontario acquired the right to dissolve marriages, the grounds were mainly covered by a single word: adultery. Only if a husband was the one being sued for divorce was that broadened to include sodomy or bestiality.

So, as Harry Worton argued, otherwise honest citizens found themselves forced to perjure themselves in order to obtain a divorce. My law practice then was in its early stages, I was involved in all kinds of cases, and I'd been in such cases myself. Every lawyer in town knew that the rigmarole was practically standardized perjury. Somebody would sue for divorce and too often the case would wind up with people perjuring themselves.

These cases almost always had the wife suing the husband, maybe not because she wanted to but because their marriage had become unsupportable and they had agreed to split the only way the law allowed. Some woman would agree for a cash fee to be seen in a compromising situation by a witness who also was in on the game, either for a fee or maybe just as somebody's friend trying to help the deal along. The woman might be found in the man's bed, or perhaps merely sitting in a chair in her underclothes with the man also there, in a hotel room or apartment. It was all a setup. When the witness turned up, on cue, and saw the man and the woman even half undressed in the same room together he'd leave and that would be it. The woman would put her dress back on, take her agreed fee, and leave.

Then when the case came to court the witness would struggle, often shame-facedly, through his story. The judge might suspect it was a setup, but how could he prove it and keep his docket moving right along? It was a scandal, plainly the result of bad law. In supporting Harry Worton's resolution, I said "the divorce law practically forces people to use the courts as a dupe." Premier John Robarts did not allow the resolution to be debated at length, let alone come to a vote. With his majority, and the government whip to order how party members should vote, he could make decisions stick.

Eight months later, when the resolution did come up again, I spoke at greater length, as did my colleague George Kerr (Halton).

A front-page *Globe and Mail* story headed "Robarts Rejects Plea for Divorce Reforms" reported part of my argument on the subject. I told about people coming into my law office and asking me if I could provide women to act as co-respondents in divorce actions. I'd go to court and watch people lie for an hour and a half, with everybody in the court knowing what was going on. It was a joke! I went to the Premier personally and argued the case for letting it come to a vote. I tried to convince him that the system was bringing the law into disrepute and that he should allow Harry Worton's resolution to come to a free vote. I knew it would pass. In a free vote, it would have been a landslide. He did not particularly disagree with me, but just shook his head. Bringing the divorce law into modern times would cause huge opposition from Catholics. He didn't want to raise a storm he didn't have to raise – in this case, particularly among Catholics who'd protested so hotly over the inter-faith adoption legislation. When I was finished talking he just let me know that he would not budge. He said quite simply that it was something that did not have to be addressed right then, and, "when in doubt, my policy is don't do it."

When a vote was called on the resolution, he used his muscle; every Tory member was ordered by the party whip to vote against. From the *Globe*, February 23, 1966:

Mr. Eagleson and Mr. Kerr faced the jeers of Opposition members as they voted with the government against an immediate vote on the [divorce] resolution. Mr. Eagleson squirmed in his seat trying to hide an embarrassed grin with one hand. When the time came to vote he got to his feet with a hand still over his face.

I hated doing that. In later years when I had become more sure of myself, I would have refused. But in the legislature you either vote with the government or you leave the party caucus. I wasn't ready for that.

The *Globe and Mail*'s editorial page cartoon that day showed George Kerr and me with a legislature bench broken over our heads. Documents labelled "Divorce speech" were scattered around our feet. In the background John Robarts, whom the cartoon suggested had broken the bench over our heads, scowlingly glanced back at us as he stomped off. Reporters caught up to him in the corridors to ask if he would let the resolution come up again later in the session. He gave no such assurance and stuck to it.

I've had to wonder from time to time about where my political career might have taken me if circumstances had been different. I suppose that if Robarts had appointed me to his cabinet in 1965, my life might have been different. That was the year when the first of the members I'd broken in with, Darcy McKeough, made it into cabinet. But there are wheels within wheels. Merit is only one of the essentials. Another is, what region do you come from and represent.

Les Rowntree, a veteran cabinet minister, held the constituency next to me. It wouldn't likely happen that two cabinet positions would go to one small section of a city. I don't think that John Robarts ever had foreseen that he was going to face a decision of that sort. The Tories, after all, had practically counted me out against Murray Cotterill in 1963. So when I won and might have been considered for cabinet, the simple regional fact of being next door to cabinet minister Les Rowntree got in the way. I thought about it. I talked about it. The argument I heard was, you have to remember that Les Rowntree is your next door neighbour. When Les is gone you will be in there. My argument to myself was that I was as capable as any of them and better than most. If I had been premier, looking at me with cabinet in mind, I certainly would have appointed me to *something*. Every time there was a cabinet shuffle in the offing and the newspapers would assess the likelies, I got glowing reviews. If there'd ever been an award for the best candidate for cabinet that never made it, I would have been a shoo-in.

I wasn't the only one consistently overlooked. Allan Lawrence was a constant gadfly to our party. If he'd been a yes-man a place in cabinet would have come earlier, I'm sure. Long after he should have been in the cabinet, he did make it as mines minister, and later he lost only by a few votes for the leadership of the party against Bill Davis.

Earlier than that when I saw Darcy go in, then Tom Wells, one of my best friends then and since, and Gordon Carton, and I was always right at the top of the list of guys who didn't make it, I began to think, well, I can't depend on politics for my career. If there ever was a crossroads for me, that might have been it. And it all became academic when I lost the 1967 election to the NDP's Pat Lawlor and had to decide whether I was content to have been a one-term wonder.

During the year after my defeat, while I was still having withdrawal pains, another political job came up, but at a different level. The Ontario Progressive Conservative Association, at the time a really tired-blood outfit, was overdue for a transfusion. For twenty-five years our party had won every provincial election, usually without any kind of real fight. The Liberals had been nowhere all that time. The CCF, predecessor of the NDP, had come close in 1943 but never since. Such walkaways don't build political muscles. A lot of us, both winners and losers from 1967, felt that the largely lackadaisical constituency approach was going to be fatal for the party down the road. The process needed jazzing up and this looked like a good time. The party

president, Elmer Bell of Exeter (which is near London, which
in turn was home base of Premier John Robarts and almost
everybody else of significance in the party hierarchy), was
intending to step down in November. His replacement had
to be a different kind of guy.

I was pretty sure I'd never run for public office again,
but this was different, a party matter. A couple of party
establishment people had already declared. Either one of
them would have meant more of what we'd been getting – domination by a London-based old guard. It wasn't
that I needed the work. I don't remember even considering,
if I win how am I going to fit all this in? I was more and
more deeply involved with the growing NHLPA. My law
practice kept growing. My family should have been getting
more, instead of less, of my time. But I figured I could
handle whatever came.

When I decided to go for it, the *Telegram* greeted me
with a top-of-the-page headline:

Rebels Force Ontario PC Struggle

"A bitter struggle for the powerful job of president of the
Ontario Progressive Conservative Party shaped up today with
a 'rebel' group's plan to nominate former Lakeshore MPP
Alan Eagleson," political specialist Eric Dowd's story ran.
"The group is unhappy with the party's London-based
establishment, and thinks the PCs should have more of an
urban tinge and a much bigger appeal to young people."

That was published September 30. For the next five weeks
I was in the middle of hockey, law, and a hot campaign
on foot and by phone across the province. I got plenty of
arguments. I enjoyed it. It was no shoo-in, but on November
5, after a three-day convention that drew about 2,000 delegates
and observers, I won on the first ballot. The margin was
just barely what you might call comfortable – 439–345.
Among those who came to shake my hand was Robert
Stanfield, elected a year earlier as national Tory leader. At

thirty-five, I read in the papers, I was the youngest president the party ever had.

I don't remember how Nancy greeted this. But for once I knew that I couldn't do it all *myself*. In my acceptance speech I told the party that what we needed was a full-time executive director of the Ontario PC Association. I even said that I had somebody in mind – Arthur Harnett from the newsroom of radio station CFRB – but hadn't offered him the job yet because I couldn't presume to do that until I won.

But right away I did offer him the job, and he accepted. His job was to organize a travelling Tory road show that I and a few others had in mind. We all would feed ideas into it, looking for headlines every weekend. Our target areas were local constituency organizations, if we could find any still alive.

My idea was basically to reorganize Tory voters or even prospects in a way similar to how I had organized the NHL players – team by team then; constituency by constituency now.

This meant being in daily touch with Harnett from wherever I was on hockey or law business, doing some of the barnstorming myself, and especially getting all the help I could from like-minded political missionaries. It was fun. We were a lively bunch. Okay, we'd say, heading for a new constituency, how will we stir these guys up? At what we called beef sessions, we'd purposely try to make people mad. The evidence indicated that we pretty well succeeded. One early headline read: "Tories' Eagleson raising Old Guard hackles."

Allan Lawrence, the mines minister, didn't raise anything so mundane as hackles. He faced the first session of the Windsor and District Conservative Council (which we had just formed, an area taking in several constituencies in which the Tories didn't have a single seat, federally or provincially), and said, "The Progressive Conservative Party is dead from the eyeballs both ways as far as organization is concerned."

That got their attention.

Almost every weekend somewhere in the province Al Lawrence, Municipal Affairs Minister Darcy McKeough, myself, and others were projecting a different kind of Toryism and getting headlines. But, a big but, by the time I won the presidency of the PC Association and hired Harnett, NHLPA work had doubled from six teams to twelve. Then the league added two more teams, to make fourteen. Orr was winning hockey awards and lucrative off-ice contracts. I was actively practising law and had been appointed to the board of Hockey Canada. All this added up to seven-day weeks, twelve-hour days, rarely spending leisure time (what leisure time?) with my wife and family, always on the run. Within a year or two we had the PCs organized into a smoothly functioning unit that was a lot of the reason for the party's new leader, Premier Bill Davis, winning the province again for the PCs in 1971.

I think that in the lull after that 1971 election, after being in the midst of such frantic activity really for years, I finally got all this overpowering *busyness* of my life in focus, at least to my own satisfaction. Maybe I was going somewhere and thinking about leaving my family behind, or coming back from somewhere and looking forward to the homecoming. Anyway, suddenly I was thinking along a new line, for me: I was going in too many directions and enjoying them, and I didn't really want to drop anything, but I wasn't doing enough about my family. I was spreading myself too thin – and it wasn't hard to count the ways. That was more than twenty years ago when, on that accurate realization of what I was doing with my life, I resolved that I must change what could be changed.

The first change maybe doesn't sound like much, but it was a start: from then on, I decided, I would avoid work on weekends, that henceforth weekends would be for the family. Around that time, maybe a little later, we asked Allen to retire from team hockey in Toronto because his games and practices impinged too much on our family weekends.

As Jill and Allen grew up and branched out on their own, this continued to mean that Nancy and I spend weekends together, summer and winter, near Collingwood. Or we simply stay at home in Toronto. We like Toronto on weekends in the summer, even though in the city there's sometimes the risk that I'll find some excuse to drop in at the office. At least I came to know that is the wrong thing to do.

One thing is sure–over the years I have kept a lot of amateur psychoanalysts off the welfare rolls. Their learned analyses in print and on radio and TV, even in a few books, you might have read. I read the stuff myself just in case I ever need any clues as to who the hell I am, anyway.

They tend to come up with such labels as "compulsive leader" (this sometimes comes out "dictator"), workaholic, impatient, pragmatic, a perfectionist. One inclination in the people-analysing line of work, amateur or professional, is that all such practitioners tend to put people in neat pigeon-holes and say, "Stay there. Don't move." Which doesn't suit my operation and never has.

For a while I was a lawyer first and everything else came second. Then hockey gradually came to dominate my life, then politics *and* hockey. In my heart I was never a Johnny-One-Note. When I became involved in organizing hockey players into a union, if they'd been demanding that I devote my time entirely to them, I would have said thanks but no thanks. I've always had certain interests that stood out above the rest, and so has Nancy, but these never were allowed to wipe out other elements that we consider to be the essential spice of our lives: foreign travel, famous and interesting people (two qualities not invariably lodged in the same person), keeping in shape and having fun skiing and playing tennis, watching great tennis at Wimbledon and elsewhere, swimming, going to movies and plays, reading for pleasure.

CHAPTER FIVE

THE ROAD TO
THE 1972 SERIES

"Please explain to the Soviets that Mr. Campbell
is the lawyer for the capitalist owners, I am the
lawyer for the workers."

–the message to Moscow that broke the old logjam.

The hockey series that most Canadians remember most clearly, right up there with falling in love or winning a lottery, was the eight-game series Canada and the Soviets played in 1972, four games in Canada and four in Moscow. The road to that series really began years earlier.

The first time I'd ever been to a world championship was the one in Vienna in early 1967, with Brewer playing for Canada. By 1969 I was beginning to get an idea. It started with a letter from Bob Wood of Winnipeg, a member of a great sporting family that included Bob's father, Canadian curling championship winner Howard Wood. By then I was on the board of Hockey Canada, which had been set up with government involvement to see if we couldn't do better in international hockey, especially world and Olympic championships. Always in earlier years the CAHA would designate some individual club, usually an Allan Cup winner, to get a team together to play in the Olympics or the worlds. We won a few, with the Warwicks' Penticton Vees in 1955, Wren Blair's Whitby Dunlops in 1958, Belleville in 1959, and Trail in 1961, but lost both the 1956 and 1960 Olympics over those years. Bobby Bauer's Kitchener-Waterloo Dutchmen were thwarted by the Soviets in 1956 and four years later a combined Whitby-Kitchener team, again under Bauer, beat the Russians but lost the gold medal to the United States in a fantastic 2–1 game.

That was the background in 1969 when Nancy and I decided that our usual spring trip that year would be to Stockholm for the world championships and then on to Helsinki, Moscow, and Warsaw before coming home.

In the back of my mind, as I told others in Hockey Canada, while I was there I hoped to get something going for the future: a team of NHLers against the Soviets' best. I figured something like that would prove that Canada had the best hockey in the world.

In Stockholm I met people from the various ice hockey federations, including the grand Pooh-Bah of all international hockey, a pompous Englishman named Bunny Ahearne.

Gordon Juckes of the CAHA was helpful, and Bob Wood from Winnipeg had introduced me at long distance to Adolph (Aggie) Kukulowicz, a tall and cheerful Winnipegger who had played some pro hockey. By then Aggie was in charge of the Air Canada office in Moscow and played on the Canadian embassy hockey team there. He had spoken Russian since he was a child and had been in charge of Air Canada's arrangements for flying teams to the world championships so knew people from other European hockey federations. Over the years, I would have hated to try to do what was done, and still is being done, without Aggie always on hand with his rare combination of hockey savvy and various languages.

I met with the Finns, the Swedes, the Czechs, and others. Now, more than twenty years later, I still deal with some of the important hockey people I met then – Miro Subrt from Czechoslovakia and Peo Wester of Sweden among them. I didn't even think until years later of the idea that became the Canada Cup but mainly talked to them about the possibility of bringing an NHL team to Europe. Everything went great until I tried to arrange a meeting with the Russians.

I kept running into brick wall after brick wall. A courtly and friendly man, Arthur Andrew, was Canada's ambassador to Sweden then and I confided to him what I had in mind. Even he couldn't do much about getting me to see the Russians. To them I was an emissary of the professionals, they were amateurs (they claimed), and that was that.

I knew we were going to be in Moscow April 7, 8, and 9 and hoped to get something laid on that we could discuss then. In Sweden in the first few days of April I managed to talk to Andrei Starovoitov, the head of Soviet hockey. With Aggie along to do the translating, Starovoitov and I had a brief talk and he said, yes, he'd meet me to talk about it at nine the following morning. I showed up at the room we'd decided on. Nobody was there except Aggie and me, but there was a message to call Starovoitov. Aggie called and was told that the Soviets wouldn't meet me without the CAHA being present. I called Gordon Juckes of the CAHA and we arranged to meet Starovoitov the next morning, again at nine. Same result: no Starovoitov. I hunted him down at the arena. He just said, "It's impossible for us to meet." He was obviously taking instructions from someone. "We can't meet you. We can only deal with Clarence Campbell, the president of the NHL."

I talked it over with Ambassador Andrew and wrote by Telex to Robert Ford, our ambassador in Moscow, asking him to help set up a meeting with the Soviet Ice Hockey Federation.

He soon replied with the same answer Starovoitov had given me, that they would only meet Campbell. That's where I got smart. I wrote back again: "Dear Mr. Ford. I will be there on April 8. Please explain to the Soviets that Mr. Campbell is the lawyer for the capitalist owners, I am the lawyer for the workers." Open sesame! The next day I got a letter saying that they'd meet us in Moscow at 9 a.m. on April 8. They would put us in the Metropole Hotel, where Aggie's Air Canada office was situated.

Ambassador Ford met us when we arrived and gave us some good advice: "Make sure everything is done in writing. Don't trust anything that is just in words." He also said that two words to remember above all were: "Be patient." We shouldn't expect just to walk in and make any firm arrangements. "It may take a year, it may take five years, but be patient."

That night, April 7, we got back to the hotel and had dinner – the typical Moscow dinner at the Metropole. You start at eight and with lousy service you finish at 11:30, and you have the same thing – the chicken Kiev and the cold potatoes and the fish. (The same meal is being served now as it was on that first trip of mine to the Soviet Union, except there was more on the plate in those days.)

We decided during dinner that in light of Ambassador Ford's advice we should get something typed out. Aggie's secretary wasn't available at that hour, but Nancy can do two-finger typing. We went to Aggie's office where there was a typewriter and I wrote out in longhand, while Nancy typed, a statement headed: Manifesto to the Soviet Union.

We got to bed about 2 a.m. About three in the morning I woke up. I have a lot of allergies and I woke with this terrible itching. I got up and flicked on the light and looked in the bed and saw about twenty bedbugs. I couldn't believe it. They had gone right up my arm and down my body and I had thirty-one bedbug bites; I counted them. I have a little pill box for carrying vitamins and other pills, which I emptied out and put in two of the bedbugs. Now I am steaming mad. I go down to the desk where the key-lady, Mamoshka, sits at all hours. I can't speak a word of Russian and she can't speak English, but she got the drift and kept saying, "Nyet, nyet," as if it couldn't happen here. I go back to the room and get the box of bugs as evidence and finally she gave us another room, and there was no doubt that we were safe from bugs there – the temperature in the room was no more than forty degrees Fahrenheit.

That night was our introduction to Soviet hotel rooms, about twelve feet by ten, one bed along one wall and another along another wall, so there's no chance of cuddling up and staying warm. We damn near froze all night.

We got up the next morning, met the Russians, gave them a copy of our manifesto. It was on old carbon paper that you could hardly read, but we gave it to them. And that, believe it or not, was the start of what became the 1972 series.

Over the next two and a half years, with Hockey Canada and world championships, I started going to the Soviet Union every three months or so just to keep the Canada-Soviet series alive. You might remember that in late 1969, with the 1970 world championships scheduled for Winnipeg, Hockey Canada had arranged with the International Ice Hockey Federation for a change in the IIHF by-laws. Starting in 1970 we could use seven pros. In preparation we took our national team loaded with seven pros on an exhibition tour to Russia and won most of the six games we played. I can't remember everybody on that team, but there were some rough and ready types, including Wayne Carleton and Jim McKenny. In Russia we got into trouble after trouble. Carleton, a big strong boy, busted a window or two on that tour. But I think it was mainly that we won four or five games that made the Russians decide they didn't want any pros. In any event, they got to Bunny Ahearne, who changed the earlier ruling and said we couldn't use any pros. In protest Hockey Canada withdrew from world competition. I guess in the circumstances we had to do it, but I've always regretted that decision. I have found that you can always negotiate better if you are participating. Once you are not participating, well – I guess no country is irreplaceable. There's no sense second-guessing it. What we did was right at the time, although Winnipeg, all geared up, was mad as hell at the cancellation after all the plans they'd made.

And I guess history showed in the end that our dropping out at the time wasn't all that bad in the long run.

Between 1969 and 1972 I kept pushing the Canada-Soviet series idea, and suddenly, after all that work, the dam broke. Charlie Hay was the chairman of Hockey Canada at the time, with Doug Fisher an important member of the board. The 1972 world championships were in Prague that year. I was intending to go over for the last three or four days to help keep my contacts alive. One day just before they were to start Doug Fisher phoned me from Ottawa and said, "I think you should get over there right away, I think something is going to happen and we have to make sure – the Russians have to know that the NHL players will agree." He meant, agree to the big series I'd been working on. That call came, I think, on a Friday. Could I be in Prague at the International Hotel on Monday? It turned out that from Hockey Canada and the CAHA Lou Lefaive, Joe

Kryczka, and Charlie Hay had been meeting with the
Russians and the deal was pretty well set as long as there
was no doubt about the NHL players agreeing.

When I got there I could give that assurance. That's when
I found out the structure of the series – four games in Canada,
four in Moscow, and one in Czechoslovakia after the main
event was over. Some parts of the deal I didn't agree with,
such as mixing European amateur referees in with our more
experienced officials, but the overall deal was good enough
that rather than try to renegotiate or change the deal, it
would be better to ride it out and maybe shift a bit as we
went along. After all, this was basically what we'd been
trying for ever since that day in Moscow when Nancy was
doing her two-finger bit on Aggie's office typewriter.

I held a press conference in Prague to announce that the
NHL players were in. Quite predictably, in twenty-four hours
the response was back from Clarence Campbell – no NHL
player would be permitted to play.

That went on back and forth for a couple of months.
In May I called Bill Wirtz in Chicago, always one of the
most powerful NHL governors, and said, "Let's get together,
I want you to meet Charlie Hay and Doug Fisher and Allan
Scott and some of the others and see if we can't get this
thing settled." Allan Scott then had the title of business
manager of Hockey Canada. He was not my type of guy.
To me, he wanted to be in a big office and delegate everything
to other people and not get in the trenches himself, like
some of the rest of us were. I found this very frustrating
because I was the one who had the commitment from the
players, and he was doing things without me knowing it,
agreeing to things with people who would come to me and
say, "Well, we have a deal with Al Scott."

I would say, well, they didn't have a deal with Hockey
Canada.

Disposal of the TV rights was only one example of his
way of doing things. In June of 1972 he led the CBC and
Hockey Night in Canada to believe they had the rights for

$500,000, which I thought was much too low. When that deal was announced I just said that they might have a deal with Al Scott, but they didn't have one with Hockey Canada. I called Harold Ballard, owner of the Leafs, and we agreed right on the phone that we could go out and sell the series for a lot more money than that. All through June that was an issue, but in the end Ballard and I won by offering $750,000 through a new entity, Ballard-Orr Enterprises, for the rights and then going out and selling commercial time.

But to go back a few weeks to Bill Wirtz, he was great. If it hadn't been for Wirtz and his influence on other governors the whole series might not have happened. In the middle of it, while we were negotiating, I got Clarence Campbell on side with the agreement that, okay, the players can play, but with the stipulation that every player must have a signed contract with his NHL club.

This was a hedge against the fact that the World Hockey Association was just getting into business, luring people from the NHL with big contracts, the main move at the time being Bobby Hull signing a million-dollar contract with Winnipeg. Bill White, for instance, just signed his Chicago contract the day before the Team Canada training camp opened. One of the reasons, maybe the only reason, he didn't jump to the WHA was that he wanted to play for Canada. We lost other players we had named to the team – Bobby Hull, Derek Sanderson, Gerry Cheevers, J.C. Tremblay, Bernie Parent. We lost those five, who would have made a big difference, but we won without them, so I guess we did the right thing.

The main frustration for me in the whole issue was Bobby Hull. I had wheedled and dealt and pushed and shoved and negotiated to the best of my ability to get Bobby Hull on that team, even though he was going to the WHA. By then Harry Sinden had been named the Team Canada coach, with John Ferguson his assistant, and we all agreed that in spite of the WHA thing Bobby Hull had been great for hockey and should be on the team.

"To hell with everything else," we agreed, "let's get him on the team and then somebody will have to kick him off, and they're not going to kick him off if we can get him on the team."

I'd known Harry Sinden in Boston because of Orr. After coaching Boston to the Stanley Cup in 1970 he had left hockey because he'd become sour with the Boston organization. For a couple of years he worked with a construction company in Rochester. When we were talking about who should coach, I wanted somebody I knew, somebody I could trust. Harry was my first choice. When I called him he said, great, and I said you have to keep it secret until I get it through the other powers that be. Mainly we didn't want to get Boston's owner, Weston Adams, all riled up.

Harry did keep it confidential, and with the help of Bill Wirtz and Charlie Mulcahy, the lawyer for the Bruins, we got him okayed by the league. When that was done and we were talking about an assistant coach Harry said, "We should get Fergie," meaning John Ferguson, the tough player who had starred for Montreal and had been out of hockey for a year. Harry wanted him as a playing coach, but Fergie said, "One thing we should get clear, I'm not playing."

It was about that time that we had other decisions to make. The big one was who would be on the team. Another was the name. We had a meeting at the Skyline Hotel and kicked names around. We talked Pro Canada, Canada Pro, and I have no idea who it was and neither has anyone else I've checked, but one of us said, "How about Team Canada?" A lot of people have used that name since, and good luck to them – imitation is the best form of flattery.

Then we had to have a design for a team sweater and that's where Bill Bremner and Terry O'Malley and others from the Vickers and Benson advertising agency helped. They came up with an exploding Maple Leaf design that made a great sweater. I decided later that it was a once-in-a-lifetime series and a once-in-a-lifetime sweater. We had it copyrighted so that nobody else can use it. I felt that the players who were in that series were entitled to be one of a kind.

That is how the team came about, a careful selection of players, some often debated among us, but when we had the list I said, "We are not naming anybody unless they agree to play. We don't want to name somebody who then says, 'up yours,' so what I want you to do, Harry, is take a bunch and Fergie will take a bunch and I will take a bunch and we'll phone them and see what the reaction is. They have to agree to play, and agree not to tell anyone."

So we started phoning.

Bobby Hull was on Harry's list, and he agreed to play. Dallas Smith was one who turned us down. Phil Esposito said he and his brother Tony had a hockey school, but he agreed anyway. The last player named to the team was Bobby Clarke.

In the end that choice came down to Bobby Clarke of Philadelphia or Dave Keon of the Leafs. I remember exactly how it went. Harry was for Keon. He was remembering what Keon had been like a couple of years earlier when Harry was coaching Boston. But Fergie was for Clarke, remembering the Clarke he had seen and played against during Fergie's last year in the league. He said, "Well, what are the stats from last year?"

We looked them up. Clarke had eighty-one points for the 1971-72 season, Keon forty-eight. Fergie said, "You have to go by the stats. And Clarke is our type of player." So Clarke got the nod, and proved himself both during the series and later when he captained Philadelphia to Stanley Cups in 1974 and 1975. He didn't have the best shot in the series but he had the most flash. In attitude he was an economy-size Ferguson. Neither ever learned to back up from anything.

So by late one week in early July we had the team selected, but we were guarding the names jealously. In our phone calls we and every player approached agreed that nobody would say a word about who was on and who wasn't until we made that announcement. If you've got something big to announce, you don't let it out in dribs and drabs. There was one other reason: Bobby Hull. The NHL had bargained with us tough and hard, and one stipulation that affected future contracts and insurance for all NHL players had been that every player we used had to have a signed NHL contract. Chicago Black Hawks claimed that Hull had one with them, but didn't have a really good case as Hull had signed, for $1 million down payment, a contract with the WHA's Winnipeg Jets. For all those reasons we wanted the team announcement to make a big splash. We called a press conference for a Tuesday at Toronto's Sutton Place Hotel to announce the team, introduce the players, and get the splash.

So we were all set until, a few days before the press conference, I got a call from Clarence Campbell. He said, "Alan, there's a story out of Nova Scotia that Bobby Hull has said he is on the team."

That floored us. Apparently at some sports celebrity dinner Hull had either announced it or had let it slip somehow. However it happened, that gave the NHL the weekend they needed to marshal their forces before our press conference. In those few days, the NHL owners decided to play a big card. They said flatly that they wouldn't stop any player from playing but the contracts would no longer be guaranteed in event of injury.

This went right against what we'd been assuring all our players. We'd told them, here's the deal, in these games your NHL contract is what you're playing under, so if you have a two-year contract or a five-year contract or whatever, you are covered in case of injury.

With the NHL ultimatum that in event of injury the contracts would not be guaranteed, we were faced with the option of getting our own insurance to guarantee contracts or leaving Hull off the team. When it came to the press conference, where we now felt we were forced to announce a team without Hull, I told Doug Fisher, "You're going to have to read this announcement and answer for it, you and Charlie Hay, because if I did it I'd be accused of kicking Hull off the team."

If Bobby Hull had not made that comment in advance and we had been able to list his name with the rest of the team at the press conference, there is no way on earth anybody could have kicked him off. The public reaction was furious enough as it was. Even the Prime Minister got involved on Hull's side. The furore was nothing to what it would have been if he had been named first and then the NHL had used that contract-guarantee ploy out of plain self-interest. Sure, the NHL was at its wits' end about the inroads the WHA was making, especially after Hull jumped. On the same grounds that Prime Minister Trudeau used patriotism and motherhood in vain, that Canadians were Canadians and any Team Canada would not be our best without Hull, I simply would not have allowed him to be left off the team. Bobby Orr was the only Canadian player who could be mentioned in the same breath as Hull at the time, and Orr was in no shape to play because he'd had a knee operation and without being able to work out had ballooned to more than 200 pounds. In effect, Hull took himself off the team. He was the only one of the thirty-odd players we called who broke the secrecy code we had asked for and, as it turned out, badly needed.

Long before Team Canada's training camp opened at Maple Leaf Gardens, Ballard and I had sold about $2 million in commercial time and CTV was all set to handle the games. I had gone to the CBC first and talked to a senior executive producer named Thom Benson.

He just sat in his office, not that interested, and told me they might take one game. I couldn't believe it. After that I went immediately to Johnny Esaw, the head of CTV sports. His attitude was the opposite of the CBC's, but he felt it was essential to get an okay from John Bassett, the owner of CTV's flagship station, CFTO. Esaw was in a sense an employee of Bassett. He said, "You call Bassett." I did, and the next afternoon I walked into Bassett's office, with Esaw. Bassett said, "Alan, nice to see you. Sit down. I know why you're here. You've got those rights. You are stuck with them. We will take you off the hook, buy you out, you are okay."

I said, "Wait a minute. That is very gracious but I'm here to buy, not to sell."

"What are you talking about?"

"I want to buy the network," I said. "We are going to run this package, so I need to know about time, line charges, everything about what it's going to cost me to put this thing on television."

Bassett turned to Esaw and asked what he thought.

Esaw already had it figured out. "I think we'd have to get about $1.1 million."

I didn't know very much about TV expenses but I knew Johnny wouldn't cheat me and also wouldn't give a figure to his boss that was incorrect.

I said, "Well, I'm paying $750,000 for rights. If I am going to pay that kind of money, I'll tell you what. How about doing it for a million?"

Bassett took one second. That's how he is. He said, "Alan, you've got a deal. Okay, get out of here and make some money."

Of course, as soon as I made that deal the CBC was all over me, hot to deal. They held a press conference and said, in effect, they'd had a deal with Allan Scott and now Eagleson had messed it up.

To make a long story short, it all worked out. Ballard-Orr Enterprises had paid $750,000 for the television rights, and $1 million for CTV. Arthur Harnett started his sales campaign with assistance from me and Ballard. Harold got Red Foster of Foster Advertising to commit some advertisers. I called Don McDougall at Labatt's, Ross Johnson at Standard Brands, and Dick Thomson at the Toronto-Dominion Bank. Bill Bremner of Vickers and Benson advertising brought Ford into the event.

Harnett eventually sold over $2 million worth of advertising for the eight-game series. All of the Ballard-Orr profit was turned over to Hockey Canada. Ballard-Orr guaranteed $750,000 and paid an additional $350,000 for a total of $1.1 million. All I could remember was that Molson and *Hockey Night in Canada* had made a deal with Al Scott for $500,000 and here we were with $1.1 million instead. It was obvious we had done the right thing.

The entire series, thanks to the profits that Ballard-Orr Enterprises had created, earned a surplus of $800,000, of which half went to Hockey Canada and half went to the NHL owners to be used for pension purposes.

A lot of people have since said, "What happened? Wasn't the profit from the series supposed to go to the players' pension fund?"

The deal was that the owners got their half and in return NHL player pensions would be increased by 40 per cent. The owners, who were responsible for funding the entire cost of the pension, in effect got a free ride that year.

What else? Well, the players were paid $5,000 each plus the right to bring their wives on the trip. Sinden and Fergie were paid I think $10,000 each, and others important in our group, assistants Bobby Haggert and Mike Cannon, could bring their wives if they wished. After the Allan Scott mix-up with the TV rights, the five of us – Sinden, Fergie, Haggert, Cannon, and I – made all the operational decisions. We called ourselves Team Five. If something came up that Hockey Canada had agreed to, or initiated, and I was told about it and it disagreed with my ideas, I would just do it my way. Hockey Canada made an airline deal that I didn't like. I said so. The airline said it had a deal with Hockey Canada. I said, "Well, you have your deal with Hockey Canada, but I am dealing with Team Canada. Do whatever you like, but this team is going on whatever flights I arrange."

To put it mildly, Hockey Canada and CAHA people didn't always like the way we did things. But a comment made two or three years later by Lou Lefaive, head of the government-supported organization called Sport Canada, sums up pretty well how the way we did things looked to him, in retrospect. In 1974 the WHA arranged a similar series with the Russians. Lefaive was part of that trip, too. The hockey was excellent – hockey always is – but from the organizational end, the press room ran all right but a lot of the rest was chaotic. Looking back on it later Lefaive said, "The difference was that in 1972 Eagleson did all the dealing with the Russians. He didn't ask us much that I remember; he would just say, 'Here's what we're going to do – do it!' In 1974 we in the Canadian group spent most of our time arguing with ourselves, when we should have been arguing with the Russians."

I guess a good example of our direct action techniques in 1972 came just before the first game in Montreal on Saturday, September 2. There'd been a big luncheon in Montreal and when I got back to my room there had been a call from External Affairs in Ottawa. I returned the call. The guy from External Affairs said, "Mr. Eagleson, I just wanted to let you know you have a problem."

"Oh, what is the problem?"

"You'd better talk to this lawyer . . . " He gave me a name. "He is acting for someone who has seized the Soviet team's hockey equipment." I called the lawyer. He talked so fast and refused to speak a word of English so it took me a while. My French is not bad but he was talking 100 miles an hour and I was only understanding at eighty miles an hour. Finally I got the drift. He was acting for a young man who had gone to Prague in August, 1968, when the Russian tanks rolled in. One of them rolled right over his rented car. The rental company sued him and recovered $1,500. He wanted his money back.

To push their case, they had seized the Soviet team's hockey equipment!

This threat was discussed very seriously by Hockey Canada, External, and so on, at a meeting, everybody with long faces.

I said, "The guy only wants $1,500, let's give it to him."

"Oh," External said, "we can't do that! Mr. Eagleson, I am instructing you formally, do not make any payment. The Russians were not there as an act of war, we recognize them as having been invited to Prague . . . " Etc. Etc. Both the Soviet and Canadian governments were afraid that if they recognized the claim by paying it, that might bring on a lot more claims. I got all this political claptrap for about ten minutes. I'm thinking, fifteen hundred dollars! And it might hold up what we've been working on for years. By then, I had been on it for months full-time, and now I had people who were spending an hour or two a week on it second-guessing me. I'm not saying anything against, for instance, Doug Fisher, who'd had to take over the top job at Hockey Canada when Charlie Hay got ill back in the middle of the TV rights battle. Doug Fisher has since come to be one of my good friends. Without him I would never have been able to structure the Canada Cup years later. In the 1972 scenario I felt I couldn't trust any of them. I figured they didn't know what the hell they were doing and that I did.

So after that meeting about the Prague case had been going on for a while I said, "Thanks very much," and went to a phone by myself and called the lawyer back and said come on over and pick up the $1,500. I submitted this on my expenses under "miscellaneous" and got my money back. I learned then that any time anybody from the government calls me and says that I have a problem, it means they have a problem they would like to drop on my lap.

Before I forget, among the things that frustrated me and turned me off Hockey Canada at that time, even though I was part of Hockey Canada, was a decision made by the board about tickets to the games in Canada. They decided to have a lottery, with coast-to-coast advertising costing about $100,000, to sell tickets that I knew I could sell in a minute. You wrote in for tickets and if your name was drawn you got your tickets for $15 each whether they were rinkside or up in the rafters. All I know is that a lot of people on the Board of Directors must have had a hell of a lot of luck in the lottery because I didn't see a damn one of them sitting up in the cheap seats.

At the same time I started making as many deals as I could, with whomever I could. I had a friend, Bob Kirby, who was a sales manager at Omega watches. I said, "How about coming up with a special watch, just for this series?" They did, and I got fifty for the Russians and fifty for the Canadian group. We'd grown by then to what some people called Team Fifty. There were thirty-five players (Bobby Orr was coming along and made it thirty-six), then doctors Jim Murray, John Zeldin, and Chuck Bull, trainers Karl Elieff, Tommy Nayler, and Joe Sgro, and Nayler's grandson, who was the stick boy.

I restricted Team Fifty to what I considered to be our family. I had to have people around me I could criticize but who wouldn't quit on me. I knew that if we kept it tight and everybody knew everybody, it would work. A man named Graeme Clark, who worked for Clarkson Gordon, was Hockey Canada's accountant, checking everything that was going on. He impressed me so much that I hired him six months later and he still does work for me. Chris Lang was with Hockey Canada and we became close friends. He was my liaison with Hockey Canada – he was invited to every meeting and kept me informed on what was going on. All this was not done without arguments. Harry Sinden's daughter was the Team Canada secretary. Somebody complained about her being on the payroll. We were paying her $50 a week for working sixty or sixty-five hours. Things like that.

All of us in the inner group met every second morning at Harry Sinden's suite. Chris Lang was at those meetings, too, never missed a meeting. He would go back and tell Doug Fisher and the other Hockey Canada people that I wasn't totally insane, that I was just half insane, and I'm

When I had my first fedora.

Aged two and a half, aiming to carry my dad on my shoulders.

In Guelph when I was eight. With two of my three sisters, Marg (left) and Carol.

My graduation photo, University of Toronto, 1954.

At twenty, I was working as a recreation director at MacTier, Ontario. Here I'm on the beach at Bala Manor.

Lake Kenogami, 1958, after I'd met Nancy Elizabeth Fisk. She is front and centre in this beach shot, with me behind her.

We were married in 1960. I had graduated in law but her salary as a teacher kept us solvent.

In the middle 1960s, with our first-born, Allen and baby Jill.

My dad, Allen Sr., and my mother, Agnes, with our kids.

Christmas at home, about 1966.

At our Lake Couchiching cottage, Allen, Jill, and dog.

The beginnings of our custom of playing together as a family.

Allen with his mother, the dance instructor.

At the same time, I was beginning to spend a lot of time on politics – being elected to the Ontario Legislature as the Progressive Conservative member for Toronto Lakeshore.

Premier John Robarts and I differed on some important issues. I think that my stands in favour of changing to a non-sectarian adoption process, and for reform of the divorce law, helped keep me an also-ran when he was appointing his cabinets.

This is rather a crowded snapshot, which was what life around our Lake Couchiching cottage was like in 1966: I'm on my back at bottom left with three children – Allen, Jill, and another child – sitting on me. To my left, also on his back, is Father David Bauer, who that summer was trying to beef up his Canadian National Team by adding Carl Brewer (on the bottom of the webbed chair) and Bobby Orr, seated behind Brewer, and soon to sign with Boston.

My intervention in a strike of Springfield Indians players got Eddie Shore out of hockey and won their case. With me here in January, 1967, are my law partner Ray Smela (seated at my left), and suspended players Brian Kilrea, Jacques Caron, and Roger Cote (with his trademark toothpick). The Springfield experience was an early skirmish in formation of the National Hockey League Players Association.

Orr's first contract with Boston, the best ever for a rookie in hockey, was signed on Hap Emms' lake cruiser near Barrie early in September, 1966. Photographer Red Favero was on hand with his camera. The following summer Orr and I played on the same ball team in Orillia, got into a fight together, and soon were being described as inseparable.

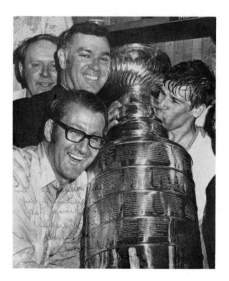

When Orr won his first Stanley Cup with Boston in 1970, I was in the dressing room. He wrote on the bottom of this photo: "Al and Nancy and kids. Your friendship is as treasured as winning the Stanley Cup. Sincere best wishes, Bobby." Later Red Berenson, who'd played on the losing St. Louis team in that series, said I shouldn't have been celebrating with Orr when other members of the NHLPA, including Red, had been among the beaten. I didn't make that mistake again.

sure that was what they must have thought because often I was going public condemning what they were doing.

Some didn't like me, and said so, because I ignored them. One of those was the late Joe Kryczka, president of the CAHA. He used to say that he and Doug Fisher and Charlie Hay had done all this and who the hell was I to be talking at all. I would just say, "Hey, if you guys want to run it, good luck. Who is going to play? If it's your tournament, count me out. But I'll tell you one thing, the players aren't going anywhere unless I say so and if you want to test it, call them."

Needless to say, it wouldn't have happened, but I wasn't going to put my credibility with the players at risk by having those other guys in charge. I trust Bill Wirtz so he became one of the inner circle. Clarence Campbell sat in finally but he still didn't like the fact that the players were even playing, so mostly he left it to Bill Wirtz to speak for the league.

During this period I was dealing not with Bunny Ahearne of the IIHF, we'd bypassed him nicely, but with a Soviet named Alexander Gresko, who was my counterpart doing the negotiating for the Russian side. This brought about one incident that didn't look good later from an RCMP standpoint. I had a call from Ottawa. Would I bring Gresko there to meet Prime Minister Trudeau in his office? So we met there and had pictures taken. Later it came out the British had kicked Gresko out eight years or so earlier as being one of the top KGB people attached to the Soviet embassy in London. When I found out about Gresko, I thought, is that RCMP efficiency? This was the man who'd been wandering around Trudeau's office taking pictures.

Which reminds me. That summer I invented a person named Ivan Slobotnik. I used Ivan fairly often on Gresko. Anytime I was having trouble with the Soviet side I would murmur darkly, "I am going to speak to Ivan Slobotnik about this. He'll help solve the problem." Or: "Wait until

I tell Slobotnik what you are doing. He will be very upset with you." Or: "That's it! I am going to have Slobotnik set up a meeting with your foreign minister."

The only ones in on the joke were Sinden, Ferguson, Haggert, Cannon, and I. For four months, from July through October, we kept the story going. Ivan was invoked in almost every meeting, one way or another, and sometimes it was hard to keep from laughing. Each of us used his name as if he were a person of consequence. The Soviet bureaucracy is such that he *could* have been, for all they knew.

Not until the series was over did Alexander Gresko ask me, "Alan, please, I like to meet your friend Ivan Slobotnik." I told him that, unfortunately, was impossible because Ivan had been transferred on a special mission to a foreign country.

CHAPTER SIX

FOUR IN CANADA, FOUR IN MOSCOW

"We've got an old rowboat that is leaking like a sieve . . . we are either going to start rowing to shore together or start hitting each other over the head with the oars, which is what we're doing now."

— my message to the team before leaving Sweden for Moscow.

Almost everybody in Canada, followers of hockey or not, knows what happened once the games started. They were all sellouts, of course, and the hockey was exciting, but in the first game we scored two quick goals and then the Russians just took over and slathered us, 7–3.

I guess my patriotism boiled over, not for the last time in that series. I met a man from External Affairs in the corridor. He said, "Gee, Al, these Russians are pretty good." I told him to get the hell out of my way. I will never forget standing in the Montreal Canadiens' dressing room with Harry and Fergie, Mike Cannon, Bobby Haggert, the original Team Five. We were demoralized, depressed. I hate to think about it even now. We had goofed up every way possible. The score was bad enough, but also we'd played chippy, belligerent hockey. For a lot of people the final stupidity was that we'd left the ice immediately at the end of the game without bothering about the traditional lineup and handshakes. I saw the Russians waiting, saw our players going off, and ran to the dressing room but I was too late. That was among the things we were criticized for in the papers and everywhere else. Even Doug Fisher criticized us. Harry probably should have realized, he'd played international hockey himself, but he'd left the bench a few seconds before the end of the game to compose himself before meeting the team in the dressing room.

After the game when we on the team had a lot on our minds, I certainly didn't appreciate the Hockey Canada people dumping on us when they hadn't done anything, either, to avoid that one mistake. That's when the split between Team Canada and Hockey Canada really widened. We had enough troubles without people on our side carving us. I know in the next two days, before the second game, I was thinking, "Damn it, we're being ridiculed by the public and in the press, we're getting hammered on the ice, even Clarence Campbell was saying we'd played the wrong lineup and let down the NHL . . . we've got big troubles."

One problem, of course, was that press and hockey people alike had specialized in picking Team Canada to win eight straight. Ken Dryden, who'd been in goal in Montreal, had a line for the post-game blues in his book on that series, *Face-Off At The Summit*: "The Eight-Straight gang was one down now and in desperate trouble." Deserters from the earlier Team Canada bandwagon were bailing out, almost to a man.

What nobody took into account was that among first-rate professionals there is a matter of pride, and that pride is never whetted more effectively than when it is being blasted unceasingly in public, with a chance coming up right away to restore it. I worked hard that weekend, and so did Harry. We got into the malarkey role as much as we could. We had lots of help – the incredibly bad press, Campbell was lambasting us, the whole world against this team. We were telling them incessantly that the way out was to jam the scorn right back in their faces with a win.

It was a different team in more ways than one that skated out in Toronto two days after the Montreal loss. There were changes on the defence, with Bill White, Pat Stapleton, and Serge Savard added, and Wayne Cashman, Bill Goldsworthy, Stan Mikita, and J.P. Parise were new on the forward lines. Tony Esposito replaced Dryden in goal.

The big New York line of Rod Gilbert, Vic Hadfield, and Jean Ratelle was dropped, which caused the first sign of dissension. Hadfield had left the practice that day, deeply annoyed at being left off the team. His fifty goals for New York that season had made him think he was unbenchable. His linemates, Ratelle and Gilbert, came to me and said that Hadfield had talked to them about them all packing it in and going home. I said, "Well, I don't think you should. I'm not the coach. Talk to Harry or Fergie." But Jean Ratelle said, "I'm staying, don't worry about me." Gilbert was more disconsolate. I told him, "Let's sit together on the plane for Winnipeg and we'll talk it over."

The changes that night did make it a different team, especially with Cashman and Parise working in the corners. Phil Esposito scored first, then Yvan Cournoyer, but with Clarke off for slashing Alexander Yakushev, made it 2–1. Then Stapleton took one for slashing and we were two men short. The Russians poured in on Tony Esposito. They had chances enough to tie the game and maybe even go ahead, and who knows what would have happened after that. But then, still short-handed, Pete Mahovlich picked up a pass from Phil Esposito and moved this way and that way with his long reach and then he was around the defence, skated in on Vladislav Tretiak in the Soviet goal, gave some great fakes, and slid a backhander past Tretiak. Frank Mahovlich scored later to make the final score 4–1.

That put everybody in better spirits. Rod Gilbert and I talked, as we'd planned. "I hope you're feeling better now," I said to Gilbert. He was. "I signed on for the duration," he said. "If they want me I'll be ready and if they don't want me that means we're winning and I'll be happy."

That wasn't the last bit of trouble. Far from it. Starovoitov had been angry at the Toronto refereeing (Steve Dowling and Frank Larsen, both Americans).

Our pre-series agreement had been that the referees had to be IIHF amateurs. The Russians could select the referees for games 1, 3, 6, and 8. We'd name them for the others, but we agreed this deal could be reviewed after the second game. Starovoitov wanted the first-game referees, Len Gagnon and Gordie Lee, back for both the third and fourth games. There was no problem about the Winnipeg game, their choice, but under our agreement, Canada was supposed to name the referees for the fourth game in Vancouver. In Winnipeg before the third game, Starovoitov phoned us after midnight, wanting assurances that they could have Lee and Gagnon for game 4. I talked to Harry and Fergie. We'd been happy enough with Lee and Gagnon, so we said okay; if we needed the referees to beat them there was something wrong with us. So I told Starovoitov okay, figuring this was a favour and maybe we'd want one in return sometime. That was a mistake. I didn't fully realize it then, but off the ice their game is brinkmanship diplomacy. Having a deal, like we'd had, you should just dig in your heels.

In Winnipeg we might have won, had two-goal leads twice, but they scored two goals in the last four minutes of the second period to tie 4–4 in a great hockey game. Then it was on to Vancouver.

The result of the fourth game, though, had nothing to do with the referees. We were never even close. The crowd began to boo us *before* the game. They booed Frank Mahovlich for sitting on Tretiak for a few seconds during one play. They booed Goldsworthy on two penalties he took, cross-checking and elbowing. We had changed the lineup a little – Dryden back in goal, Hadfield and Gilbert back in the lineup, but when it was over, 5–3 for them, Harry just said, "The score was closer than the game."

After that game Phil Esposito was on television. He blasted the Canadian press, the Canadian public, and everyone else he could think of for the way Team Canada was being treated.

His message was that all these Canadian players had given up their vacations to play this series, were doing their best, giving their all, and did not deserve to be treated this way. "These Russians are great hockey players," he said. "Why not give them credit and stop blaming us?" I chipped in, too, with a blast about the booing Vancouver fans, which I hope by now Vancouver has forgiven me for.

So that was the Canadian tour: two wins for the Soviets, one for us, one game tied – and now four games coming up on the Russians' home ice. Starovoitov got me a message through Aggie Kukulowicz that they'd like to see me after the Vancouver game about arrangements for Moscow, ice time for practice, and so on. Of course, I'm lower than a snake's belly and they are as high as kites – although they didn't really show it. We got through what our setup would be in Russia. When the tough part of business was over they loaded me down with twenty or so jars of caviar, their best vodka, champagne, you name it, three big boxes of goodies. That was the kind of thing they'd do, tough as hell in a meeting, and then that kind of a surprise at the end – things that sometimes knocked me off balance.

Back in Toronto when I had time to think about the big picture, I kept hearing what Phil Esposito had said on television. A lot of us will never forget it, Esposito with the sweat pouring down. We needed somebody to say what Phil said. I think a lot of people in Canada listened to him and finally thought, these players are in trouble, we should be helping them. When Phil Esposito made that impassioned straight-from-the-heart speech, it changed the whole way Canadians were looking at us. At that moment Phil, a great player who'd always been second banana – to Bobby Hull in Chicago and then to Bobby Orr in Boston – no longer was anybody's second banana. He had become the leader on one of the greatest hockey teams ever put together, and he was going to show it in Moscow.

In terms of fan reactions, player reactions, a little mild infighting with Starovoitov and company, and the often irascible conflict between Team Canada and Hockey Canada, the first four games had their good points and their bad points. In a sense it was a training camp for me and everybody else. After those games we knew that the fans were with us, win or tie. Pride-related tensions among the players we'd been more or less prepared for, but not on the scale we eventually faced. Maybe there could not have been any other result when you have thirty-five of the best hockey players in the NHL competing for nineteen lineup places per game. In differences with Hockey Canada, we declared a policy of "no surrender" and more or less made that stick. The matter of dealing with the Soviets *off* the ice we'd managed to keep pretty well on an even keel in Canada. When we left Canada it didn't take long before we were embattled off the ice as well as on.

The plan had been for both teams to take a rest before the second half of the series in Moscow. The Soviets hadn't wasted a minute. They flew from Vancouver to Montreal, then home and right back into training. Our plan couldn't be that rigid: we'd built in a week of home rest for everybody before we assembled at Labatt's brewery near the Toronto airport and caught a plane for Stockholm. Stockholm? On a trip that Team Five had made to Europe that summer to check out all arrangements, we'd decided on a stopover in Stockholm to get acclimatized in various ways, including time zones and European referees. We'd figured on a couple of tuneups against the Swedish nationals, which would send us on to Moscow raring to go.

Instead, Stockholm was close to disaster.

Before our first exhibition there, I had a call from a quite senior and responsible player. Could he come and talk to me? Sure. Could he bring along a couple of others? Sure. I'm not naming them. Maybe I would except that every one of them stuck to the end, some playing exceptionally well, none being among the players who did soon fly home from Moscow. In fact, I'm grateful to those players. They did come to see me instead of bitching and brooding where it would infect others even more than was already the case.

These three players came into my room in Stockholm and told me that they and some of the other players had been saying that the way things were going, we wouldn't win another game.

I said, "Who are we talking about? We might as well get them all in here." So in came three or four more, mostly senior players, people I knew well. They were frustrated. Some of their complaints were legitimate, including things Harry and Fergie and I had said or done as well as general attitudes they didn't like at the team management level.

Apparently because of our years together in the players' association, these few felt they could trust me not to go straight to the coaches and blow the whole thing wide open. I listened for nearly two hours. Of those players, three ultimately played very important roles in the next four games, but of course we couldn't know that at the time.

When they were finished talking, I replied with a statement about what this team was all about, who we represented – Canada for one thing and the NHL for another – and I said, "if there is still one among you who thinks we're not going to win another game, I'd like you to get out of here. I have enough trouble without losers. If you think we will lose, then it's for sure, we will lose. I'm willing to listen to you and do what I can for you, but if we lose every goddamn game, I'll go into the last game vowing we're going to win. Unless you are prepared to believe that, then you can save a lot of time – just get going back to Canada right now."

The team went out that night against a good Swedish team, half a dozen of whom later played in the NHL. They were so good against us that I thought maybe the Team Canada players who had come to see me were right, that we weren't going to win another game. But that night we played a lot of guys who hadn't played much, if at all, in Canada – Brian Glennie, Dale Tallon, Eddie Johnston, Mickey Redmond, Marcel Dionne – and they played great hockey. We won 4–1, but the next day the press reaction (including from some Canada reporters) was vicious. The Swedish writers especially said *we* were brutal, gangsters, murderers. They couldn't find enough nasty names to throw at us. They didn't then or later ever notice the many times our players were fouled.

In the second game Cashman got a badly gashed tongue when speared in the mouth by Ulf Sterner, who didn't get a penalty. Lars-Erik Sjoberg took a cross-check across the nose that made all the front-page pictures, although he was walking around after the game while Cashman (without any newspaper pictures) couldn't even eat and was in hospital being fed through a tube. It went on and on – the papers had a field day over Hadfield cross-checking Sterner on the

face, nobody mentioning that just before that Sterner had
pole-axed a couple of our guys. Not that one should have
resulted in the other, but there were lots of things going
on that the referees ignored while, with the frantic approval
of the crowd, they were giving us thirty-one minutes in
penalties to only four minutes for the Swedes. That high-
lighted the worst omen from our standpoint. The referees
were two Germans, Joseph Kompalla and Franz Baader,
who were going to referee some of the Moscow games. Not
all their bad calls were against us, but that didn't help our
peace of mind, either.

In the last minutes of the second game Esposito scored
a shorthanded goal to tie the game 4–4. The pass from Tallon
to set up the goal was fifteen feet offside. We all saw that,
grateful as we were to get a tie. The referees never batted
an eye. Anyway, we *stole* that tie, and I was the first to
admit it.

Then, of course, there was politics. Canada's ambassador
to Sweden, Margaret Meagher, apparently had been primed
by reports of rough play in Canada as well as what she
saw in Sweden. She came out and blasted our team, said
we played like animals. I don't remember what I said in
reply, but Ken Dryden wrote later that I told her, not politely,
to mind her own business. Smooth passages obviously were
not for us.

All this time, although we'd beaten and tied a pretty good
Swedish team, certainly not looking like world beaters, I
kept thinking about the group who had come to see me
earlier. I had kept that confidential, apart from telling Harry
and Fergie some of the complaints, without names or much
else in the way of detail. I was still stewing about it. At
the end of our last practice in Sweden I went into the dressing
room and called a team meeting of everyone – players,
doctors, coaches, trainers, everybody. I had set this up for
a room at the arena where there were Cokes and coffee,
a sort of team lounge.

I told them in the dressing room, "We'll get the arena staff out and close the doors and we're going to stay in there until we solve a few problems."

This was done. First, I announced that when we got to Moscow the wives would be there.

"Now," I said, "one other item. Six players in this room came to my room the other night and said they were speaking for three or four more, and I'm sure they were, and told me they were convinced that we can't win a game in Moscow unless there are some major changes.

"I just have to tell you this. There are going to be no changes! We are stuck with what we have, with the five of us running this from the management side, and you players, and right now we have a choice. There's still a lot of crying on this team. Too much! As far as I'm concerned we've got to get this crying over and done with.

"We've got an old rowboat that is leaking like a sieve, and our choice is this. We are going to need every man. With this old rowboat we are either going to start rowing to shore together or start hitting each other over the head with the oars, which is what we're doing now. If enough of us get to the oars and start rowing and the others start bailing, we're going to make it. Otherwise we're going down, and we're all going down together. As far as I'm concerned, if you don't want to row this boat to shore, get out now. Don't come to Moscow. Let me know how you feel."

Everybody took this in. Nobody opted right then for abandoning ship. As it turned out later in Moscow, not everybody was convinced.

The first to go was Hadfield. The fifty goals he'd scored for New York the season before were very much in his mind. In Canada he had played two games without scoring and with a total of four shots at the goal, two of them on the net. Really, no coach could ignore that. He'd scored once in Sweden. After his first threat to leave the team in Toronto, he'd seemed to be in a mixture of good and bad moods as he went along. But the crunch came at our first workout in Moscow.

When Harry was making up line combinations, Hadfield wasn't on any of them. That was a mistake, an unfortunate but honest mistake that Harry had made. If it had been any player but Vic, there would have been no problem. With that crowd of players, it is easy to imagine someone being overlooked.

Fergie noticed that. He went to Harry, who said Hadfield should take turns on line rushes with other left wingers among the spares. When Fergie relayed that, Hadfield said he didn't have to take that crap and sat on the bench reading a newspaper. At that point Harry went to him. You can imagine the pressure on Harry, too. He didn't apologize, but told Hadfield that sitting there reading a newspaper looked a little silly. They argued back and forth. Harry told Vic he wasn't playing well enough to make a place on the team, and that a player basically played his way on or off the team. Maybe he'd thought Hadfield would get mad and go out and show him, I don't know.

I got to the practice late, after a go with the Soviet organizers. Hadfield, sitting there, said flatly, "Eagle, get me out of here. I'm not staying." I said, "Hey, calm down, we need you." But he wasn't in the mood. He asked me if I didn't think he was better than Dennis Hull or J.P. Parise. I told him it was his problem to convince the coach that he was better. That didn't do any good. He wanted the first flight out. I pointed out that his wife had just arrived with the other wives. Shouldn't he wait and think about that before he made his decision? "I've thought about it. Get me out of here."

That was it, for me. I went to Mike Cannon and told him to get on to Air Canada and get the Hadfields out as fast as he could. That was set in motion. But we weren't out of the woods. Hadfield talked to Dennis Hull and Rod Gilbert and others, telling them they should leave, too, they weren't playing, etc., etc. Most of them just said they were staying but Jocelyn Guevremont also left. Too bad about Hadfield. He had a lot of hockey in him if he'd chosen to use it, but as in the case of Bobby Hull being dropped from the team, this was substantially Hadfield's own doing. His angry departure just at the time when public opinion was about to swing over to our side caused headlines in Canada that he had to live with for a while.

The four games in Moscow could be summarized in two ways, what happened on the ice and what happened behind the scenes. The game results make a short summary. The behind-the-scenes material takes a little longer, so we'll start with that.

Confrontations became a daily occurrence once we landed in Moscow. We'd even had a foretaste in Sweden. The day before our last game in Sweden, word came through that there were no hotel rooms reserved for the wives of players and others in what we called Team Fifty. I don't remember how we got that word, but it was a portent of psychological warfare to come. Through our Swedish ambassador, who didn't like us much, if at all, I advised the Soviet Ice Hockey Federation that if the situation was not remedied pronto we would not be travelling to Moscow and the four games there would not be played. Suddenly the rooms were available. What had been "not possible" in our first communication on the subject suddenly became "no problem."

From then on those two phrases came up on a daily basis. If something was all right, it was "no problem." If it was not all right, it was "not possible." There was nothing in between those two positions – at least nothing we didn't have to fight for.

When we turned up at the Luzhniki Ice Palace, which included two arenas, one small and the other big, the Soviets told me that our dressing room would be in the small arena. I had a look at what they were offering and said, "No way," which soon became my version of their "not possible." We argued for twenty minutes. They relented. That was the good news. The bad news was that the dressing room we did get was still a long way, I once figured more than 150 yards, from the ice. Our players had to walk 50 yards from the ice, turn left, and go more than 100 yards down a dank, dreary corridor to a stinky, smelly, small dressing room.

At first, it was full of junk. When we tried to remove it, we were informed by a burly police or militia we couldn't move anything. We solved that problem by coming back late at night and clearing it out, leaving everything in the hallway.

The next confrontation was on rooms. The wives, going to their rooms, had found that all beds were perpendicular to one another rather than side by side, where they could be pushed together. When the players got there they fixed things on their own, pulling the beds away from the walls and putting them side by side in the centre of each room. The hotel manager informed me that this change would cost us another fifty rubles for the stay! After a lot of hot arguing, we lost that one and agreed to pay the extra fifty for each room for the duration of our stay.

Meals were another problem. In an earlier visit we had been assured of a separate dining room for players and wives. But the food was the same as was served elsewhere – hard-boiled eggs, bread, jam, some thick peach juice for breakfast. We had foreseen some of that and had shipped our own kind of food, juice, soft drinks, and beer. Now we were told that the hotel would only keep some of our supplies in refrigerated rooms. The rest would be stored elsewhere. They brought a limited amount of our food to use each day.

After a few days it became clear that what we were getting was not enough. I then met with Gresko and arranged for all our food to be shipped to the hotel so that we'd have proper servings of what we wanted. At that point they said, "Very sorry, not possible," that our beer and Coca-Cola and other stuff that had been stored outside of the hotel was no longer there. They didn't know how that had happened, but it had been "stolen."

After a lot of my ranting and raving suddenly they found some of the beer and some of the soft drinks but we never did track down the big supply of steaks that, through a friend, Frank Bonello, had been shipped to us by Canada Packers. As a result our gang had to live on rubber pork and rubber veal and rubber chicken from then on. Fortunately they were able to wash it down with Labatt's Blue and Coke.

That wasn't the only thievery. When we left our locker room after a practice or game all our sticks, skates, and other essential equipment were thought to be safe enough behind a locked door. We were supposed to have the only key to the lock. Still, every night stuff was disappearing, including several sticks and skates. We finally had to mount a twenty-four-hour vigil. Someone from our training staff watched during the day. For night duty we hired a young Soviet who worked part-time at the Canadian embassy and had him sleep in our dressing room. After that, whoever was doing the thieving left our goods alone.

Then there was practice time. It seemed that whenever we arrived for our appointed practice time, the ice was unavailable. It was either a fifteen-minute wait or a twenty-minute wait and sometimes they said it was simply not available, that it was being used by school children. The first time this happened was at the Luzhniki Sports Palace on the morning after game 5. Our practice time was supposed to be 10 a.m. Now it was 9:55, our team was out of the dressing room ready to go, and the ice was full of kids. I went for the nearest Russian official I could find and demanded that the ice be cleared right then so we could get on with our workout. All I got was a shrug, the "Not possible" line, and that the kids on the ice weren't finished and couldn't be moved. I solved that one by getting Dennis Hull and Rod Gilbert to throw a couple of pucks on the ice and practise their slap shots.

After a few booms off the end boards, the wide-eyed kids – it wasn't their fault – were shepherded hastily off. But that kind of harassment, not having our practice ice ready when we were ready, still kept on happening now and then.

The next confrontation was on tickets to various Moscow events. We'd been advised that the wives, because they'd paid tourist charter rates, would get tickets to the Moscow Circus, ballet, Kremlin, and other standard tourist stops. There were none for the players.

The Soviet Ice Hockey Federation said they didn't have the money to pay for player tickets. I asked how much this would cost. They said 300 rubles per player. With thirty-five players, we were looking at about 10,500 rubles. This was approximately $15,000–$20,000 Canadian. I had no intention of paying that much but thought I'd have some fun negotiating with them. Over two days I got it down to 100 rubles per player. Then I offered fifty. We finally settled at sixty, or a little more than $3,000 Canadian.

Having done that well at negotiations, I decided to take it one step further: to the black market, one of the great no-nos in the Soviet Union. There I found I could get five or six rubles for every dollar, and eventually for about $300 Canadian I obtained rubles to cover the player tickets. When I started to pay in rubles they said, "Oh, no, Mr. Eagleson. The tickets can only be paid for in foreign currency." I pulled out some tickets to the circus, marked around five or six rubles each, and said, "Then someone must be telling lies because these tickets were bought with rubles."

They argued. I said I would have to take the matter to our ambassador. They quickly agreed to take the rest of the cost in my black market rubles. I never heard another word about it. I think they were trying to pull a fast one to get Canadian currency from an unsuspecting tourist. When they found they didn't have an unsuspecting tourist in their clutches, that was that.

Tickets to the games brought approximately the same difficulties, except that the game tickets were more important to us. The wives had tickets as part of their tourist packages, so that was no problem. But many people who arrived in Moscow, friends of mine or the players or others with the team, wanted to see the games. That happens in every major sporting event, everywhere – people involved, like us, needing tickets for late-arriving friends.

We went looking and found that tickets priced at five or six rubles were available, all right – at anything from $25 to $40 U.S. We had no choice. We wanted to look after these late arrivals and the only way to get tickets was on the black market through our "close friends" in the Soviet Ice Hockey Federation. It was as if you go to a Stanley Cup final and go to officers of the NHLPA or NHL and get the tickets – but at scalpers' prices.

It never seemed to end. Then we ran into problems involving seat locations for the games. Although Nancy and I had identical tickets every night, right behind the timer's bench, for the first couple of games we were taken to different sections – pretty good seats, sometimes on one blueline, sometimes on another, but not as shown on our tickets. When I asked the Russians why, I was told, "Oh, the numbers on your tickets don't mean anything. Just sit where you can find a seat."

Oh, yeah? I made it clear that I was going to sit in the seats provided for me. A member of the embassy staff who could read Russian showed me the seats I was entitled to. About fifteen minutes before the game Nancy and I went to those seats and found them occupied by Russians. I showed them my stubs. They pretended they didn't know what I was getting at. I got Aggie Kukulowicz over and through him told the Russians to get out of the seats.

They got out and we never saw them again.

Another confrontation would take place about three times a game. At the end of a period I liked to go and visit in the alleyway leading to our dressing room. Every time I did this I was stopped by two rude police or militia officers. Even though I'd seen them only twenty minutes before, they'd stop me, make me come out with an identity card or passport, plus someone from the Soviet Hockey Federation who would vouch for me. I got to know those cops very well – but every twenty minutes I had to go through the same rigmarole, as if they were just trying to frustrate me; if so, it worked.

One other incident might have been funny if it hadn't seemed so much part and parcel of the whole bug-the-Canadians campaign. The late Thereza Ford, wife of Ambassador Ford, was small, fiery, excitable, and Brazilian. She was also a great Canadian fan, and when sitting in official Russian boxes, as she sometimes was, she had been known to scream insults at the referees when Canadians got a penalty, or even (this did happen) bonk a senior Soviet, the deputy minister of foreign trade, over the head with her handbag. After one period she and Nancy went down behind one of the goals to cheer our players as they came off the ice. A police officer gave them a healthy shove out of the way. Mrs. Ford wasn't having any. She said to Nancy, "Come with me!" and they marched into the main VIP lounge area. It was full of big-deal Soviet officials and army officers. Mrs. Ford screamed at them in Portuguese, getting well ahead of her translator, but the message got through. Nancy stood there with her, supporting the Portuguese imprecations with some English. It was quite a ruckus – enough that an official apology was offered within minutes. Ambassador Ford had been watching the game on television at the embassy and had not seen the incident, but he was telephoned immediately and appeared for the last few minutes of the game to lend his weight to his wife's eloquent protest.

So that's some of the behind-the-scenes stuff. Now to the main events, and their aftermaths – some of them also behind the scenes.

In game 5, we had three-goal leads twice, 3–0 at the end of the second and 4–1 early in the third, but they got four more against Tony Esposito to win 5–4, their third win, meaning they only had to win one of the next three and they had the series.

Game 6 we won, Paul Henderson getting the winning goal, but it really should have been a 3–3 tie. With us leading 3–2 and playing two men short, Yakushev got the puck to Kharlamov at the side of our net. He tried to flip it up and in. It hit Dryden's pads and deflected upward. Dryden thought it was going in. I was standing right behind the net. I knew it was in. But it hit the netting inside the net very softly as Dryden was wheeling, glove out. The puck dropped into his glove and he pulled it out. The Russians thought they had scored, but the light didn't go on and the referee whistled the play dead, no goal. The Russians argued only a little, and the 3–2 win stood up.

Game 7 we won, 5–4, tied almost all the way before Henderson got his second consecutive winning goal with 2:06 to play. That tied the series, three wins each and one tie.

With everything riding on game 8, the score was knotted at 1–1, 2–2 and again at 3–3, but late in the second they scored two to make it 5–3. The score was a fair one and could have been higher. Once a puck got past Dryden but Phil Esposito got his stick on it and cleared safely. In the third period, though, Esposito slapped one in to make it 5–4. Cournoyer made it 5–5. Then in the dying seconds Paul Henderson scored to win it, 6–5, his third winning goal in the last three games. That gave us the series.

When we blew our big leads to lose game 5, oddly enough that produced something that I saw later as one of three turning points.

The first was Esposito's tour de force on post-game TV in Vancouver. The second was our team meeting in Stockholm. The third came when we were going off the ice after game 5, beaten and with our heads down, and the 3,300 Canadians who had flown to Moscow on special charters surged to their feet and cheered and shouted their heads off. A standing ovation! I went into the dressing room expecting to see a bunch of guys just broken up. They weren't. Everything was, "Did you hear those people cheering? We're going to show them!"

The only one feeling really depressed, in fact, was Tony Esposito. To me and everybody else on the team, it had been our best game ever. In the first two periods we could have been leading 7–0 and holding it because of his stupendous work in goal. Now I tried to say that he'd really kept us in it but he just kept shaking his head and saying, "Al, I stunk. I blew it. There's no way they should have got five goals in one period. I'm the one to blame. Dammit, we *can* beat them and would have tonight if I hadn't let you down."

He was normally not one to take more than his share of any blame, so what he said was good for everybody – both the part about we *can* beat them and blaming himself for this loss.

After the game Gilbert Perreault (who'd played well and set up the first goal) and his Buffalo teammate Rick Martin decided, as Hadfield had, that they weren't playing enough. Both young players, only twenty-one, Perreault two years in the NHL and Martin one, they felt they'd be better off back in Buffalo getting ready for the NHL season. I talked to them in their room and thought I had Perreault convinced to stay, but the next morning he said he was going. He and Martin were the last players to leave.

Punch Imlach, their coach in Buffalo, later was criticized for giving them bad advice about leaving, but he always contended, correctly, that it was a bum rap. They had made up their own minds and indeed had gone home before he even got to Moscow as a spectator. Punch agreed with their decisions, he said, young guys really just getting started in the NHL who didn't want to waste their time being spectators.

Anyway, at that point, down three wins to one with one tie, we were beleaguered. Something had to be done, hard and fast. On my side, I decided that in future conceding anything to the Russians at the committee-room level, as I had in Canada about the referees, was over. From then on I was damned if I was going to lose any argument with them or anybody else. I might even do so while keeping my cool in all things. That turned out to be a hard resolution to keep.

I remember an incident after that game 5 when they'd come from behind to beat us. Irv Ungerman had sent over some smoked turkeys with his brother Karl. I was taking about half of a big smoked turkey into our dressing room when I ran into Trent Frayne, the Canadian writer.

He said, "Alan, this is going to be tough, they are great hockey players, we may not win another game." I'd heard that too often. I blew up and called him a Commie bastard and some other things and grabbed a drumstick and said, "I'll shove this drumstick right down your throat, get out of here." He has told his version of this story a few times himself, but that's the way I remember it.

Still, at that point, we were so close to being out of it that the dirty tricks hadn't really been moved into high gear. That happened after we won game 6. Until then, the Russians had been thinking it was in the bag. Now, suddenly, they realized that we might win!

Then we win again and square the series. For the final game we had changed the original plan and were supposed to have the choice of referees. We picked a Swede, Ulf Dahlberg. We were supposed to name the second referee from among Eastern bloc officials, so we decided on Rudy Batja from Czechoslovakia and went to give the Russians our two nominees.

We met them that morning at about 10 a.m. in a bare room with a few chairs, a table with a jug of ice water on it, a few glasses: Harry, Fergie, Aggie, I, Starovoitov, Gresko, and some other Russians. When we named our choice of referees, Starovoitov said that Dahlberg was sick and wouldn't be able to work the game.

I said, "Just a minute, I had breakfast with him at eight o'clock and he was all right then."

Starovoitov said, "Well, he's sick now."

I stepped out of the room and called Dahlberg and asked what was going on. He said, "Alan, I am sick because Starovoitov said if I ref this game, I will never referee another international game, and he is head of international referees for the International Ice Hockey Federation."

I went back into the room. I knew that what Dahlberg said had the ring of truth and that this was a ploy to foist another Eastern bloc referee on us, one that they wanted and we didn't. We argued. They didn't back off. At that point they were planning to dump both Joseph Kompalla and Franz Baader on us. We'd seen those two before, in game 6. We called them Badder and Worser. Fergie had a way of arguing that was even more direct than mine. He grabbed the pitcher of ice water and threw it against the wall. Glass and ice and water went all over the place. I think the Russians were wondering if they were going to be next. One thing sure, they knew we weren't going down without a fight.

That night we were all at the ballet. I don't remember who heard me, but I did say that if we didn't get the referee matter resolved, if they were going to keep on jerking us around on it, we wouldn't play the last game, that we'd tied it up, we could get out of there, all that kind of stuff. It got back to the Russians, of course, and the press, and Hockey Canada, and everybody else.

That was our position when another stupid thing happened. Prime Minister Trudeau had sent Senator Arthur Laing over to be head of the Canadian delegation. One of the Canadian reporters came to me and said, "I just wanted you to know that Senator Laing has met with the Soviets and assured them that no matter what they'd heard, we would be playing game 8 as scheduled."

Well, most of the Canadians, including Senator Laing, were at the ballet, *Anna Karenina*, that night along with wives. At intermission I got together with the players who were still there. Several had gone back to the hotel but there

were about twenty of them in the Bolshoi foyer. I told them
what was happening, and then I went to Senator Laing.
Here is a senator coming over and undercutting all my
negotiations, in effect telling the Russians I was only bluffing.

"Senator Laing? Alan Eagleson. I just want to let you
know, you better be ready to play tomorrow night because
these players are not going to play if we get two Eastern
bloc referees. So don't you be telling the Russians that you
are in charge of this team."

"Oh," he said, "I didn't mean that."

I stomped off. But I do give credit to Senator Laing. Within
minutes he apologized to our team and said that if we felt
we had to withdraw because of unfair tactics by the Russians
he would be prepared to support our position.

The day before the referee matter had been settled, a bunch
of us were in the hotel lobby. The press were always after
me, and to make contact easier I'd put many of them in
the same hotel we were in. I'd spent much of the previous
twenty-four hours fighting with the Russians about the
referees, talking about maybe going home and not playing
the eighth game.

Columnist Eric Whitehead of Vancouver was there. He
went on and on at me, saying you don't really mean this
and you don't really mean that.

I say, "Just a minute, ask me the question and I will
give you the answer, but don't you give *me* my answer."

Red Fisher and a lot of other guys standing around knew
what I was trying to say, but Whitehead kept on that I
didn't mean this and I didn't mean that.

Finally I couldn't take it any longer and I said, "Eric,
bugger off! You are a pain in the ass!"

He kept right on yapping and right in front of the whole
crowd I was going to whack him. This was one of my berserk
times, but I'll never forget, Herb Capozzi from Vancouver
saved me. He grabbed my arm and said, "Alan, don't, he's
not worth it."

I guess it was soon after that when we did thresh out the deal to take their man Batja and name our reluctant choice, Kompalla. It would have been better, as it turned out, if we'd taken somebody else. Before that game started, there was another clash with the Russians. We had taken over with us a totem pole given to the Soviet Union by British Columbia. Everywhere I went for about ten days I'd carted this damn thing around. It had been in my room and in the training room. I wanted to get rid of it. We were supposed to present it and now it was the last game and we'd better get it done.

I tell Joe Kryczka of the CAHA to get ready. Then we went to the Russians and said we were going to present the totem pole before the game.

"Oh, not possible! Not possible!"

They said something about not wanting to disturb their team before the game with anything extra. The game must go on time, on the button, without any (what's the Russian word for bloody?) last-minute presentation.

They were serious, and normally they ran the place. So I went to our players to tell them not under any circumstances to let the game start until we'd presented the totem pole.

By then we had the totem pole at the timer's bench. When the time came I told Joe Kryczka, "Come on." So we step on the ice, pushing this totem pole. We present it. The game got going.

Right away we get a penalty – Bill White. Thirty-six seconds later, another – Pete Mahovlich. Two men short. Yakushev scores. Then they got a penalty so we're only one short. All this happens in less than four minutes. I know that because at 4:10 we have the J.P. Parise incident. He's called for interference by Joseph Kompalla, *our* nominee. How you could call interference on a man who's trying to check the puck-carrier, I don't know. I guess Parise didn't know, either. It meant we'd be two men short again. Parise ran at Kompalla with his stick raised. Pretends he's going to hit Kompalla. All hell breaks loose. Kompalla gives him a match penalty.

Our players and coaches and fans were in a turmoil. From the bench, two chairs were thrown. That was the first time that night that I left my seat. I went to our bench on the other side of the rink and told them to cool it. At that point, suddenly 500 soldiers are marched in, surrounding the rink in the waste space between the seats and the ice.

Anyway, the game goes on, very tight, 3–3 near the end of the second period when the Soviets break it up with two quick goals and I thought we were dying. I actually thought, oh boy, it's over. Between the second and third periods I see Gresko. I said to him, "Alex, maybe this will be like Winnipeg – you were two goals down and tied it. We could do it in the third period and then everything would be tied, the game and the series, everybody happy."

He looked at me with steely cold eyes. I didn't even see it coming. "Alan, I must tell you, if we tie, you lose. In international hockey with no overtime the team that has the most goals in the tournament wins, so we will win."

That totally ended peace and good will to men, for me.

"Alex," I yelled. "Up yours!"

That was the only time I went into the dressing room during the progress of a game. I was livid. Maybe that had something to do with the much publicized incidents that later involved me in the third period. Red Berenson has told me he had never seen anything like it, before or since. I repeated to the team what Gresko had said, that if we tie, we lose, and called the Russians every name in the book. I ranted and raved. "All I can tell you is if we are going to lose we might as well kill a few of these bastards and take them home as trophies." That was pretty extravagant, even for me, but then I must have calmed down a little. "I don't care what you do, but if we can get a fast goal these bastards will fold, I can see it."

Then I had enough sense to get out of there, disappear, and leave Harry and Fergie with the mess.

In the third minute of the third period we did get that fast goal. Pete Mahovlich fires the puck to Phil Esposito. Phil tees it up. Damned if he doesn't whiff! But the puck stays there, Phil has time for another shot, and bang, it's 5-4.

Now we're looking a lot better, starting to get a fair bit of the play. I'm sitting right at centre ice, a few rows behind the timer's bench – the timer being from Edmonton, the only person who ever defected from Canada to Russia, chief announcer in all our games there because of his English. We're still down a goal. I remember noticing that when we score, the light goes on, snap, and off just as fast, while when they score, it stays on for about ten seconds. Anyway, that was vaguely in my mind, a mild irritation, when around the twelve-minute mark there's a scramble in front of the Soviet net and Cournoyer gets his stick on it for the tying goal, and the light doesn't go on! At all!

I see the referee pointing in the net so I know it's a goal. But no light. What the hell was going on?

I'd been listening all night to Canadians in the crowd chanting, "Let's go home! Let's go home!" Our fans have seen the puck go in, and no light, and they're going nuts. In the heat of the moment I think if we're going to be cheated out of that tying goal that's what we're going to do, go home.

I want to get the goal announced so I jump out of my seat. I'm in about the third row. I get almost to the timer's bench where the announcer was. Then one soldier puts a half-nelson on me and another one grabs me around the neck and about four of them start beating the blazes out of me.

Some of our players, Marcel Dionne, Bill Goldsworthy, and others not playing that night, had been sitting behind me. I can see them coming to help, but I'm being dragged, maybe ten feet or so, and finally . . . Well, until that game my favourite hockey player always was Bobby Orr, but as of then it was Pete Mahovlich. He was the one tall enough to see above the crowd what was happening. He jumped right over the boards and hit one soldier with his stick and speared another one holding me and I'm free. By now all the players in the stands behind me have come down and the players from across the rink have raced over. So I jump on the ice and with them all around me I slip and slide across to our bench, on the way shaking my fist at the goal judge. If he'd signalled Cournoyer's goal, none of that furore would have happened. I didn't give anybody the finger, as some accounts had it. I shook my fist. I've seen the replays often enough to know. But everyone is sure I gave the Russians the finger. So I just agree and tell them I was letting them know that Canada was number one, and I used the wrong finger.

All this time the Soviets in the crowd are going mad whistling (their way of booing), the Canadians not far behind them in noise with their cheering. Anyway, that was my international television debut.

And then I'm behind our bench, standing there for the longest eight minutes of my life watching the play go back and forth, back and forth. With about seventy seconds left Brad Park and Gary Bergman go in and Gary shot point blank – over the net! He could have been the national hero right then instead of Paul Henderson.

The Soviets swarmed into our end and missed, then it's back the other way and we get the Paul Henderson goal. Even after that the Russians had one good play on the net. Then the guys just kept kicking and shooting the puck away from our zone until it was over.

So then there is a big party, planned well in advance. Before the last game I had told all our guys that whatever happens in the game, we show up at the party. I had told Gresko, too, we'll be there, win or lose, count on that. We get to the party and there is not one Russian player. Only Bobrov, the coach, showed up. Gresko came in while I was thanking our team and making a little speech, so then I call on Gresko to speak for the Soviets.

He steps up, looking very sombre. Then instead of saying thanks and good luck and God bless you and congratulations, he starts making a political speech. When he got to, "Until the third period Alan Eagleson was my friend, but the way your team played hockey is very disappointing," I reached over and grabbed the mike and pushed him away and said, "Folks, this is Russian hospitality at its best. Let's us and our wives get out of here and back to the hotel where we'll be having our own party."

As I was leaving with the team, the whole big crowd of us, wives, friends, people connected with us, Gresko caught up to me.

"Alan, you were very rude to me," he said.

I guess he was right, but I pushed him up against a post, called him every name I could think of, and said I didn't ever want to see him again.

Then we had *our* party. Nancy and I landed back in our room at 4:30 a.m. At 5 a.m. I heard a noise and sprang out of bed. Someone was in the room. I grabbed a couple of bandy sticks to do battle–but it turned out to be the security man from the hotel. He was looking for me. Nobody has signed for the champagne! I told him to sign Doug Fisher's name for Hockey Canada.

When we got to our bus the next morning someone hadn't turned in a key. That cost us time and rubles.

You might think after all that, peace would break out and I could just go around smiling and patting guys on the back. All we wanted to do is get home and celebrate the victory. There was still the game in Czechoslovakia, part of our original agreement. At the Moscow airport, everybody had a passport except Rod Gilbert. He had packed his. We stood around while the authorities pawed through Team Canada's forty-eight identical bags to find his and let us go to Prague.

Meanwhile, as it transpired, Nancy was assembling a few warm memories of her own. She wasn't coming to Prague but was going with a group to Kiev, leading to contretemps

Number One. When the players' wives had been leaving Canada for Moscow, Wayne Tanenbaum of one of Toronto's wealthy Jewish families came to the airport carrying twenty-five Bibles and prayer shawls. He asked Nancy if she would ask the players' wives to carry them to Moscow, where he planned to present them to Russian Jews. The ladies obliged.

In Moscow he picked up his contraband and headed out. There was only one synagogue in Moscow, and at the time no cab driver would take a passenger there. The common ruse was to take a cab to the offices of *Sovietski Sport* magazine, next door to the synagogue. That was what knowledgeable Jews did when heading for the synagogue for services or hoping to contact relatives. Whatever the case, Wayne's present-laden visit was noted by the state police.

He wasn't stopped at the time, but after the series was over and the players' wives were leaving with Nancy and some other Canadian tourists, customs officers pulled Tanenbaum and his wife aside from the others for a body search. Nancy put up a furious battle, refusing to let the others board the aircraft until the Tanenbaums boarded as well. To this day Wayne Tanenbaum sends Nancy a gift at Christmas with the message, "To Nancy, thanks for '72."

Nancy's contretemps Number Two also had its excitements. On September 29 when the hockey team headed for Prague for our postscript game with the Czechs, Nancy and about ten others went to Kiev for a brief Intourist tour. One, Belle Grubert, had relatives she wanted to see in Kiev but figured she couldn't dodge the Intourist guide on the afternoon part of the tour to do so. On the morning part of the tour Nancy suggested that Belle feign illness at noon and cancel out for the afternoon. Then she could go and find her relatives, who were at that moment only a few minutes away from the hotel.

"Refuse lunch," Nancy counselled. "Remember now – you're too sick to eat!"

Trouble was, when Belle was faced with a spectacular meal she forgot the plan, ate, and in the washroom told

Nancy, "It won't work!"

"Lie down," Nancy ordered. "Pretend you can't move."

The Intourist guide argued, did her best, but finally decided to leave Belle to suffer in peace. When the tour bus pulled away Belle staged a miraculous recovery and had the two hours with her relatives that she'd been hoping for.

We flew to Prague, let a couple of players go home, and in the game against the Czechs dressed all the ones who hadn't been playing. It was hard to get up for that one in Prague after the tremendous tension of Moscow. Serge Savard had to score with four seconds left and our goalie out to salvage a 3–3 tie.

Enter Hockey Canada again. There was a party after the Prague game. We're supposed to leave for home the next day. Then suddenly somebody is telling me about flight arrangements. An awful lot of people were in a hurry to get back to Canada, planes crowded, all that stuff, but here I'm told that half the players would go via Paris and the other half via Amsterdam or Frankfurt or London or somewhere.

I said, "Just a minute! This team after all it has done is going home on the same plane! There should be fifty seats set aside for our gang, especially the players and others of us who have been in it all the way."

I was told no, you can't do this and you can't do that. I got on the phone to my friend Jack Callen, a vice-president at Air Canada, and said I wanted to charter a plane over here, and here's why. I gave him the whole story and he said, "Alan, I'll need somebody from the government to say yes." So I got on the phone and tracked down John Munro, then the sports minister.

He came through. He got the authority. So I go back and tell Hockey Canada. They are really angry with me. Again. "You can't do that, what if it costs us more money?"

I said, "Listen, we are going on this special charter. The media can come and you can come. By the time we get other tickets rebated it isn't going to cost us more than five thousand dollars to do it right."

So by putting up one final fight, we all came back together.

In Montreal we were greeted by Prime Minister Trudeau at the head of a cheering and applauding crowd. The players climbed on the backs of two fire engines for a run around the airport through fans as excited as we were. Then we went back to the plane and parted company with those players who were leaving us in Montreal to go directly to their NHL training camps.

It was a sad farewell, suddenly knowing that this team that had come together so well from August 5 to October 2 was now breaking up, would never be together again as a team. I think because of that we were all a little subdued when we boarded again for Toronto.

There was a wonderful welcome for us there, too, in pouring rain. A police escort met us and led our fleet of cars to the welcome at City Hall. I remember the funniest part of the ride in from the airport. I was riding with Phil Esposito and Wayne Cashman. Cashman had had a few drinks on the flight, augmented by the fact that we'd been travelling since 3 a.m. Toronto time and now it was 10 p.m. He had a balalaika and all the way in from the airport he was playing the balalaika and singing over and over the only two lines he knew from the song "Me and Bobby McGee." He was no Kris Kristofferson but it was a happy ride through the city. We were met at the City Hall parking lot by Toronto police chief Harold Adamson, who escorted me to the podium. There I joined the others, including Premier Bill Davis and local officials. Thousands of others stood in the rain, cheering our team for the job they had done for Canada. That was a great thrill.

However, I have to admit there was one disappointment in the days that followed. Wilder Penfield, the famous Montreal neurosurgeon, obviously had not been in any of the cheering crowds. He wrote a letter that was published, saying that our team had been very bad for relations between Canada and the Soviet Union.

He wrote that the Soviets were good people and that we, I particularly, had maligned them, treated them in an improper manner. My disappointment with that was ameliorated a little later when Harry Sinden wrote a reply to Penfield and everybody else saying that it couldn't have happened without me. Harry knew everything we had gone through.

Two other events helped me feel that we had done something right, besides winning. Nancy had come back home a day before me, and a few days later our family, Nancy and I, Allen, who was eleven, and young Jill, eight, went to spend a quiet Thanksgiving weekend in Cornwall, Ontario. We went to Upper Canada Village and one wet evening we went into a shopping mall in downtown Cornwall and found a table in a small restaurant. As we sat there I noticed four or five young boys in a nearby booth. One little red-headed youngster kept sticking his head up and looking and finally he came over and asked if I was Mr. Eagleson. I said yes and he called his friends over.

Within a few minutes everybody in the mall seemed to converge on us, making us feel that we were the toast of Cornwall. I felt right then that the way the people of Cornwall thronged around us, wanted to hear everything, just wanted to be near someone who had been there in Moscow, was more important than Wilder Penfield.

In the next few days there were many supportive individual letters from players. I particularly remember one from Red Berenson. Also, later there was a paragraph in the book Ken Dryden wrote about the series: "I don't know anyone else who could have led us through this series as well as Eagleson. Sure, maybe some of his public actions were questionable, but it is unfortunate that the public never got a glimpse of what he did behind the scenes."

I think the public perception of me is that anything I undertake I go at full speed ahead and don't second-guess myself. That is true in some things, but the 1972 series is different. I needed that kind of reassurance. I know what we did and that we had to do it that way. I would not do anything differently if I had to do it all again. We would not have come out winners otherwise. Still, obviously, I wanted some balance to the criticism, the reinforcement of people I respect. Those who stood with me, as is clear from the above, helped erase the confusion in my mind between the cheers and the criticism.

Finally, there was something that I carried in my wallet for a year or two, until it was almost worn out, a letter from Ambassador Robert Ford in Moscow. Soon after returning home I had written to him to say thanks for everything the embassy had done. This was his reply:

Canadian Embassy   Ambassade du Canada

Moscow, December 15, 1972.

Dear Mr. Eagleson,

        I was about to send you a Christmas Card when
I received your letter of November 28. So I take this
opportunity to send you and your wife all the very best for
next year. Whether that will include another hockey series
in Moscow is, I presume, in the lap of the gods.

        In retrospect I think we can consider the
hockey series a great success and I have so assessed it in
my report to the Government. In spite of the many snide
remarks made by Soviet officials and the press about our
type of hockey I think the important thing is that maybe
as many as 150 million Russians saw the games and were
able to appreciate the high standard of Canadian hockey.

        I don't need to say how much of the success
was due to your unstinting efforts. You know it much
better than I do but I got pretty angry when I began to
receive the Canadian papers and saw some of the unfair
comments made about your role. However I have no doubt
of your ability to defend yourself.

        All in all, it was a great experience and we
do hope we can see you and your wife again sometime.

With very best regards,

Yours sincerely,

F. A. D. Ford
Ambassador

R. Alan Eagleson, Esq., Q.C.,
    365 Bay Street,
       Toronto 1, Ont.

CHAPTER SEVEN

LIFE AND DEATH OF THE WHA

"Hey, Al, what the hell is going on? This is our deal and you're sitting in the good seats with all the big wheels and we're up with the flunkies in the last row."

– *WHA's Ben Hatskin in Moscow.*

When Bobby Hull made his sensational leap away from the Chicago Black Hawks to sign with Winnipeg for those big dollars in the summer of 1972, got his cash, and other World Hockey Association clubs anted up their $100,000 each to enable Winnipeg to make the deal – that's when I realized the WHA was for real. At the league's formation in 1971, a year before play was supposed to begin, the question naturally came up, "Where are you going to get players?" The most important answer turned out to be by raiding the NHL. The WHA simply claimed that the NHL reserve clause was illegal and that any player ostensibly bound by it was fair game. Even before Hull's decision, other people of respectable capability had joined up – players Johnny McKenzie, Wayne Connelly, U.S. Olympic team goalie Mike Curran, and goalie George Gardner, along with a few experienced hockey executives such as Glen Sonmor and Harry Neale. Veteran NHL referee Vern Buffey signed on as referee-in-chief. But Hull's signing for a $1 million signing bonus, plus $250,000 a year for five years as a player or player-coach, plus another $100,000 a year as a good will rep for the league, opened the floodgates.

The most publicity at the time concentrated on the NHL losing its first wave of stars – Derek Sanderson, J.C. Tremblay, Ted Green, Bernie Parent, Gerry Cheevers, and others. Approximately seventy NHL players eventually took the leap. From the NHLPA standpoint, it was a dream situation for players.

Those players who flocked to the WHA got much more than they'd ever made in the NHL. Those who didn't make the jump could demand and get big pay raises. For an agent, who could ask for anything more? For once, the owners didn't have the whip hand.

At one time, no less than seven Leafs were eligible for new NHL contracts – Norm Ullman, Paul Henderson, Ron Ellis, Darryl Sittler, Jim McKenny, Brian Glennie, and Mike Pelyk. Other NHL clubs faced roughly similar situations.

For anyone who didn't get what he wanted from his NHL club, the WHA was right there waiting.

Sometimes when clubs from both leagues were going after the same player the process took on some aspects of poker, a series of bluffs and calls on both sides.

John Van Boxmeer had been a first-round draft pick by Montreal in 1972. He played most of his first two years in pro in Halifax but it was obvious that he had enough talent to be a star in the WHA. John would be a free agent in the summer of 1975.

In June of 1974, Bill Dewitt came to see me. Dewitt was the owner of the Cincinnati WHA team that would start up in 1975. Dewitt was looking for a defenceman for that team and wanted to sign Van Boxmeer for delivery one year later. Van Boxmeer and I talked over Dewitt's offer, which was astronomical, and John decided to stay with the NHL. He said he wouldn't feel right signing for Cincinnati while still under contract to Montreal. I agreed.

Dewitt still wanted a defenceman. Who was available? This gave me a chance to do some creative planning for a Leaf player I liked, Mike Pelyk. I told Dewitt he could sign Pelyk, loan him to another WHA team for the 1974-75 season, and then get Mike to start off the 1975-76 season with the new Cincinnati Stingers franchise.

"Okay," Dewitt said, "let's see what we can do."

He offered Mike three times what the Leafs had been paying him and Mike accepted. Dewitt arranged to loan Mike to the Vancouver Blazers of the WHA for the 1974-75 season and everyone was happy.

But there was one other factor. Mike had been born and raised in Toronto, played in the huge Toronto Hockey League for Shopsy's (a young club with several teams for kids, supported by the Leafs). From there Mike had gone onward and upward in the Leafs' minor system until he made the big team. In short, he wanted the money when he jumped to the WHA but he didn't feel good about leaving the Leafs.

"You know," he told me, somewhat troubled, "I've been fifteen years with this organization."

That kind of loyalty is found in hockey players more often than you might suppose – allegiance to the team that brung them, as the saying goes.

The Leaf general manager in 1975 was Jim Gregory. Harold Ballard had been left the sole owner after Stafford Smythe died. I said to Mike, "If you feel that way, write a letter to Jim Gregory and Harold Ballard just outlining your feelings about being sorry to leave, but that you have to make this move for economic reasons." He wrote in that vein. That honest declaration of regret came back to help him. After the two years with Vancouver and Cincinnati, Mike still missed Toronto, missed the packed rinks that he rarely saw in the WHA, missed the Toronto fans who'd known him from childhood. Jim Gregory must have heard something to that effect. He called me and said, "Do you think Mike would come back?" We made a buyout deal with Cincinnati and back he came to the Leaf organiza-tion – first in Dallas of the Central League and then up to the Leafs again. Leafs had refused to look again at some other players who'd gone to the WHA and would like to return, but they took Mike back because of that letter he'd written. So he finished his career in the NHL, where he wanted to be, later established himself in the real estate business in Toronto, and has done well.

To go ahead a few years to 1977, the whipsaw technique was still part of the negotiation game. Brad Maxwell that year was a top draft pick by both the Minnesota North Stars and Johnny Bassett's Birmingham Bulls (previously the Ottawa Nationals and Toronto Toros). I hadn't been able to get Minnesota's bid up high enough, but Jack Gordon, the general manager at Minnesota, kept after me. Finally I told him on the phone, "Brad and I are going to meet in Chicago and go on to Birmingham for a press conference lined up there to announce his signing. This is your last kick at the cat." Jack flew to Chicago bearing a new offer. We signed it in the Chicago airport and, instead of going to Birmingham, flew to Minnesota.

We had our press conference there instead. Bassett, a good friend of mine, often reminded me of that deal, but it was my job to do the best that I could for the player. That kind of thing was happening those days. The WHA always was sitting there in the wings, not always winning but helping to get salaries up and, in effect, changing the hockey world forever.

Measuring the WHA's effect in the seven years it survived, it's strange to think that the whole WHA idea sprung from two men, Gary Davidson and Dennis Murphy, a couple of hucksters who never put up a nickel and yet formed the new league and got it going.

I give them all sorts of credit. Of course, they had the example of the American Football League in the early 1960s going from a laughable, joke-producing start to, within a few years, forcing a playoff with the National Football League and then winning the Super Bowl and going on to make millions for the AFL's original owners. The highly publicized signing of quarterback Joe Namath for the New York Jets, followed by his sensational Super Bowl win, was one of the gospel texts used in getting the whole WHA to round up enough money to attract Bobby Hull. Using the AFL example to the hilt, Davidson and Murphy were able to convince people to lay out good money to buy WHA franchises. In the end they walked away from the operation with handfuls of money, made from scratch.

On the other hand, Ron Roberts, head of the WHA players' association, had nothing but problems with the WHA owners. As he was my WHA counterpart, I tried to find out things about WHA pensions and benefits, but never did manage to. I tried to help him, for the good of my clients and other players who were going to the WHA, but it was a losing battle. All Ron Roberts seemed to want was a front seat on the bus. He didn't seem to care that much about what he might do, or not do, to get there.

From the start in my dealings with the WHA, my principal aim was to protect the players. With some WHA franchises immediately folding and others not looking too solid financially, I would not permit anyone I was representing to go to the WHA unless his contract was prepaid. I demanded and usually obtained either cash front money or letters of credit from banks. Because of this give-no-favours approach, many WHA people claimed I favoured the NHL against the WHA. That's baloney. Mike Walton, Paul Henderson, Normie Ullman, Rosaire Paiement, and maybe forty or fifty of my other clients went to the WHA when the conditions were right. The only thing I demanded was that money for my clients was properly guaranteed.

Some WHA people I dealt with I enjoyed. Benny Hatskin, a big happy fellow from Winnipeg – I could never get mad at Ben Hatskin. But it wasn't like dealing with an NHL owner. I couldn't always get Ben to acknowledge what day it was, let alone that the WHA wasn't as safe a haven for a hockey player as he contended.

Then there was Nelson Skalbania. He's the man who beat everybody in the hockey world to put Wayne Gretzky under a personal services contract to play for the WHA's Indianapolis Racers. He parlayed that into the deal with Peter Pocklington, another high flyer, that sent Gretzky to Edmonton, then still in the WHA. While Nelson Skalbania was operating in the WHA, or anywhere, for that matter, he was a media delight. He was either up $10 million or down $10 million, depending on what day it was. He eventually became involved in hockey out of Vancouver, football in Vancouver, football in Montreal, disaster after disaster.

He did one very slick thing in hockey, in 1980. Typical Skalbania. The Atlanta Flames were for sale. Tom Cousins was their owner.

Tom offered the Flames to a Calgary group headed by D.K.(Doc) Seaman, who bid $12 million. Tom wanted $16 million. That's where Nelson checked in. "Tom," he said, "you've got a deal for $16 million." Nelson then went to Molson's. My understanding is that he got $10 million prepaid for a television contract. He still needed $6 million, which he borrowed or got by taking in partners. Then he flipped the deal to Calgary and Doc Seaman's group and, however the details worked, walked away with $3 or $4 million profit from a few days' work. That's Nelson. Knowing Nelson, it would be gone within a week, into another deal.

Johnny Bassett was great to deal with, a close friend. To establish the Toronto Toros, he'd taken over the original Ottawa franchise from a fellow named Nick Trbovich, the first owner. Nick had a company out of Buffalo, where he lived and worked. As far as I could learn, he must have run the Ottawa team from Buffalo by sleight of hand. It miraculously survived one season in Ottawa. Johnny Bassett bought Nick out and moved the team to Toronto, where, despite a brave try, he foundered on the rock of trying to compete with the Leafs. Then Johnny took the club to Birmingham and quickly set up what in hockey became known as the Baby Bulls. This was because Johnny and his people did a good scouting job on juniors and soon started signing eighteen-year-olds. They were too young to be eligible for the NHL draft but couldn't legally be prevented from playing pro hockey if they wanted. Many of the best of the Bulls became NHL stars after the two leagues merged.

Another memorable WHA character was Jim Pattison, who owned the original Vancouver Blazers (after the Blazers moved from Philadelphia): short, slight of build, I'd say about 120 pounds, a born-again Christian who drove an old Cadillac that looked about fifty feet long.

He always wore a watch with two time zones on it, Toronto and Vancouver, where his favourite stock markets were. He had money, plenty of it, and wanted to keep it, which is why he soon moved his team to Calgary and eventually dropped out of hockey. His gamble from the beginning was knowing that the only way for WHA owners to make money, or even to get some back, was to merge with the NHL. Once around 1973 or 1974 he offered me $2 million if I could swing a merger. He came to the wrong person and I told him that frankly; I wanted the WHA alive for as long as possible as an alternative for contract-hunting players.

I found it rather amusing a few years later, while the WHA was still in business, when Glen Sather and Peter Pocklington from Edmonton came to see me. I like Sather, a fringe player who became one of hockey's top executives. As a player he was never my client – said he never made enough money to justify having an agent – but always gave 100 per cent playing with six different NHL teams before landing as coach (and eventually general manager and president) with Edmonton. Anyway, he brought Pocklington to see me and after a few preliminaries said, "Here's the deal. If you can help us get an expansion or merger or whatever with the NHL, there's a million bucks in it for you in fees."

I just looked at them. "Have I gone downhill?"

I think they thought they'd insulted me somehow. "What do you mean?"

"Five years ago Jimmy Pattison told me he'd pay me $2 million if I could get the WHA and NHL together. Is it only worth a million now?"

We laughed about it, but I told them, as I had told Pattison, that as long as the WHA was reasonably healthy and continuing to operate, I didn't plan to intercede in any fashion whatsoever.

Speaking of Pattison reminds me of the 1974 Canada-Soviet series. The WHA had seen how well we'd done both financially and artistically in 1972 and wanted a re-run against the Soviets for an all-star WHA team. That was fine

with me. I was on the board of Hockey Canada, which
would have to handle the nuts and bolts of the deal. The
only cavil I had was from experience: I said there's going
to be money in this, and the players ought to share it as
we had in 1972, through an increase in their pension plan.
The WHA, I forget exactly who was doing the talking, said,
"Oh, no, no, we'll handle it our way."

In June or July of 1974, just before the WHA was going
to announce their team, Doug Fisher and Chris Lang of
Hockey Canada came to me with the message, "This thing
is going to be a financial flop. Can you help bail us out?"

It seemed that the only sponsor of consequence the WHA
had was Carling O'Keefe. I made a couple of phone calls,
one to Standard Brands to get a promise of about $800,000,
the other I think to Coca-Cola for about $200,000, a million
dollars worth of sponsor time on two phone calls. I thought
I could find another million or so, but I stipulated to the
WHA that all profits must go to the players' pensions, which
I suspected had not been funded properly. That was the
only condition I was imposing. Jim Pattison and Ben Hatskin
got right back to me: it's none of your business, it's not
your deal, you won't tell us how to handle our money. Get
out of our hair.

Fine. So they phoned Coca-Cola and Standard Brands
and were told that the deal was only available if I was involved.
In the end they didn't do well at all financially, but even
though they lost the series it was an aesthetic success. Bobby
Hull, Paul Henderson, Gordie Howe and his sons Mark
and Marty, Frank Mahovlich, Gerry Cheevers, and other
great ones pretty well upheld the eminence of our kind of
hockey.

I must admit I enjoyed that series not only for the hockey
but for the rather amusing level of frustration among WHA
people once they got to Moscow. I had been invited by
the Soviet Ice Hockey Federation to come over for the four
games there. I got to Moscow and was met right at the

aircraft with a car and driver and various officials. They had arranged that I didn't have to go through customs, where huge WHA lineups had developed. They drove me to the Intourist Hotel, where I was given the best suite (as opposed to the cramped rooms in the Rossiya where the WHA people were billeted), told me the car and driver were at my disposal, and gave me ten excellent seats, some of which I gave to some Canadian students and to friends at the embassy.

After the first game Ben Hatskin came to me in good fun – not mad, that's not the kind of guy he is – and said, "Hey, Al, what the hell is going on? This is our deal and you're sitting in the good seats with all the big wheels and we're up with the flunkies in the last row. You've got a car, I haven't. You've got a suite, I've got a dump."

All in all, I think the WHA owners would have been pleased if I'd been overcome by carbon monoxide in Moscow. Every time they saw me I was going somewhere with a big shot and they were going somewhere with a lesser light. I heard that one of them said, "Geez, next thing we hear will be they're asking him to drop the puck."

The reason for all this was that while the Soviets were talking to the WHA as hosts, they were meeting with me about future international hockey, including creating what became the Canada Cup. That meant I had more time with the high-level Soviet Ice Hockey Federation people than the WHA did. In fact, when a big problem came up in one game – Rick Ley hammering their great star, Valeri Kharlamov – the Soviet Federation people came to me to complain before they went to the WHA.

This was very upsetting for Hatskin and his friends. As you can imagine, I revelled in it, felt it served them right – they'd turned down the opportunity I'd presented to them to make that series financially successful so my compassion for them, if any, was minor.

One other thing, I guess, has to be said: they were inexperienced in dealing with the Soviets, which meant that time and again they were hung out to dry. It was a good, exciting series, but they spent too much time fighting among themselves, leaving nobody free to fight the Russians.

Over years when the NHL and WHA were involved in court battles, and sometimes some owners met secretly (they thought) to discuss merger, I always stated that merger was the last thing our players wanted. I wanted the WHA as competition in the job market as long as possible, and I knew there were enough NHL owners who hated so much what the WHA had done that they'd fight merger all the way. Among them were Bill Wirtz and Harold Ballard. I felt part of my job was to keep all the anti-WHA elements well stimulated.

On the other side were certain business-oriented people such as Jacques Courtois in Montreal, Ed Snider in Philadelphia, and Bill Jennings in New York who felt that enough blood had been spilled between the two leagues. Early on, the NHL and WHA teams made a deal to drop their suits against one another in return for a payment to the WHA for legal fees. That went through, but later any time they were talking I was on the case. One of my successes in that regard was to find out about a secret merger meeting involving some NHL owners and Ben Hatskin and other WHA people. When I got wind of it I just called Bill Wirtz and said, "This has got to stop," and the roof flew off at the NHL offices.

Along with other anti-WHA owners, Clarence Campbell and Bill Wirtz were livid, Campbell particularly because it was personal to him – he felt the WHA had done nothing less than stolen players from his league.

To sum up, my overall feeling was that we had to keep the NHL and the WHA apart until it was obvious the WHA was dead. In my opinion we succeeded in that. So we didn't kill the WHA, quite the reverse. The real finish came after the WHA's 1978-79 season. That's when the Cincinnati and

Birmingham teams had come to the end of the road. That would have left the WHA with only four teams remaining of the original twelve, so in 1979 the WHA died a natural death.

Once that was obvious, there was no reason for the NHLPA to prevent a merger from taking place. Picked up from the ashes were the four remaining teams, Winnipeg, Edmonton, Quebec, and Hartford. It really was a merger, but the NHL labelled it expansion because each of the WHA four had to pay a $6 million fee to join the old league.

When the merger/expansion came I still had to jealously protect the position of the NHLPA, whose agreement to the NHL's new twenty-one team setup obviously became a matter for negotiation. We used the altered circumstances as a reason to re-open the collective bargaining agreement we'd thrashed out in 1975 when Pit Martin was NHLPA president. On individual player contracts, I don't like signing and then renegotiating when the player has a good year. From the perspective of the whole union, any time you have a reason to re-open a contract it can only be of benefit.

There was a precedent. In 1977, we had re-opened the agreement. That time it was by request of the NHL owners. It resulted in something the NHLPA can be proud of, done strictly in the interests of the game. That year some clubs were in serious financial trouble – Cleveland, Atlanta, Minnesota, and Pittsburgh.

Ticket sales in those cities were way down, partly because some NHL payrolls were overloaded with fringe players as a result of the WHA raids. The owners came to us and said they had three teams that might not be able to start the season. What could we do to help?

What we did late in August of 1977 was make a deal that would relieve the NHL clubs by allowing them to buy out players they didn't want to keep. In such cases they would pay one-third of the balance due on a signed contract after the players involved had cleared waivers (by which other clubs could pick up players they wanted). That one-third buy-out for players was still better than what prevailed in other pro sports, where players who cleared waivers could be dropped without any payment.

That was one deal we made. For the Cleveland Barons an immediate relief package, something like $1.6 million, was needed. To raise that, the NHL put up $800,000 and the NHLPA put up $800,000, on a note guaranteed by the NHL. The NHLPA in effect loaned $800,000 to the NHL owners, who loaned it to Cleveland to get them through the year, which was their last. In 1978 their player roster was merged with Minnesota's, leaving one team less in the league, but with the survivors stronger.

All this had come about by us re-opening our collective bargaining agreement in 1977 at the owners' request. Normally that 1977 rewritten agreement would have run until 1982. The merger/expansion deal in 1979 gave us another opening – this time at our insistence. New circumstances, new agreement. In return for going along with the new situation, we negotiated a substantial increase in our league-supported benefits. I was happy with that result, no matter what criticism came ten years later from some of hockey's most noted begrudgers (agents Ed Garvey, Rich Winter, Ron Salcer, and company), who thought we should have been tougher.

I predicted at the time that within two or three years NHLPA players would have most of the jobs on those four WHA teams. It really didn't take that long. Within eighteen months most former WHA players were phased out. Meanwhile, the fact was that no one with an NHL club ever missed a paycheque during the WHA years. The same could not be said for many players with WHA clubs.

At the Stanley Cup parade that
June in Orr's home town, Parry
Sound, Allen and Jill rode
with him.

In 1971, when Orr was twenty-
three, we worked out a contract
with Boston that would pay
him $1 million over the next
five years.

Orr and Mike Walton. Their
close friendship had started at
our cottage in the late 1960s.

This is Team Canada, 1972. Some played more than others, some contributed more than others, but we couldn't have done it without all of them. The names: FRONT ROW: *left to right:* Tony Esposito, Brad Park, Stan Mikita, Phil Esposito, Harry Sinden (Coach & General Manager), Alan Eagleson (Executive Director NHLPA), John Ferguson (Assistant Coach), Frank Mahovlich, Jean Ratelle, Bobby Orr, Ken Dryden. SECOND ROW: *left to right:* Bob Haggert (Executive Assistant), Dennis Hull, Mickey Redmond, Paul Henderson, Gordon Berenson, Wayne Cashman, Vic Hadfield, Ed Johnston, Bill Goldsworthy, Ron Ellis, Rod Gilbert, Mike Cannon (Administrative Coordinator). THIRD ROW: *left to right:* Joe Sgro (Trainer), Yvan Cournoyer, Gary Bergman, Dale Tallon, Bill White, Peter Mahovlich, Serge Savard, Jocelyn Guevremont, Gilbert Perreault, Pat Stapleton, John Forristall (Trainer). FOURTH ROW: *left to right:* Karl Elieff (Physiotherapist), Marcel Dionne, Bobby Clarke, Don Awrey, Brian Glennie, Rod Seiling, Guy Lapointe, Rick Martin, Jean-Paul Parise, Tom Nayler (Trainer).

That summer of 1972 some of us went to Moscow weeks early to meet our Soviet counterparts and iron out kinks, if any. (There were plenty). Standing in front of me is Andrei Starovoitov, head of Soviet hockey. My favourite linguist Aggie Kukulowicz is directly in front of us, *Toronto Star* sports columnist Milt Dunnell at the extreme right. Soviet coach Vesevelod Bobrov second from the left, our coach Harry Sinden six from the left.

Before the first game in Montreal. I'm shaking hands with Vyacheslav Tretiak, Soviet goalie. The *Globe*'s Dick Beddoes, recognizable for his distinctive hat and jacket, is behind me; the *Star*'s Jim Proudfoot on my left, Jean Béliveau beside him.

Phil Esposito, the team's inspirational leader.

In Canada, crowds gathered on their lunch breaks to watch the games on window-TV. We couldn't have been winning this one – not a smile.

But we did win in the end and came home to tumult. Prime Minister Trudeau met us in Montreal.

Backing him was a wildly cheering crowd.

The players climbed aboard fire-engines to tour the airport's cheering throng.

In Toronto's rain-swept welcome, including officials led by Premier William Davis, Tony Esposito and I carried winning-goal hero Paul Henderson on our shoulders.

In 1968 Orr and Mike Walton opened their sports camp near Orillia. This is Mike and Bobby with my son Allen in 1969.

Looking back, Orr had become like part of our family.

In 1976 when Orr's contract with Boston was up, in our negotiations for renewal Boston wouldn't come up with the right deal. I believed Orr deserved better than Boston offered. Bill Wirtz, the Chicago Black Hawks' owner, agreed. Chicago general manager Tommy Ivan is holding a contract calling for $3 millions over five years, with $1.5 millions guaranteed. Shown in a Chicago sweater for the first time, Bobby wrote across the photo, "Al, thanks." But he went on to change the contract on his own, costing him needed money. Recurrence of previous knee injuries eventually caused his retirement from the game.

The Canada Cup trophy, first played for in 1976.

When we won the first Canada Cup – Orr's last and maybe greatest series ever – Pierre Trudeau and his wife Margaret, held a reception for our players and their wives, followed by a dinner for about 500.

Five years later we were slaughtered 8-1 by the Soviets in the 1981 Canada Cup final. Valery Vasiliev receives the Canada Cup. I'm trying to smile.

I thought Trudeau showed his mettle that year when he came to comfort Wayne Gretzky and the rest of us in defeat. Not all that many politicians come to say hello, win or lose.

Canada Cup, 1984. We're back on top again, here with Rick Middleton, Kevin Lowe, and Doug Wilson. We won again in 1987.

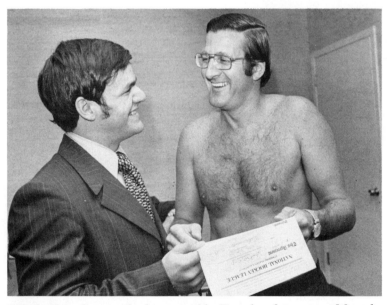

I like hockey players to look respectable. But when future great Marcel Dionne came to my office to sign his first pro contract with Detroit, an event to be shot by a *Star* photographer, Marcel didn't have a shirt, jacket, and tie with him. I whipped mine off me and on to him. As we joked forever after, I gave him the shirt off my back.

CHAPTER EIGHT

THE CANADA CUP

This was an idea I had while up a ladder painting
our cottage, listening to the World Cup of
soccer on radio.

In the summer of 1966, before Springfield, before Orr's signing, when I was still a lawyer first, we were at our cottage near Orillia, taking it easy. One Saturday morning I was painting the cottage and listening to the final of the World Cup of soccer being played in London between England and West Germany. The tremendous excitement of the crowd, sometimes drowning out the commentators as England won 4–2 in extra time, was my introduction to what happens in competition between countries at the highest level of a team sport.

I didn't fall off the ladder yelling, "I've got it! I've got it!" But later I realized that right then, painting the cottage, the first tip of an idea came to me: why not a hockey world cup?

I thought little more about it and did even less. Taking any kind of action never even occurred to me. I had no status whatever in hockey. That soon changed. Less than a year later I had negotiated Orr's first contract, wangled Carl Brewer's freedom to play for our national team, freed the slaves in Springfield, and was stumping North America laying the foundation for the NHLPA. Established over the next year or two as the man who spoke for the players, I was appointed to the board of governors when Hockey Canada was formed in February, 1969. That put me right in there with everybody who was anybody in Canadian hockey: the long-running (since 1912) Canadian Amateur Hockey Association, Clarence Campbell, club owners Stafford Smythe (Toronto) and David Molson (Montreal), political columnist and former MP Douglas Fisher, publishing millionaire Max Bell, oilman Charlie Hay, other major financiers and industrialists.

They were all powerful Canadians and it was a proud moment for me when I was invited to join the Hockey Canada board.

I was carrying a fair load of Canadian hockey credentials barely two months later, in April, 1969, when Nancy and I travelled to Sweden for the world "amateur" hockey championships. The word "amateur" was part of the championships, an arguable term considering the way some countries, especially the Soviet Union, financed their national teams. These championships had been running for several decades under the aegis of the International Ice Hockey Federation, headed then and for years earlier by an obnoxiously arrogant English travel agent and hockey executive named Bunny Ahearne. What I noticed that year in Sweden, with the games being a double round-robin, was at least a vestige of parity among the hockey nations. The Czechs defeated the Russians twice, the Russians defeated the Swedes twice, and the Swedes defeated the Czechs twice. Canada was never really in it. We won only four games. When the Czechs, Swedes, and Soviets wound up tied on top, the Soviets won the championship on goal averages, mainly because of eleven goals they'd scored in the two games against Canada.

The Canadian national team had nothing like the power it would have had if we'd been able to use the country's best hockey players, the pros. Exclusion of our best gave every other team an unfair advantage, which I and most others on Hockey Canada knew should be changed.

When I went on to Moscow at the end of the tournament what I worked on first was not a Canada Cup but the first step toward our best, a team of Canadian pros, playing the Soviets' best. That idea, as I've related, took three years to bring about – the eight-game 1972 series.

When I was planning the 1972 trip, I'd kept the other top hockey countries in mind, too, setting up two games in Sweden after the four Canada-Soviet games in Canada and before the four in Moscow, and another in Prague on the way home. They were all good games, close enough that the world cup idea grew a little in my mind.

In the years between 1969 and 1972, when the Winter Olympics were in Sapporo, Japan, I had been attending world championships – even though after 1969 Canada was refusing to play until they could use pros. My aim on those trips, including one early in 1972 prior to the Sapporo Olympics, was simple: to expand my relationships with International Ice Hockey Federation people. Bunny Ahearne was still in charge, trying his best to ignore me. Others helped. Billy Harris, a friend and client of mine when he was in the NHL with Toronto, Oakland, Philadelphia, and Pittsburgh, by then was coach of the Swedish national team. He had introduced me to the main people in Swedish hockey. Also, I'd made a point of cultivating contacts with people from all the other hockey federations.

The Canada-Soviet series in the fall of 1972 naturally attracted the IIHF's attention, along with everybody else in the hockey world. In the middle of the tremendous homecoming welcomes, seeing those huge, tumultuous crowds in Montreal and then in Toronto, I was sure that international hockey would become the dominant feature of the North American hockey scene and that fans would not be denied that special kind of exhilaration that comes when nation faces nation, each represented by its finest players.

By 1973, when the world championships were in Moscow, I unofficially sounded out a number of people on the idea of a world cup for hockey. It wasn't until the 1974 Canada-Soviet series, another eight-gamer but with the Canadian team made up of WHA players, that things really started to move.

In Moscow that time, 1974, WHA people had their noses a little out of joint because of the breaks I was getting from the Russians – better hotel, official car and driver, best seats in the rink while they sat up in the rafters. The explanation was simple: the Russians knew me and didn't necessarily like me, but they respected the fact that I spoke for the NHL players. Old animosities sometimes don't last long when there's something big at stake. I met with Alexander Gresko, my old sparring partner from the 1972 series, exploring the idea that the now successfully established Canada-Soviet clashes could be expanded to include other nations. Gresko and other main movers in the Soviet Ice Hockey Federation, knowing their country's own huge attention to the soccer World Cup, were positive about extending the concept to hockey. On the way back from Russia I let Jim Proudfoot of the *Toronto Star* in on the idea that I was thinking of trying to organize a world cup of hockey.

I don't remember if he, then, or someone else later, was the first to ask, "What will you call it?"

Whoever and whenever it was, I eventually came up with the answer: "Canada Cup."

In the next few months of 1974 and 1975, I discussed the idea with fellow members of Hockey Canada. They shared my enthusiasm. The chairman of Hockey Canada then was Doug Fisher. He had differed with me loudly and often over my self-appointed role as supremo for the 1972 series, but now he was the most important ally I had in seeking an official government reaction.

In the late fall of 1974 I was called to Ottawa to meet with the head man in Canadian sport from the government side, Marc Lalonde, Minister of Health and Welfare and also responsible for Fitness and Amateur Sport.

Because he was both a close friend and cabinet colleague of Prime Minister Pierre Trudeau, it was generally considered in those days that if you had Lalonde on your side, the political side of any project was as good as won. Anyway, never mind the politics, it was a hell of an idea. When I was asked to outline what I had in mind, I did so enthusiastically, and Lalonde said he'd take it to cabinet. In a matter of weeks, still before the end of 1974, I heard back from Lalonde: the government approved the idea, committed itself to support the world cup of hockey concept, and I was named Hockey Canada's chief negotiator for international hockey.

I heard later that the only dissent from that decision in cabinet was from a tall and eloquent lawyer originally from the Ottawa Valley, Joe Greene. He was categorically opposed to any so-and-so Tory like Eagleson getting an appointment that would enable me to sell the Liberals down the river every chance I had. He didn't prevail (and a couple of years later he came to me and said he was happy to have been proved wrong).

With the government support behind me, I discussed the idea with everyone involved in hockey at that level, some club owners, NHL president Clarence Campbell, and naturally the players.

I made one important decision that avoided trouble. Apart from the Olympic gold medal at Squaw Valley in 1960 and the silver at Sapporo in 1972, the U.S. hadn't been prominent in world hockey. Because of the growing number of U.S.-born players in the NHL and the number of U.S.-based teams in the NHL, I determined that the United States should automatically be counted in, along with Canada. We'd start with those two countries and then add four from Europe. There weren't any specific guidelines but it was generally agreed that we would invite the top four European finishers from the world championships in the year immediately preceding the Canada Cup.

With all that in mind, I travelled to the 1975 world championships in Munich and Dusseldorf to spread the word further and do some dickering. Remember, after the bitter cancellation of the 1970 world tournament scheduled for Winnipeg, Canada had refused to compete. They missed us. How they missed us! Some hated to admit it, but they knew that any world championship without Canada wasn't really a world championship. They had tried every year to get us back in, but we'd hung tough on our contention that we should be allowed to use at least some pros.

I'd been opposed to withdrawing. You're always better off to stay in and raise hell than to be bitching from afar. Hunting for a compromise, I'd developed in my own mind an idea that was not a retreat but more like a flanking movement. It was at least a new proposal: that the university-based Canadian national team that Hockey Canada put together for the Olympics every four years could be beefed up for world championships by pros whose teams either missed the Stanley Cup playoffs or were knocked out early. As long as Bunny Ahearne was running the IIHF, such revolutionary ideas always got the cold shoulder, at least by him and the majority votes he controlled. Just at the right time there was a major breakthrough.

Dr. Guenther Sabetzki, a silver-haired, courteous modern man – or, I could say, as different from Bunny Ahearne as day and night – was elected as president of the IIHF to succeed Ahearne. I'd met Guenther along the way. I went to him with my Canada Cup plan. He supported it immediately. He wasn't one of those old-time hidebound European hockey people looking down their noses at reality. You might get his measure from what he said in a luncheon address to open the first Canada Cup nearly two years later.

He spoke bluntly to the European countries, especially those in what was then the Communist bloc, to the effect that their players were as professional as outright North American pros. They could be classed as army officers, engineers, or whatever method of masking their true jobs was used, but: "The fact is that these men, regardless of what occupation they have, are being paid by the state to play hockey. So they are as professional as any."

We in North America had been waiting for such a breath of fresh air from our European hockey counterparts for years. That might give you a hint as to why I supported him then, and ever since.

The NHL involvement was tricky, especially on the issue I'd insisted on and had sold the European countries on – that in the Canada Cup all NHL players would play for their own countries. In 1975, when the plan had to get past the NHL clubs, there weren't as many Europeans playing in the NHL as is now the case. Borje Salming was the most prominent of them, but several were playing with the WHA or even in minor pro and the prospect was there'd be more. Of course, most players with U.S. clubs were Canadians and under my plan would play for Canada. I had begun writing contracts providing that in international competition a man would be able to play for his home country without the club's consent.

That was fine with the players' association, but it took some doing with some U.S. owners, who wondered why they should permit their U.S.-based assets (players) to be loaned to foreign countries. The Canada Cup concept, as far as I was concerned, was etched in stone in August of 1975. Clarence Campbell and the owners and players at the time were deep into plans for some Soviet teams to tour some NHL cities. They wanted to get that done. I said fine, I'm in total agreement, but the trade-off is the Canada Cup.

I can remember Gil Stein, who was then the lawyer for the Philadelphia Flyers and is now the general counsel for the NHL, getting up and giving a dissertation on why no Philadelphia player was ever going to be loaned to Canada for any such event. They were playing in the U.S. and being paid with U.S. dollars. He went on and on for five or ten minutes until I stood up and let him know in no uncertain terms that his type of American bullshit was unacceptable.

"We're going to have the Canada Cup," I said, "and I have the support of the Canadian government and have been going around to other countries with a personal letter from the Prime Minister, and the Canada Cup is going to take place in 1976."

Another item up for discussion at that meeting was a new collective bargaining agreement between the owners and the players. I said if the Canada Cup concept of players joining their own national teams wasn't acceptable to everybody right then, there would be no collective bargaining agreement and that was the union's position.

Suddenly Bill Wirtz from Chicago stood up and said to Stein, "Gil, you'd better just relax, we need Canada to be dominant. What Alan has done is put the NHL in indirect control of international hockey by his own involve-ment – meaning we don't have a third party, Hockey Canada, in the driver's seat.

"Eagleson is one of our partners at the joint venture level. It is better to have our partner there running it than a stranger. In 1972 the stranger was Hockey Canada. They put the whole thing together and then dumped it on our plate for us to digest. In contrast, now we are participating in how the tournament is structured, where it's played – we can play in some American cities – how we can help, are our players insured, and what's our share of the profit. It's a business relationship." That pretty well wiped out the U.S. clubs' opposition.

To go back to Guenther Sabetzki's 1975 election as IIHF president, one of the first things he and I did together was to call a meeting of the IIHF at the Canadian embassy in Stockholm that autumn, specifically to deal with the Canada Cup. Not the least of our purposes then was to smooth the way across the only visible speed bump (apart from raising the money) we had left, the Canadian Amateur Hockey Association.

Until the 1969 creation of Hockey Canada and my appointment as negotiator for international hockey, the international side of the game had been the CAHA's baby. Some CAHA people still resented what they saw as encroachment on their traditional territory.

Our good fortune was that the CAHA president, a roly-poly Newfoundlander, Don Johnson, was gung ho for the Canada Cup idea. In the Stockholm meeting he stood up for me and my idea all the way in spite of criticism that he created for himself with the CAHA. His support was absolutely crucial. Under the constitution of the IIHF, the CAHA – and nobody else – could cast the Canadian vote. Don Johnson, the most important CAHA figure, took his critics head on.

Back in the days when the CAHA was composed almost entirely of volunteers working at it part time, and the rest of the international hockey world (except the Soviets) was not all that different in style, the CAHA in the driver's seat had been fine. Don Johnson was the one who could see the new facts, that world play had outgrown the CAHA and that in spite of the CAHA's historic and sometimes glorious past, this idea was too big for that organization – but Hockey Canada and I could do it.

At that meeting I also produced my trump card to enable Guenther Sabetzki to deal with possible dissidents in the IIHF ranks: I promised that in return for the untrammelled support of the IIHF for the Canada Cup in 1976, Canada would return to the world championships with NHL players for the following three years, 1977 to 1979. After that, and depending on developments, we could plan for the future.

That was a busy winter in other respects, not the least being the tour of NHL cities around Christmas and New Year's by two Soviet teams, Central Red Army and Wings of the Soviet. Red Army beat New York Rangers 7–3. Wings beat Pittsburgh 7–4. Red Army went into Montreal New Year's Eve and tied 3–3. Then Punch Imlach's Buffalo Sabres got some revenge for the NHL, hammering the Wings 12–6. That, and a game in Philadelphia against the Army team a few days later, are the two of the tour I most vividly remember.

The Flyers were in their heyday as the Broad Street Bullies. They had won the Stanley Cup the previous spring, and from the start against the touring Soviets played very tough, sometimes dirty, hockey. This eventually involved me. The entire Red Army team left the ice after a vicious check by Ed Van Impe on Valeri Kharlamov and refused to come back. The television commentators were going mad with the prospect that the game would be cancelled. Clarence Campbell and I went to the Soviet dressing room together and told them they had to return to the ice or the future of these series would be in jeopardy. Campbell was even more vocal in his exhortations. Finally we put it in terms they would understand: we both said that they had better get back on the ice, there was a lot of money at stake here,

and "if you don't play you won't be getting any money."
At that point we had not paid them for the games and they
were looking at a couple of hundred thousand dollars going
down the drain.

They said, well, that was a consideration but they still
wanted assurance that the Philadelphia hooligans were going
to clean up their act. I told them I would go and speak
to the Flyers, which I did. In the Philadelphia dressing room
I spoke to Bobby Clarke, Bill Barber, and the rest. I told
them, too, what was at stake.

"Play as tough as you can but you don't have to be dirty,"
I said. "Just play the game. I think they are scared skinny
of you now. Let's not have anything drastic occur. We don't
want a huge black eye to what so far has been a pretty
interesting series."

For both teams, the message was that discretion was the
better part of valour. On that basis, the teams went back
on the ice and there were no more incidents. I think the
fact that both Clarence Campbell and I, the owners' man
and the players' man, stuck together on the financial issue
was enough to let the Soviets know that we weren't kidding.
The experience geared me up for what was left to be done
about the Canada Cup.

Gordon Juckes was then secretary-manager of the CAHA,
which controlled the only Canadian vote in the IIHF. He
and I travelled the European hockey capitals together. As
I'd told the NHL owners, Marc Lalonde had arranged for
me to present a letter from Prime Minister Pierre Trudeau
to each of the national sports federations we visited. This
letter confirmed on his authority that I was the Canadian
emissary and negotiator for the proposed tournament and
had full government support. That had a powerful impact
in the task of bringing any remaining doubters into line.

Back home with Europe on our side, it was a matter
of organizing the structure responsible for the team. Sam
Pollock was general manager of the Montreal Canadiens,

one of the best hockey men anywhere, ever. In February of 1976 I went to Montreal to ask him if he would take the job as general manager. He agreed.

Sam and I then set out by car for Ottawa. There, his appointment as general manager was to be confirmed by Hockey Canada. We had a media conference planned and ready.

We almost didn't make it. Sam was driving. Suddenly we hit an icy patch, spun around twice, and wound up in a snowbank on our side of the highway. I'll never know how long it might have taken us to get out of that fix if a trucker had not been travelling behind us. He saw the accident. He parked his truck and walked over, then stared at us incredulously and shook his head.

"Well!" he exclaimed. "I never thought I'd meet Sam Pollock and Alan Eagleson this way!" Then he hauled out a rope or chain and pulled us back onto the highway. After we thanked him and bade him farewell, I said, "Sam, I think I'll drive the rest of the way."

After that, we got to Ottawa without incident.

Don Johnson and I went together to the 1976 Olympics in Innsbruck (a Soviet win), answering questions about money, arrangements, referees, everything they needed to know – except exactly what teams would be invited, which would be decided after the world championships. Don sat in on every meeting. Between times he helped me a lot in another way. He sat in the hotel lobby watching the passing hockey people and letting me know who was talking to whom, a great help in negotiations.

Finally we travelled to the world championships (a Czech win) in Katowice, Poland, and while there got everything arranged with the teams we were inviting: Finland, Sweden, the Soviet Union, and Czechoslovakia, to go with Canada and the U.S. Then, back home, I knew finally that I had a tournament. There was only one more tiny blip. A lawyer named Guy Bertrand, no doubt with separatism on his mind, suggested there should be a separate Team Quebec. I replied that it was either Team Canada or no team at all.

Fortunately, or maybe even naturally, all of the Quebec and French-speaking players who might have been eligible for a Team Quebec stood up for me. I told Guy Bertrand to stuff his idea.

The next major consideration was the financing. My first call was to Johnny Esaw of CTV. I told him I'd like to buy the network again, as I'd done in 1972. One problem did come up. CTV covered 90 per cent of Canada. The other 10 per cent could only get the CBC. The government insisted that Hockey Canada arrange a feed to CBC to cover that 10 per cent of Canadians. The feed cost Hockey Canada $250,000, but it had to be done. Once that was out of the way, to make it another profitable financial venture for Hockey Canada and the NHLPA, all I had to do was sell the advertising.

I was pretty sure that I could simply call Labatt's and sell the rights, but it wouldn't do to make a private deal with Labatt's, then have some other company say they would have paid more. So I invited bids from not only Labatt's but Molson's and Carling O'Keefe, the other two major competing breweries. Molson's said no. Its commitment was to *Hockey Night in Canada* and the NHL, and international hockey did not fit into their plans. I called Don McDougall, president of Labatt's and a personal friend, who had helped out with heavy financial support in 1972. He offered to buy approximately $2.4 million of Canada Cup television time.

I thought that would be more than enough to be top bid. I was wrong. Through Arthur Harnett, whom I'd retained to handle all bids because he'd done such a good job in 1972, I was approached by Wilmat Tennyson, president of Carling O'Keefe Breweries. His home was three or four doors from me in Toronto's Rosedale district. One night he came over to our place and said he understood that we had $4.6 million worth of advertising for sale. He only wanted about $2.3 million for Carling O'Keefe "but if you can't sell the rest and I can't sell the rest then I guarantee you I will buy the whole amount."

The next morning I got on the telephone. Arthur Harnett did the same.

I had a good relationship with Standard Brands and its president, Ross Johnson. He committed about $1 million to the project from O Henry, Planter's Peanuts, and other Standard Brands products. Within a few weeks Arthur Harnett and I had sold about $2 million to go with the $2.3 million Carling O'Keefe wanted. In the end, what we sold totalled about $4.6 million.

Then there was the matter of designing the Canada Cup trophy and the team sweaters. Industrial designer Chris Yaneff, recommended to me by Ross Johnson, came up with a sweater design that was simple and clear but I wasn't entirely happy with it. Then Wilmat Tennyson came to me with the Carling O'Keefe designer, Rolf Huecking. Rolf's half-maple-leaf design for the Cup itself had an immediate impact on me. Within another week he was back with the Canada Cup sweater design, which I thought was spectacular – a half maple leaf with the word Canada at an angle. It has been our sweater in each successive Canada Cup. Then we dealt with making the Cup itself, the trophy. I went to Scott McCann, president of Teledyne Canada, and Johnny McCreedy, president of International Nickel, who had played for the Leafs when they won the 1945 Stanley Cup. With their help and at Inco's expense, $50,000 brought the original Canada Cup trophy into being.

At the same time that we were selling advertising and ordering the uniforms I was negotiating for arenas. Sam Pollock helped in Montreal, Harold Ballard in Toronto. Those were the main venues. There would also be a game in Ottawa so that the nation's capital could trot out diplomats, cabinet ministers, senators, MPs, and other notables, as well as some people who bought their own tickets. Two games would be in Quebec, one in Winnipeg, and two in Philadelphia.

The coaching staff and team makeup were next. Canadiens had won the Stanley Cup that spring over Philadelphia. Our first approach was to the Montreal coach, Scotty Bowman. At first he replied that he'd had a long year and would prefer not to be involved. Next on our list was Philadelphia's Fred Shero, but he was in Europe and we couldn't find him.

At the NHL's June meetings in Montreal Sam Pollock and I tried Scotty Bowman again. This time he agreed, on the understanding that we would line up assistants to help him.

We went for the best: Don Cherry from Boston, who needs no introduction, Al MacNeil, whose Nova Scotia team had won the American Hockey League Calder Cup that year, and Bobby Kromm, who'd won that year's WHA championship with Winnipeg. We invited two widely experienced hockey men, Keith Allen and Toe Blake, to sit in as assistants to Sam Pollock.

Our plan was that these coaches and managers, with me sitting in as adviser, would meet on the day before each game was played and meet immediately after each game as well. The other teams arrived and on September 2 at the Civic Centre in Ottawa, with the best and brightest of the nation's capital packing the rink, the Canadian and Finnish teams on the ice, the fans accepting fairly politely the idea that they had to stand through the national anthems of all six teams, Governor General Jules Leger declared the Canada Cup open for business.

Right away Bobby Clarke, Bill Barber, and Reggie Leach set up shop in Finland's end, followed on the first line change by Bobby Hull, Phil Esposito, and Marcel Dionne. Just think about those forward lines. Canada slaughtered Finland 11–2 in a decidedly undiplomatic manner. After that we moved along quite well in the early part of the tournament, beating the U.S. and Sweden before we lost 1–0 to Czech-oslovakia in a brilliant game played in Montreal, dominated by the Czech goalie, Vladimir Dzurilla.

That one has several memories for me. Even I, even in losing – and magnanimity in defeat is not one of my strong points – recognize greatness when I see it.

Also one memory, secondhand, tells you something about Guy Lafleur, one of the Team Canada stars who then was in his prime. A friend of mine, travelling up in a hotel elevator with Lafleur after the 1–0 loss, kept quiet about the game. He felt that every Canadian player would be feeling in the pits, and especially wouldn't want to discuss it in an elevator. Just as the elevator stopped, Lafleur glanced at him and said quietly, "Beautiful game, eh?" Not many players, however great, can see the beauty in a contest when losing.

Another half-humorous memory from that 1–0 night is of Sam Pollock, coming into the room after the game with that little smile he sometimes has, and saying, "Well, we sure as hell made a tournament out of it, didn't we?"

We certainly had. That loss meant we had to win or tie our next game, against the Soviet Union in Toronto, to make the final. We won 3–1, Orr playing one of his greatest games ever, though he didn't figure in the scoring. Against the Czechs in Toronto for the first game of the two out of three final, we won 6–0. When we moved to Montreal for the second game we figured we could beat them just as easily. We should have had more sense. We were losing 4–3 late in the third until Billy Barber scored from Leach and Clarke at 17:48.

In the first ten minutes of overtime each team almost lost it and almost won it. The near miss by the Czechs provided Rogie Vachon with a memory for life. Vladimir Martinec was wide open in front of him with a rolling puck at his feet. He lashed at the puck as it danced around. Because the puck was spinning, Vachon couldn't anticipate where the shot would go. The puck came off Martinec's stick rising fast. All Vachon had was his reflexes. He threw his hand up and caught the puck that would have gone under the crossbar and won the game, forcing a third final game. What happened next, he said, he'd remember best about the whole tournament.

"Martinec skated up to me and patted me on the back. I take the sudden-death winning goal away from him and he pats my back."

So that was the chance the Czechs couldn't cash. We're still in the first ten minutes of overtime. Lafleur scored but it was ruled no goal because the net was off its moorings. Guy Lapointe scored, but it came a split second past the halfway point in the period–when under IIHF rules the teams had to change ends, which we did.

The winning goal came on a play that I visualize every time I think of Darryl Sittler. The Czech goalie, Dzurilla, had a habit of coming out to challenge and stop what looked like excellent scoring chances. Once he'd beaten Reggie Leach, one on one, charging straight at Leach and taking the shot on his pads. Don Cherry, from his observer perch in the press box, had seen something extra in that save. Before overtime started, he arrived in the dressing room with an urgent message. "Anybody getting a breakaway from now on, try delaying a bit," Cherry said. "Take an extra stride or two. Try to get around the goalie a little so that you got something to shoot at."

About ninety seconds after we'd changed ends, a passing play from Marcel Dionne and Lanny McDonald moved the puck to Sittler, playing left wing on that line. He shifted to his left to beat a defenceman, Milan Chalupa, and outskated a diving check from Marian Stastny. Then he was skating in clear on Dzurilla, who came out to meet him. Cherry's advice had been to try delaying a bit, get around him a little. Sittler faked a slap shot that made Dzurilla lunge to his left. Sittler kept going. Now he could see the goal. The angle was still sharp.

He took one more stride. Two would have put him too far past.

Dzurilla had recovered now and was leaping desperately to his right, reaching out with his big goal stick to deflect, intercept, block. Sittler shot. The puck passed a fraction of an inch under the heel of Dzurilla's flailing stick and caught the far side of the goal.

When the light flashed, Dzurilla skated to his net and put his head down on the crossbar, a teammate's arm around his shoulders. Canadians on the ice, on the bench, and some from the crowd, including me, charged across the ice to mob Sittler.

That's the way we won the first Canada Cup.

A few moments later came an interesting and controversial decision. Rogie Vachon had played every game in goal for Canada, losing only to Dzurilla's 1-0 shutout. By vote of a media committee he was named the outstanding Canadian player. But Bobby Orr, beaten out by Rogie as the outstanding Canadian, was chosen by the IIHF's Guenther Sabetzki as the most outstanding player in the whole tournament.

Obviously, there was a contradiction. Rogie's wife felt that Rogie deserved both awards and that I had fixed it with Dr. Sabetzki that the major one went to Orr. I didn't fix anything. I was happy for Bobby but thought that despite the apparent contradiction, both awards made sense. Rogie was absolutely at the top of his form, but Bobby had never played better in his life, and that is saying something. Even with his switch from Boston to Chicago in the big contract he had just signed, there was a sense that his time in hockey was winding down. MVP of the first Canada Cup was the last major award of his award-filled career.

People sometimes ask me how I calm down after the tensions I've just described. That night I was with my friend Ross Johnson pacing the suite at the Quatre Saisons when Jan Starsi, the Czech coach, came in for a glass of champagne. He spoke no English, but reasonable French. We talked until about 3 a.m. Then Ross said, "Let's get Desmarais out of bed and over here." We phoned. Half an hour later

Paul Desmarais, a financier not known for 3:30 a.m. strolls, was walking through the lobby with a topcoat over his pyjamas. He and Ross and Starsi and I talked until five, then I went to bed.

I think maybe this is the time to say something more about that team. It might have been the greatest lineup Canada ever assembled. I'd hate to have to pick a better one.

Goal: Rogatien Vachon, with a 1.39 goals against average.

Defence: Denis Potvin and Bobby Orr (each had nine points), Serge Savard, Guy Lapointe, Larry Robinson, and Jimmy Watson.

Forwards: Bobby Hull, thirty-seven years old, nineteen years after his first NHL game, with five goals, tops for Canada and tied in the tournament only by the Soviets' Victor Zhluktov and Czechoslovakia's Milan Novy; Gilbert Perreault, Richard Martin, Peter Mahovlich, Phil Esposito, Marcel Dionne, Guy Lafleur, Darryl Sittler, Bob Gainey, Steve Shutt, Reggie Leach, Lanny McDonald, Bobby Clarke, Danny Gare. Some played more games than others, but remember their names; they were the best.

In the end, the financial statements looked as good to me as the hockey had been. We paid approximately $1.3 million to the CAHA, the balance shared by Hockey Canada and the NHL players' pension plan.

Equally or maybe even more importantly, for the third time (the 1972 and 1974 series being the first two) the hockey public in many nations, but especially in Canada, had shown enthusiasm for great hockey even if it was played before the normal breeding places of the game, the frozen ponds and sloughs and flooded vacant lots that once produced the greatest players, were showing any ice at all. At one time, even in the 1960s, September always had been reserved for football and baseball. Back in those years the Stanley Cup rarely went beyond mid-April, and now rarely ends until late May. Stanley Cups late in May and the pre-season competitions of 1972, 1974, and 1976 had shown that if the hockey was good enough, almost any time of year would do.

*

I was sure that after that great and successful start, the Canada
Cup would go on every few years as an IIHF fixture, as
special an event in hockey as the World Cup is in soccer.

The Canada Cup still is – but it has not been without
problems. No one could have foreseen those problems.

Negotiations for planning future Canada Cups started two
years later, in 1978. At the IIHF meetings in Sermione,
Italy, I asked for approval of two more dates, in 1979 and
1982. Both those were non-Olympic years and were years
in which the world championships, always held in the spring,
would build up a head of competitive steam that would help
the Canada Cup in the fall. In both cases we could raise
a lot of money to help Canada's world championship and
Olympic hockey programs. The IIHF voted in favour and
we seemed to be all set for 1979.

Neither worked out that way. The 1979 Canada Cup had
to be postponed, partly because of troubles I was having
with the CAHA. I'd had that all along. This time Don
Johnson was no longer CAHA president, not there to help
head off the bitterness and envy of those within the CAHA
who couldn't come to terms with its international role having
been pre-empted. It seemed a matter almost of hatred. Some
members of the CAHA, obviously out to get me, leaked
improper and untrue information to the newspapers over
spending Carling O'Keefe money on the 1977 and 1978
world championships. They wanted to discredit me, and
in some ways they did that job too well. They suggested
that I was ignoring amateur hockey while spending CAHA
money.

There was another major hitch. At the time of the first
Canada Cup or shortly thereafter I made a deal with Carling
O'Keefe to fund our world championship teams in 1977
in Vienna, 1978 in Prague, and 1979 in Moscow. Suddenly,
along with the CAHA's attack on me, there was a change

of attitude at Carling O'Keefe. Just before the 1979 championships, the company hired Jim Taylor from Molson's. He didn't think the Canada Cup was a good vehicle for the brewery to support. He felt that his former employer, Molson's, had a lock on hockey sponsorship because of its long association with *Hockey Night in Canada*.

He preached in the boardrooms that Carling O'Keefe was wasting its money – even though the record showed that the brewery had increased its share of the beer market in 1976 and there was no reason why it shouldn't do the same in 1979.

No one will ever know. With the Canada Cup's main financial prop removed and the CAHA howling for my blood, we had to cancel in 1979 and reschedule for 1980. We had to cancel again in 1980 because of the Soviet invasion of Afghanistan that caused many countries to boycott the Moscow Olympics that year. The Canada Cup was also a victim. Although I still had hopes for 1981, with Carling O'Keefe out as the major sponsor I knew it would be a tough sell. Sometimes when we were trying to put the deal for that year together I felt that maybe the first Canada Cup had also been the last.

I'd been able to count on Arthur Harnett for sales promotion and ideas from 1972 to 1981. Arthur had spent a lot of money buying rights to the 1981 world championships. With TV sales limited and few sponsors, he had lost about $200,000 and as a result was in no financial position to buy rights for the 1981 Canada Cup. Not wanting to lose his expertise, we hired him on a commission basis. He went back to Labatt's, helped by an amazing coincidence. Sam Pollock had left Montreal Canadiens and now was a director of Labatt's. Sam and Harnett, helped by Labatt's president, Sidney Oland, a friend and sometimes tennis partner of mine, put the whole relationship of Hockey Canada, international hockey, and Labatt's back together.

Then came more problems. We had to move some games out of Quebec for lack of support. Winnipeg couldn't get

the crowds: some were less than 1,800. For a while I wondered
if we'd be able to show any kind of a profit.

On the ice, we were great – wound up undefeated in the
round-robin games to finish in first place. We beat the U.S.
in one semifinal while the Soviets took out Czechoslovakia
in the other.

That meant the sudden-death final shaped up as yet another
classic Canada-Soviet summit. Instead, it was a massacre.
When it ended – Soviets 8, Canada 1 – the patriotic side of
me, my love for Canadian hockey against all comers, made
me terribly depressed. On the financial side I had worked
so hard for so long, got it together, only to lose on the
ice. I said, and not only to myself, that's it, I've had enough.
If I'd had anybody to resign to right then, I would have
resigned. I was still in that state when Sidney Oland
came over. He must have heard about my decision to
quit.

"Alan," he said, "I know you're downhearted but think
about it for a few days. I want to tell you right now that
Sam Pollock and I and Labatt's will figure out a way to
get the financial burden totally off your shoulders, if you
will agree to go on with the next Canada Cup."

I was still way down, but it was good to know that people
who knew me were refusing to count me out. I said okay,
I would think about it.

When we did the final arithmetic we found that on the
financial side, I'd been too pessimistic. I still deemed the
Canada Cup a failure because we had lost so badly in the
final, but on the other hand we had turned a profit of
approximately $1.5 million. By agreement between the
NHLPA and the NHL, the first $600,000 went to Hockey
Canada and the rest was shared 50-50 by the NHL owners
and the NHL players, going directly into pension contri-
butions by both clubs and players.

Over the next few months I began to look ahead again.
As Sidney Oland had said, he and Sam Pollock did find
a way to relieve me of the financial burden. Labatt's saved

the day by agreeing to buy all rights to future Canada Cups. All I had to do was put the team together, help see that it was managed properly, and get people to come and watch the games.

That may sound like enough for one guy to do, but it was a lot easier than the whole load I'd handled before. Out of those decisions came the Canada Cups of 1984, 1987, and 1991.

In 1984 Glen Sather was the general manager. Before we get into what happened a memory comes to mind that tells you something about the most famous brother act in modern hockey – the Sutter brothers. Fairly well along into the camp, we decided to add a couple of players to the roster. One of them was Brent Sutter, who had just turned twenty-four a couple of months earlier. When the time came to decide on a final roster, one of the last cuts made was Brian Sutter, Brent's brother, four years older. Brent was close to tears to learn that he might well have been the player who replaced Brian. He told Sather that he would prefer to forgo his own chance and let Brian stay because it might be Brian's last chance to play in a Canada Cup. Brian quickly interjected, "They're going with the best team and you are the better player – you're staying! I'm going!" They gave each other a hug, with tears included, and I thought to myself, "There is one hell of a family!" Brent was outstanding in that Canada Cup and the next one, while Brian – as well as his brother Darryl, now assistant to Mike Keenan in Chicago – might have Canada Cup victories in future, from behind the bench.

At first that year we didn't play well, finishing fourth in the round robin – barely making it into the semifinal. As it turned out, we'd just been getting warmed up, as hard as that might be on nervous bystanders like myself. Our semifinal was against the Soviets. We beat them 3–2 in double overtime on an amazing goal by Mike Bossy, set up by Paul Coffey. The final was two out of three. We beat the Swedes in two straight games and at the end of the tournament again had earned for Canadian hockey and NHL players' pensions more than $1.5 million.

Originally, we'd planned the next Canada Cup for 1988, another Olympic year. In 1986 Labatt's asked me to consider moving the tournament up a year to 1987 because of a possible and even probable squeeze on sponsors by the 1988 Summer Olympics. I was happy to agree.

For 1987 Mike Keenan was our coach, Serge Savard and Bobby Clarke the general managers. The dates were from August 30 to September 17. It was an absolute gem of a tournament, but very hard on the heart. I don't know about other people, but as it was the last Canada Cup before 1991, which was in the planning stage as this is being written, every game in 1987 is clear in my mind. I get nervous retroactively even thinking about it.

In the first game we tied the Czechs 4–4 (there's no overtime in the round-robin) but should have won. We handled the Finns all right, 4–1, in our second game. But from then on we were *always* coming from behind.

We were losing 1–0 against the U.S. before we managed to pull it out, 3–2.

We fell behind 2–1 against Sweden in a really tough game but managed to come to life in time to win 5–3. Against the Soviets, we got a 3–3 tie with about five seconds to go. After all that travail and close calls, with three wins and two ties, we'd even finished on top, still unbeaten! In our semifinal against Czechoslovakia we were down 2–0, and could have been down by a lot more, but won 5–3. In the other semifinal the Soviets knocked off the Swedes. Once again it was the old scenario: Canada versus the Soviet Union. As usual, in spades.

The first game of the final was in Montreal on a Friday night. At the end of the second period we were down 4–2. In the third we came back, even led 5–4, but the Soviets tied it 5–5 with about a minute to go. In the overtime, a Soviet shot from the blueline deflected into our goal off Doug Crossman's stick, we lost 6–5, and we're in big trouble.

The second game of the final was in Hamilton, a beauty that went to double overtime before Mario Lemieux scored the winner, 6–5, on a pass from Gretzky. The third game was again in Hamilton. After eight minutes of the first period we're down 3–0. I could see that slaughter of 1981 coming at us again.

Then our players came back in what I have come to think of as being their typical manner, designed to drive me nuts. We not only tied the game but were ahead 5–4 going into the third period. The Soviets tied it 5–5 with three or four minutes to go. The way the game had been going, I sure didn't want overtime. I sure didn't want to lose in regular time, either.

I remember very clearly, with about ninety seconds to go there was a face-off in our zone and I couldn't believe what my eyes were telling me. Mike Keenan had been juggling lines left, right, and centre. Now he put Dale Hawerchuk at centre. Put Mario Lemieux at right wing. Put Wayne Gretzky at left wing.

Three of the best centres in the world, not one of them noted for defensive prowess, handling this face-off in our zone!

Not only that, but on defence he has Larry Murphy, another offensive-minded player who usually spends half his time in the other team's zone, along with Paul Coffey, another dedicated attacker. I couldn't believe what was right there before me. I thought of the millions of Canadians watching on television what had been one of the best Canada Cups ever and saying, as I was, "Okay, we're still in there, but who is going to do the checking?"

Suddenly, bing-bing-bing, from the face-off and off the boards Hawerchuk gets the puck to Gretzky and he's away with a three on two. Larry Murphy dashes to the front of the net. I thought Gretzky would pass it to Larry and Larry would be the hero. Wayne didn't do that. He just waited and waited and then made a drop pass to big Mario, who came in right at the face-off circle, cut toward centre, and snapped a shot over the goalie's left hand – 6–5 for Canada.

It all happened in seconds with that powerhouse that Keenan had put on the ice. We played out the last sixty or seventy seconds and had won the Canada Cup.

One extra-nice part to remember about that series, especially the uphill finish, is that to my mind it gave the same feeling to young Canadians that other young Canadians had had in 1972. Mario's goal in 1987 closed the generation gap all the way back to Paul Henderson's goal in 1972. The young ones had seen it once again, just as in 1972 – you're behind, in this case down 3–0 early in the game, but you keep on coming and don't quit.

The ones who don't remember how it happened in 1972 sure remember how it happened in 1987. If you're as lucky a man as I am, you remember one as clearly as the other.

So now, as this is written, we're into the Canada Cup for 1991, the fifth. I imagine it'll be over by the time you read this. It has been no easier to swing than any of the others, in some ways harder. On the ice the European players are getting better, and more plentiful, every year. We've done that for them – the ones who now play in the NHL. The Americans are also surging ahead in both skill and numbers. So are the Canadians. For this Canada Cup, I'm happy that several games were played in Toronto, not because I want to deprive any other city's fans but because I live here and work here. Partly because of Harold Ballard banning Soviet teams from Maple Leaf Gardens, I hadn't always been able to go away from great international hockey and be only a few minutes away from my own front door.

I've spent a lot of time going through the pleasures and perils of making the Canada Cup's balance sheet live up to the games themselves. For 1991 something new was added. Until now, we handled all Canada Cup financial and commercial matters in Canada. Nobody in Europe argued that we shouldn't. This year's change might not have been visible to the fan in the rink, or in front of TV, but part of my deal with the IIHF for this year's Canada Cup was based on Guenther Sabetzki's insistence that Cesar W. Lüthi, the IIHF's licensee in charge of television, radio, and board advertising in all international hockey (except, until now, the Canada Cup), should be part of the overall Canada Cup sales force.

This really is a natural outgrowth, but it brought more complications both in Europe and at home. I spent months and several trips to Europe working out the details so that everything sat well with the IIHF, Lüthi, and John Hudson of Labatt's. When we got that behind us just around Christmas of 1990 and finally were able to announce that the 1991 Canada Cup was on track, I for one got that old feeling that it was all worth doing, always had been, I hoped always would be.

One of the first things I did after the way was finally open was to go over a lot of financial details. Sam Pollock, always the loyal friend, helped with this. In reviewing the 1987 budget and inflation since then, it was obvious that I would have to reconstruct the tournament to keep expenses down and revenue up. For instance, looking at the figures for 1987, I found that the Soviet-U.S. and Finland-U.S. games, played in Hartford, showed a surplus while the Czech-U.S. and Sweden-U.S. games, played in Canada, showed a deficit. I decided on those grounds to put all U.S. games in U.S. cities, except Canada-U.S. I made a lot of related decisions on both pre-tournament and tournament games, arranging that in some NHL cities these games would be on the season ticket package, assuring gate receipts in the $200,000 to $300,000 range.

Labatt's wanted to include at least one western Canada city and one or two in Quebec, plus Toronto and Hamilton in Ontario. I promised Saskatoon a six-game package if they could sell 5,000 packages of tickets at $150 per package. That would create income of about $750,000 for six games that brought in less than $500,000 in 1987. Those are simply examples of a new approach, but similar or better package deals were made for games in Toronto, Montreal, Quebec, and Hamilton, as well as U.S. cities. There were complications. I was afraid that the Persian Gulf war would make our expensive insurance coverage unavailable or simply prohibitive in cost, but even before the Gulf war ended I was assured by our broker in London, Bernie Warren of Crawley, Warren, that we'd be given rates not too much higher than 1987, which was done.

All this essential negotiating, from insurance rates to prices for individual packages, is far from the games themselves but had to be managed, mainly by me with the help, this time, of my son Allen and Team Canada '72 star Ron Ellis. Just when we thought all the loose ends had been tied up securely, we were faced with the world-wide shock of the Moscow coup against Gorbachev. For three days Soviet participation in the Canada Cup hung in the balance even though my contacts in Moscow assured me their team would be coming, as usual. It is only a tiny footnote to that cataclysm in Soviet history, but my contacts were right; the team came.

Maybe the Canada Cup, or something like it, would have happened anyway in the passage of time and the growth of the game. One has to have his little (or my critics would say, not so little) vanities, and the fact remains that the germ of the idea came when I was up a ladder painting our cottage and listening to a soccer game on radio twenty-five years ago.

CHAPTER NINE

ANOTHER SIDE OF
THE COIN

When I was signing the guest book I noticed that two guests a few days earlier had signed in as "Elizabeth and Philip."

BE WARNED: some of what follows is plain name-dropping, mainly not about hockey stars. This is going to go a bit back, and a bit forward, some at home, some on the road, some personal and some reflective. Mostly, one way or another, personal.

Thinking, as I often do, of the first years after we married, before the NHLPA, it seems so simple a life to have led. Maybe Nancy doesn't see it that way, but in the early 1960s all I had to do all day, besides the sports I played and loved, was law and politics, along with accidentally getting involved in advising hockey players on a few investments. Then it got more complicated.

By the time I won the PC Association presidency in 1968 we were eight years married, had moved a few times, and owned a four-bedroom house in the Kingsway. Because of law, politics, hockey, and business, we entertained a lot. I still have a newspaper clipping of that time from the *Telegram*, showing Nancy, "the vivacious dark-haired wife of the new PC party president," at home with Jill, who was four (our son Allen was seven that year). We liked that house. Nancy's paintings lined the recreation room walls. The other rooms reflected Nancy, too – full of antiques, including a beautiful pine corner cupboard I'd given her for Christmas. Maybe Nancy had found it someplace and pointed it out to me. That had been known to happen.

I read a 1971 clipping the other day that said I had decided to step down from the players' union. That long ago! I don't remember what caused that impression to get around, but I'm sure it was true at the time. After only the first couple of years, when the NHLPA had been well launched, I would tell the players, "maybe it's time you got somebody else." They'd say no. Still, when the union began to demand more and more time that I felt might be infringing on family and professional concerns, that 1971 clipping indicates that it was hockey that I considered giving up, not law, politics, business, or other interests, including many good friends who are totally unrelated to hockey. Nancy I thank as prime mover, I a willing participant, in keeping that private side of our lives in place.

All along, in law, politics, and hockey, I was always looking for ways to build a secure future for Nancy and our family. As it turned out, and I certainly didn't have any grasp of the ramifications at the time, real estate almost accidentally helped us a lot on our road toward financial security. We moved a lot, but there was never a time when profit was the motive. As is the case with almost everybody who has a strong family life, our moves were always made because, as our family grew, we wanted a bigger place, a better place, a place closer to downtown. As it turned out, financial gain was usually a by-product. Luck, and simply Toronto, played a part. Good Toronto real estate had just kept rising in value. I've often thought that if I'd been living and working in almost any other Canadian city, that financial growth would not have been anything like the sure thing it has been for us, while always helping to give our home life the kind of interest and comfort that we wanted. Eventually, I also bought property in the Collingwood area, Nancy's home town, but even that was close enough to the city to feel the Toronto growth effect.

I treat money, my own and anyone else's, with great care. I often take the subway to work. Generally we have trained our children to take the same care about money. I sometimes tease Nancy about being the spender in the family, but three out of four in the family isn't too bad a success rate.

I may tease her, but since she has taken the bulk of the abuse of living with me, she's entitled to that luxury. She spends wisely, an expert in so many fields that sometimes it just brings a smile of pride to my face. I hear professionals talking to her about furniture, modern or antique, and know she has as much firsthand knowledge as any of them, has read books where some have just read pages. The same thing applies when she's discussing art with curators and others prominent in that field.

She subscribes to and devours thirty or forty magazines and books a month. Our home sometimes looks like a magazine warehouse, but they feed her special range of interests. She reads every movie review and has seen every quality movie for the last twenty years. Neither of us watches television very much. I watch the odd sports event, but Sunday night is reserved for dramas. I think of *Masterpiece Theatre* and *Mystery Theatre*. That's the one time during the week that we almost always spend at home. Usually we will be together in the family room, but in the unlikely event that one of us doesn't want to watch what's on, I'll watch a set in the bedroom. The other television that we regularly share is *Saturday Night Live*. If we're too tired to watch it in full, and somebody falls asleep, we tape it to watch later through the week.

From the time when we could afford to travel, our choices were, and are, rarely at random. Nancy always has a list of interesting prospects, with guide books and maps to back them up, parts of the world we both want to see: Europe, the Far East, the Mediterranean, Scandinavia, the Soviet Union. Our travels over the last twenty years or so would fill a book on their own, with the sports side of my life sometimes, but not always, involved. Invariably, in every country we find someone we know. I usually wind up doing some business on the trip, helping to pay at least some of the travel expenses.

We try to go in comfort. Our homes away from home are part of making travel a good deal more pleasant: a shared flat in London, a house in Palm Beach, an apartment in New York City, a cottage near Thornbury in Collingwood township, a farm nearby as well as our house in Toronto. When I, or we, have to be in New York City for four or five days it's a lot more comfortable to spend the time in our own small condominium apartment than in a hotel. The same applies to trips to Europe. We always stop in London for a day or two on our way to and from European destinations. We sometimes just go to London to relax in the flat, see the shows, visit some people. We were in Israel for the Macabee Games in 1973. We have been to Egypt and travelled the Nile. We have been to all the countries in Western Europe and most in Eastern Europe.

Sometimes we enjoy the cities and sometimes Nancy's main aim is to visit ruins – in which case I keep her company. The only continent we've not visited yet is South America. Our favourite country to visit is Italy. We usually take a week a year just to travel through Italy, sometimes by car, sometimes by train. We settle in the best hotels in the centre of Italian cities or small towns and roam out from the centre. The only way to see a city is on foot. When we travel we do more walking than most people, and love it.

As I mentioned, such trips are rarely at random. One exception was a trip we made to China in 1973. We were living in Mississauga at the time but had bought a house in the comfortable downtown area of Rosedale and were about to move. A neighbour called to say that there'd been a cancellation by someone on a trip to China organized by the Canadian Importers Association. Would we be interested in replacing them?

I wasn't really an importer of anything but hockey teams from time to time, but did qualify because I'd been part of a group that had organized a company, Pony Sporting Goods. (Our first ad featured Bobby Orr walking on a beach; Pony became a strong shoe company internationally, eventually taken over by Japanese.) We decided that the China trip was the chance of a lifetime, we could move into the new house on our return, so we went. Through our embassy I arranged meetings with Chinese sports federations, suggesting that Bobby Orr might come to China to help their hockey program and that Karen Magnussen, another client, might help their figure skaters. Canada was sending a hockey team to China later that year, the UBC Thunderbirds, so these contacts in other fields of sport made the papers.

Then I did, unhappily, become a real importer. Of a serious case of asthma.

On our last day in China, Nancy and I went for dinner with *Globe and Mail* correspondent John Burns and his wife. Something in the incense being burned in the restaurant bothered me some and was still a problem when we left for Canada the next day. As we moved straight into our new house, the asthma attacks were getting worse.

Forgetting that this had started in China, I suspected the culprit was something in the new house. I lost fifteen pounds in the next ten days, was very sick, went down to 157 pounds, couldn't work, and, even worse, couldn't handle the worry and stress of being choked up all the time, trying to breathe.

Eventually I was referred to Dr. Elie Cass, who since has become a close friend. Elie tried antibiotics on me for three weeks, but I wasn't getting any better. Late in November I'd been planning to fly to Montreal for the wedding of Syl Apps, Jr., a friend and one of my hockey clients. Feeling as I did, I figured I'd have to cancel.

That day I was in Elie's office early, feeling terrible.

"Let's try acupuncture," he said.

Right then I was ready to try anything. I knew he was vice-president of the Acupuncture Association of Canada. He picked a book out of a case and started flipping through the pages as if looking for something.

"Hold on!" I said. "You have to look it up in a book? Are you telling me you've never done this before?"

He glanced at me briefly. "No, what I'm telling you is that I've never done acupuncture for asthma before."

He did it. In five minutes I felt so much better that I called Nancy and told her I was flying to Montreal for the Apps wedding. I did, flew home the next day, and later would go in every month or two for "a little tuneup," as Elie calls it. From that time on I haven't had major asthma problems. We figured eventually that my first reaction to the incense in China had been the cause of the asthma all along.

On many such foreign trips, beginning when Mitchell Sharp was External Affairs Minister, Canadian embassies or consulates along the way would be told to expect us so we might be included in any dinners, luncheons, or other social events. I'd let Mitchell Sharp know how this embassy or that impressed me or not.

Along the way, in Canada and elsewhere, we met many memorable people, often more or less by chance. One I remember with particular warmth was Queen Elizabeth at an Ontario Place reception. Claude Bennett, the minister responsible for Ontario Place, was walking with the Queen. He stopped in front of me and said, "Your Majesty, may I present Alan Eagleson, the president of our party?"

She said, "Good day, sir." Maybe what I did then was brash, but it just seemed natural, as are most things I do on impulse. I immediately took the opportunity, not common among many who meet her at such seemingly casual but actually closely regulated functions, to introduce Allen and Jill. (Nancy was inside with my parents holding seats directly behind where the Queen would sit later.) So our kids met the Queen, too. Might not have had another chance! At the same time I introduced a friend of Allen's, Bruce Johnson. That just happened. I wasn't trying to combine business with pleasure, although Bruce *is* the son of Ross Johnson, whose company, Standard Brands at that time, is now R.J.R. Nabisco – holder of one of the more lucrative contracts I later negotiated for Bobby Orr.

One early experience that resulted in a friendship I value came in 1964. Flying to New York, and with a window seat, I noticed that the man sitting beside me was trying to look over my shoulder to see out. I gave him my seat and we chatted a while and introduced ourselves. He said his name was Paul Metternich. I thought no more about it right then. The only time I could remember seeing that name, and that vaguely, was in history books.

I later found that he was president of the German Automobile Club, a car racer, and the great-great-grandson of the Austrian statesman Prince Klemens Wenzel Nepomuk Lother von Metternich, dominant figure of the 1814-15

Congress of Vienna, which was assembled to determine details of territorial resettlement and restoration to power of the crowned heads of Europe after Napoleon's banishment to Elba. On that first meeting we shared a cab into New York. He invited me to visit him, the verbal invitation being followed by letters and a definite invitation to call next time I was in Europe.

When I did so I found he had one of Europe's most beautiful homes, a veritable palace on the Rhine, Schloss Johannesberg, where he produces a white wine among the world's finest. Paul's wife, Tatiana, is the daughter of the last Minister of Education in pre-Soviet Russia. Her book *Five Passports Through Europe* describes the way she and her family escaped from Moscow after the Communists seized power. So from a chance encounter came a friendship that has lasted now for more than twenty-six years. On one of my subsequent visits, when signing the guest book, I noticed that two guests of a few days earlier had signed in as "Elizabeth and Philip."

In 1966 when I was a young member of the Ontario legislature, I travelled to Australia, visited the parliament buildings in Canberra, and met Prime Minister Harold Holt. While in his office, his predecessor as Prime Minister, Sir Robert Menzies, dropped by – so that day I met them both. (A few months later Harold Holt disappeared in a swimming accident, his body never found.)

Nancy and I, travelling through the Greek islands by ship, met a couple from South Africa – Peter McLean, publisher of the *Durban Daily News*, and his wife. They said, "Come and see us." We don't turn down such invitations. A trip anywhere gets better when you are guests of someone who knows the country.

When we did go to Durban, Peter took two weeks off to give us a tour through South Africa, including a few nights at Kruger National Park in Swaziland.

British Prime Minister James Callaghan I met at the first Canada Cup in 1976. He invited Nancy and me to visit him sometime at 10 Downing Street. We took him up on that a year later. Although he'd been called out of the country at the last moment he arranged for his aide to have us over for tea. I found it fascinating to stand near the cabinet table, small in comparison to the many momentous events decided upon there – including declarations of war.

That same year I met Margaret Thatcher, my kind of operator, at the Toronto home of the consul-general for the United Kingdom. It was obvious to me from our conversations that she had a brilliant future in war and peace, as well as politics. This was not long before she became Britain's Prime Minister.

That same year, at the Innsbruck Olympics, I was sitting in a hotel lobby when I noticed a man having difficulty getting a door open: pushing instead of pulling. I walked over and opened the door for him. He thanked me. We chatted for a few minutes about the Olympics. Then he gave me his card and I found that he was the president of Austria, Dr. Rudolph Kirchschlager. Very friendly and easy to get along with, he suddenly asked, "Would you join me in my box for some of the events?" For simply opening a door for him I wound up watching hockey and figure skating from what had been known from the time of Austria's emperors as the royal box.

At the world championships in Sweden in 1979 our seats were directly in front of King Gustav and Queen Sylvie and their two children. Over the course of the games we were just plain excited hockey fans together. The King gave me a souvenir from Sweden and I gave him one from our country – naturally, a Canada Cup pen!

In February, 1982, we were invited to the White House to lunch with President Ronald Reagan and his Nancy. My immediate companion at the table (Table #11, according to the invitation, which I have saved) was Vice-President George Bush. I got to know the future President as much as one could over the course of an hour or two while President Reagan kept us laughing with stories of his radio-announcing days and his work as a film star in New York's Hell's Kitchen area, where (if you'll pardon a social note) NHL star Joey Mullen was brought up.

Which reminds me of another encounter, this one expensive, with former U.S. President Gerald Ford. Peter Pocklington of Edmonton had arranged an NHL-NHLPA tour of the Betty Ford Clinic in Palm Springs, California. We thought we might want to support the clinic financially. Our group included Ed Snider from Philadelphia Flyers, Morgan McCammon of Montreal Canadiens, John Ziegler, and I, all of us with our wives. We toured the clinic with the Fords, played golf at his golf club, and when we were checking out of the pro shop that day, John Ziegler said, "Well, that's the most expensive round of golf I ever played."

Somebody asked how much. He said, "Guess." The replies were around the $200-$300 range.

I said it probably cost $15,000.

John said, "Exactly! But how did you know?"

I knew because Gerald Ford came to Toronto that year to make a speech. His fee was $15,000. I figured he'd want the same for the golf, the cocktails at his house, and the dinner at his golf club. At that price, we didn't mind putting him through a photo session so that all of us would have mementoes to take home for the family albums.

While making presentations on behalf of the NHLPA to U.S. Senate banking committees and legislation committees, I met several senators well known far beyond committee work. One was Ted Kennedy. I met him again years later, with his then wife Joan Kennedy, at a fund-raising function that included Bobby Orr in Boston. The Kennedys invited Bobby and me to a private room with them for more leisurely conversation. I remember thinking at the time, which one is the principal celebrity? In Boston then, it was a toss-up between Kennedy and Orr.

Of course, at home I'm on a first-name basis with a lot of the well-known people in politics – by no means all of them Tories. One of my prime memories is of a time in

1966 when Nancy and I spent a full day with the Dief-
enbakers at their home. He then was Leader of the Opposition, his Conservative prime ministerial years gone but not
forgotten. We had a great lunch with The Chief and his
wife Olive and a wonderful afternoon talking politics, law,
his feisty career as a criminal lawyer in western Canada,
and his involvement in the early 1960s, by no means always
amicably, with U.S. President John Kennedy.

Liberal Prime Minister Lester Pearson was a firm friend
to the NHLPA. Of course, he had a keen interest in many
sports. He'd been known to check out of a Commons debate
to catch baseball on television. When he retired as Prime
Minister in 1968 he agreed to sit on the board of Sports-
men's Mutual Fund Limited, which we'd set up to help
hockey players with their investments. His involvement was
engineered through my friendship with Senator Keith Davey,
then a heavy hitter with the Liberals. Mr. Pearson also
approved the use of his name for the Lester B. Pearson
Award for the player chosen each season by his fellow
members of the NHLPA.

He came to Toronto to make the first presentation. That
was to Phil Esposito, the forerunner of a string of great
nominees. If you guessed Bobby Orr, Bobby Clarke, Wayne
Gretzky, Mario Lemieux, and Steve Yzerman, you'd be
on the right track – that's the kind of quality the Pearson
award personifies.

A few years later, in 1976, Prime Minister Pierre Trudeau's
letter of support helped get the Canada Cup established.
In November that year, after we'd won the first Canada
Cup, he and his wife Margaret threw a grand cocktail party
just for our players and their wives at the prime ministerial
residence on Ottawa's Sussex Drive. This was followed by
a dinner for 400-500 people. Five years later he showed he
wasn't just a fair-weather friend: he turned up for breakfast
the day after we'd been threshed 8–1 by the Soviets in the
sudden-death final of the 1981 Canada Cup. To me, it's
always a good sign to see politicians show up when times

are tough. When there's nothing but cheer in the air, it's easy. That morning he told Wayne Gretzky, Larry Robinson, and the others how sadly he felt about Canada losing after the players had given their all for their country.

Back to the Tories. In 1967 when I worked on Davie Fulton's campaign for the leadership of the federal Progressive Conservative Party, my co-workers included two future Canadian prime ministers, Joe Clark and Brian Mulroney. In this connection, I can prove that if political conventions were horse-races, which they sometimes resemble, the pari-mutuels would have nothing to fear from me. In 1976 I worked for Brian Mulroney in his first, unsuccessful, bid to succeed Robert Stanfield as leader. That year Joe Clark won. In 1983 I worked for Joe in his unsuccessful bid to retain that leadership. The victor at that time, as we all know, was the same Brian Mulroney, for whom I'd worked seven years earlier.

A lot of people wondered if Brian would still treat me as a friend after I'd worked for Joe Clark. That was a matter solely between me and Brian, solved without a problem. I had a stronger personal relationship with him than with Joe, but for the party's sake I'd felt it was necessary for some of us to stay with the leader in that particular battle. He accepted that. It never made a difference to our relationship.

Whether it's Pearson or Trudeau or Mulroney, access to our country's Prime Minister has always been a benefit to me and the people I work for. When Brian called to congratulate me on the 1987 Canada Cup victory I asked him, "What would you think about giving a party for our team?" He gave an instant okay. He and Mila threw open the doors. Good party, full of warmth.

Finally, when Brian held a luncheon in honour of Mikhail Gorbachev's visit to Canada in the summer of 1990, he introduced me. "This is the man who handles all of our international hockey negotiations," he said. "He has set up all those exciting games between the Soviet Union and Canada. Right back to 1972."

Mr. Gorbachev shook my hand warmly while looking me straight in the eye, a smile touching the corner of his mouth. I had a feeling I knew what he was thinking about. I felt like asking, "Did you see Paul Henderson score that goal, sir?" but didn't. One time I kept my mouth shut when maybe I shouldn't have.

CHAPTER TEN

BOBBY ORR – THE BREAKUP

"That guy is going to do to you what he has done to my brother . . . he shouldn't badmouth my brother."

– *Tony Esposito, pointing at Bobby Orr, who was then a Boston teammate of Tony's brother Phil.*

Among the most unhappy events of my life – and there haven't been all that many – I'll always remember Wednesday, August 29, 1979. Nancy and I were taking a few people out to dinner, including Ron Ellis and Paul Henderson and their wives. They were friends of ours stretching back a dozen years or more to when Henderson and Ellis were in the NHL and I was the more-or-less rookie executive director of the NHLPA. For about the same period I had been personal representative, friend, and in general considered myself and tried to be something like an older brother to Bobby Orr.

We were having a pre-dinner drink when Bobby phoned. We talked for a few minutes in a way that was obviously not in the pal-old-pal line that had been our norm in the years after I negotiated his first contract with Boston in 1966. For a year now relations had been showing some strain. That started after he'd gone to the management side with Chicago Black Hawks. This day he ranted a bit and I ranted a bit. In a few minutes Nancy appeared in the doorway urgently pointing to her watch to remind me of the dinner reservations. I'd had enough of the conversation, anyway, so I said, "Look, I'm busy. I'll get back to you." I did call him back a couple of hours later. He might have had a drink or two and I'd had some wine with dinner. He said he had tried to tell me before, but now, "I just want to tell you that I'm through with hockey and I might as well be through with agents and representatives. Let's get everything separated and let's split."

When we hung up I assumed that, as had happened during earlier differences, this one would disappear within a week and he'd think differently. That didn't happen. What did happen was that for a brief period the Eagleson-Orr split, making redundant all those dozens of magazine covers and hundreds of news photos and articles over the years depicting the two of us as being inseparable, was the big sports-page news.

It took us until April 2, 1980, to finalize the split, and those months were the toughest time I had experienced. In August Bobby said good-bye and the hockey world was shocked. In December I fell playing tennis and reinjured an old back injury that dated back to my lacrosse days in the late 1950s, making it impossible for me to sit, stand, lie down, or move in any way without pain. In March, 1980, Bill Watters, who had worked with me in hockey agenting for years, left me, stimulated by Orr's departure. At the same time Mike Milbury was mounting the first real attack ever made on my stewardship of the NHLPA.

Of all those difficult times, the most difficult was the Orr situation. It was a divorce that came absolutely out of the blue. I couldn't believe it when it happened. I still have difficulty believing it now. It hurt me a lot, still does, partly because it was also hard on my family. Bobby had been something like a big brother or uncle to our children ever since Allen started to school and Jill was in rompers. Now he suddenly pulled himself entirely away from them. That bothered me as much as his leaving me. His career was over in hockey, but the business relationships I had created for him were quite extensive. Years later, some are still operating positively to his benefit. Bobby was saying some hurtful things to which I, at the time, did not reply. It was like a one-sided divorce.

It was quick and it was, or seemed to be, clean, but I am sure it hurt Bobby, too. With all the media rumours and guesses swirling around, I actually can remember only one bright spot from that winter. It was a hand-written letter from Darryl Sittler, who was then in a running battle with general manager Punch Imlach and owner Harold Ballard of the Leafs, with me on Sittler's side. It was on Air Canada stationery, dated Remembrance Day, 1979, about two months after Orr had told me to get lost, and Sittler told me that he felt I had "been very fair, helpful and important" to him, thanked me for what I had done for him, and signed it "Sincerely, your friend and client, Sit." Although Orr was never mentioned in that letter, he was certainly there between the lines.

Orr never gave me a reason for demanding our split during that call in 1979. He paid accountants and lawyers for six months of work going through all my files that pertained to him.

We gave them full access. For months an accountant named Ed Hanley, hired by Orr, sat in one of our back offices – which were on Queen Street in downtown Toronto at the time – sifting through documents. I said to Hanley, "There are the files. Go through whatever you like. Photostat whatever you like."

Their aim on Orr's behalf was to find out if all money due him through the operations of his company, Bobby Orr Enterprises Limited, had actually been paid. All they found out was what I had told them in the first place. The books and records were as clean as a whistle.

Marvin Goldblatt, my accountant, said to me, "Do we need somebody in there with Hanley?"

I said, "Who cares as long as he doesn't take anything out?" and told Hanley, "Here are the books and here are the cheques. You notice the name on the bottom of the cheques. Robert Orr. Not Alan Eagleson."

So Hanley plugged away through details of various arrangements and deals I had made on Bobby's behalf through Bobby Orr Enterprises Limited. Where did the money go? The records showed lines like these: Robert Orr – $10,000 a month; $5,000; $12,000. Too often, when we'd get to the end of the Bobby Orr Enterprises Limited fiscal year we'd find that the gross intake, less tax, left a sum *less* than what Bobby already had drawn in shareholder advances. I had remonstrated with him about his spending. Years later he admitted that he should have taken more interest, should have known what was going on, but "that was Al's side" – blaming *me* for *him* not listening to me. Did I take the cheques he was taking as shareholder advances and cash them? No, Bobby Orr did. He took all the money coming to him, and more, and spent it all. Years later he's still trying to make out that the reckless things he did with his money were my fault.

I should point out that Bobby Orr Enterprises Limited, his umbrella company, was never intended to be, and never was, an investment company. It was strictly for income management, under a widely held concept common among tax consultants of the time. He was president and I was vice-president and directed that company. We had a good group of people on the board – among them Walter Bowen, a senior counsel around Toronto, and Keith Davey, for many years a name to conjure with in the Liberal Party. These men gave their time because they felt it was to the benefit of Bobby Orr that things should be done the right way. There was nothing wrong with the concept of Bobby Orr Enterprises except for Bobby Orr's spending habits. My wife Nancy once told him, when we used to discuss such things, "Bobby, you can't spend the money and have it too." If he had spent the money the way I spent money or Darryl Sittler spent money, there would have been in that company right now probably $2 million.

When he dropped that bomb about us splitting, he did not give me specific reasons. I didn't know what he was trying to accomplish or what was behind it, except that he wanted to get rid of me. The more I thought about it the more I have come to believe that when he came to that autumn of 1979 and was out of hockey but secure financially because of contracts I'd made for him, security and a safe future weren't enough. He might not even have realized this consciously, but one of the big changes in his life was that he'd been slowly but surely sliding out of the limelight, losing the public attention that had been part of his life for so long – books, magazine covers, reporters lined up in the dressing room to hang on his every word, if he deigned to say any.

Once in the late 1970s when Orr and I were still together, I hosted a reception for Ontario Premier Bill Davis. The

Toronto Sun used a front-page picture of the Premier, Darryl Sittler, and me. Orr at the time was in Chicago, unhappy, missing Boston, the public and media interest in him pretty well in eclipse compared to what it had been. On the other hand, Sittler and his battles with Punch Imlach and Toronto Maple Leafs' owner Harold Ballard were at the top of the sports-page menu. I was never particularly aware of any animosity between Orr and Sittler. Both had starred in the Canada Cup of 1976, Orr the dominant player and Sittler scoring the final's winning goal. Sittler's one appearance as the NHL's second-team all-star centre in 1978 was nowhere near Orr's dominance of individual awards.

Bobby had a possessive streak. I'd seen it in action before and would again even after our split. When he saw that *Sun* picture he phoned me. "What are you doing? You spend all your time with Sittler, with no time for me." I said, "Hey, Bobby, you used to be there but you don't come to those functions any more. I don't cancel the function just because you don't come."

I should interject here that all through it, and to this day, I was and am still partial to Orr as a hockey player. I had too many great memories of him to follow any other course. I have never stopped making that plain in such things as comparisons between him and the star of the 1980s and beyond, Wayne Gretzky. To me, the difference between them as hockey players was that any time Bobby Orr picked up the puck behind his own net and started up the ice, I *always* felt there was a chance at the end of it that he would score. He often did. As great as Gretzky is, he didn't have that overpowering capability. In some ways, I think I remember Bobby Orr the hockey player more clearly than he does himself.

On the more personal side, for years I tended to play down the problems his proneness to knee injuries presented. I'd lived with them for a long time – in fact, I was at the game when he first injured his knee. When he was hit and went down I knew he was hurt badly. I rushed to the dressing room and was there before the club doctor arrived. Hap Emms blew a gasket when he found that I'd been in the dressing room talking to the doctor even before Hap knew how bad the injury was. It was my argument that Bobby Orr right then should have been put in the hands of the best doctors in the world, he was such a great asset. The Boston Bruins decided that their club doctor could do the job and I think to this day that was the beginning of the end for Bobby's knee. After only two NHL seasons he'd had two knee operations, the second before the end of the 1968-69 season. The knee was still weak enough that it bothered him in training camp before the 1969-70 season, but it got stronger as he worked at it. That year he played Boston's entire seventy-six-game season, but it kept getting hurt from time to time. He had another operation in the summer of 1972 and wasn't fit to play the first Canada-Soviet series in September of that year.

I always thought that one of the problems was his stubbornness. All along, he resisted going to a doctor he didn't know.

In 1976, just before the first Canada Cup, when I was negotiating with both Boston and Chicago for his next contract, there is no question that we were trying to create a media impression about Bobby's knees being better than was justified. We had pretty solid advice from medical experts that he wasn't going to be able to play much longer. But I didn't feel that it was incumbent on me to make that announcement at a press conference. I felt that it was better for me to say, "Hey, we want the best deal possible for Bobby Orr." Also, people had been wrong about his knees before. Going back to 1972, orthopedic surgeon John Zeldin, one of our Team Canada doctors, told me, "Alan, I don't think Bobby Orr can last three more years and he's a young man, he's going to hurt himself, maybe he should consider

Sure, it was just a 1970 skate promotion, but with men I liked: Bob Nevin, Tim Ecclestone, Lou Angotti, Rick Ley.

Lester B. Pearson award winners are picked by NHL players, hockey's ultimate jury of peers. The first one, 1971, went to Phil Esposito.

I don't have photos of them all, but Bobby Clarke got his in the Philadelphia Spectrum in 1974.

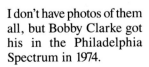

In 1974 I had six first-round draft choices to negotiate contracts for. From the left, Jack Valiquette went to Toronto, Dave Maloney to New York Rangers, Lee Fogolin to Buffalo, Rick Hampton to California, Bill Lochead to Detroit, and Wilf Paiement to Kansas City.

An international day at the Hockey Hall of Fame, 1977: with the International Ice Hockey Federation's Guenther Sabetzki, Anatoly Tarasov, Curt Berglund, Gord Renwick.

Wayne Gretzky, sixteen, was player of the game in the 1978 World Junior Championship at Cornwall.

Mom and Dad's fiftieth wedding anniversary, 1979, with my sisters Frances Eagleson Dawe at Dad's right, Carol Eagleson Ruse and Margaret Eagleson Hooey to Mother's left. Ten years later we had a bigger one, the sixtieth.

Among friends:
Maureen McTeer and
Robert Stanfield.

Sarajevo Winter
Olympics, 1984:
Aggie Kukulowicz,
Sam Pollock, Lorne
Greene.

With former U.S.
president Gerald
Ford, in his Palm
Springs home. Mr.
Ford's fee for a day
of golf, dinner, and
bon mots with hockey
leaders was $15,000
(U.S.).

Proud moment in 1989: I was made an officer
of the Order of Canada, presented by Governor-
General Jeanne Sauve.

After we won the 1987 Canada Cup on Mario Lemieux's goal after a pass from
Gretzky, the Mulroneys said, "Come on over."

Robert Marvin Hull, my pal. Both smiling. That year, 1988, he and I were among those inducted into the Canadian Sports Hall of Fame.

In 1991, Brett Hull and his old man's onetime sparring partner.

In 1989 when my job in the NHLPA was under attack by dissident players and agents and for a while the long knives were everywhere I looked, the *Hockey News* published this Elston cartoon. The situation in a nutshell. Couldn't have said it better myself.

The happy day when Jill graduated in law, with her mother, dad, Allen and Yasmine there to cheer.

Nancy and I and the Great Wall, China, 1973.

Thanksgiving, 1984.

On a river-raft trip in Utah, 1978.

Aspen, not long ago.

retiring now." Well, Bobby had great years after 1972. Also, the magic of his name and skills, what he could do when healthy, made him sought after. So we were trying to get everybody cranked up about Bobby, and the potential $3 million contract we signed with Chicago (half of it guaranteed, whatever happened) was the result.

To get back to the 1979 breakup, naturally our deeply meshed business and other associations couldn't just end with the wave of a magic wand. There was hardly an item that didn't take negotiations back and forth. There was his unilateral, personal, and drastic rearrangement downward of the hockey contract I negotiated for him with Chicago. There was a disagreement over disposition of the hockey camp property that he and Mike Walton, mostly Walton, had worked at. There was the matter of who paid (eventually, I paid) for what started out being called the Bobby Orr Sports Injury Clinic at York University.

I was fair and straightforward about this. Letters back and forth between me and his lawyer in Boston, Jack Herlihy, gradually settled most of the items. One of the reasons the business changes went relatively smoothly was because of Jack Herlihy's respect for me and mine for him. That had begun years earlier when Don McKenney, who had started out with Boston, took a court action against the club. Herlihy was McKenney's lawyer. The Bruins' lawyer was a man named Bob Quinn, an unsuccessful candidate in a recent election. In my view, Boston was simply trying to renege on a contract it had with McKenney, so on behalf of the NHLPA I was called as a witness. On one memorable occasion, in cross-examination Quinn tried to convince me and the court that I was not telling the truth. I told him if he was calling me a liar we should step outside, or I should just step outside the witness box and punch him on the nose.

At that point the judge, trying to control his laughter, said, "Mr. Eagleson, please calm down and just answer the question, and for you, Mr. Quinn, ask the question in more temperate fashion so that Mr. Eagleson won't get upset again."

McKenney won the case hands down and to this day Jack Herlihy insists that he would not have won without my testimony. Any examination of letters between Herlihy and me over the Orr situation years later would indicate that mutual respect paved the way for solving contentious issues.

Most of what I've talked about so far is hockey-related. There is a whole different field, nothing to do with knees, but about the difficulties in representing him on business sponsorship matters. When he had a big and lucrative deal with General Motors, he said he wanted a Mercedes. I said, "Bobby, you can't drive a Mercedes! I won't let you get it." With some control over his spending I thought I could enforce that. He turned around and made a deal with a friend of mine whom I called and burned for letting himself be persuaded to sell Bobby his Mercedes. Endorsing Chevs and Buicks and driving a Mercedes!

Then there was another deal, for Bobby Orr Pizza Places. Oscar Grubert is a really successful restaurateur of the chain variety. He owns the rights to several of them, all big – Cavanaghs and Kentucky Fried Chicken in Winnipeg, Mother Tucker's in other places. When his deal for Bobby Orr Pizza Places was launched in the Royal York Hotel, a lot of celebrities, from Pierre Berton to Robert Fulford, were on hand, as well as all the sportswriters. The fanfare was for a new Bobby Orr Pizza Place to open in Oshawa. Oscar set them up and they did well, except Bobby didn't want to have anything to do with them. He'd say, "I never eat this stuff," that type of thing, and wouldn't go to an opening. So Oscar finally said, "We might as well get out of that deal." If Bobby had co-operated he'd be making hundreds of thousands of dollars from that business right now, but he just kissed off an association that could have been a long-time money-winner for him.

Another example. We set up a company called Bobby Orr Inc. in Boston, owned 20 per cent by David Landay and Alvin Wolfe of Brookfield Athletic Shoe Limited. Bobby owned the other 80 per cent. They decided they were going to market a Bobby Orr line of skates and other equipment, and Bobby was going to tell them how to develop it.

We made $100,000 the first year with them. We could have been making more. But Bobby would denigrate the product. They'd bring the product in. It was quite good quality for kids but he'd say, "I wouldn't put that junk on my kid." They'd phone and say, "Bobby, we've got an important customer," and he'd say something like, "Sorry, I'm busy." After five or six meetings it came to the point where he said, "I don't like those two guys, screw 'em, I'm not going to their plant."

Eventually they just got tired of him.

When I'd bring up and develop these opportunities by which he could ensure his financial future, which I saw as part of my responsibility, sometimes I would have to do a selling job on him, but I never forced him into anything. All he had to say was no.

From time to time through the six or seven months when we were painfully amputating our version of Siamese twins, sometimes I would think of a conversation I'd had with Tony Esposito in the plane on the way back from Moscow after the '72 series. Tony had had a couple of drinks. I'm walking up and down the aisles talking to the guys when Tony says, "Come here. Sit down."

Bobby Orr was sitting about four rows ahead. "See that guy," Tony said. "He shouldn't be here."

I got mad. I'd got Orr there, specially. "What do you mean?"

"What the hell did he do for this team?" Tony demanded. "Couldn't play, couldn't skate, and he's a goddamn whiner."

The more he says, the madder I get.

He went on. "I'll tell you one thing. You just remember this conversation. That guy is going to do to you what he has done to my brother."

"What's he done to your brother?"

"My brother is a good hockey player. That guy up there," pointing, "is a great hockey player, but he shouldn't bad-mouth my brother."

I was getting hotter and hotter. I did remember times when at two or three in the morning after a game I'd get a call from Orr and he'd be talking about what he'd done that night and say, "Esposito always makes just one extra pass so I don't get an assist."

I didn't take that seriously at the time, just figuring that all Orr wanted was to play well, but it was what you might call a straw in the wind.

"I'm just telling you," Tony said, "I don't trust that guy and you shouldn't trust that guy." And that was in 1972, long ago, but I remembered that conversation when I was working my way through that part of the Orr trouble in 1979 and 1980. A year or so ago I asked Tony if he remembered what he'd said.

He said, "Yes, I remember that."

CHAPTER ELEVEN

THE UPRISINGS

"Hey, Al, there's something I think you
should know . . . "

*—former adversary Mike Milbury, tipping me off about
the secret 1989 attempt to get rid of me.*

In the earliest days, it seemed that when any dispute arose, large or small, that involved our members, the reaction was, "Phone Al." I scan twenty-year-old clippings about player-management frictions that were sports-page sensations for a day or two and have to work hard to remember what this one or that one was really all about – but I was always aware that from the middle 1960s to the beginning of the 1990s, each year hockey grabbed more and more of my time. Over that period the difference was that in the early years I rarely had any opposition within the NHLPA that couldn't be handled by chewing things over and reaching one of our long series of unanimous votes. I had stage-managed the 1972 series, the players all with me but several people in Hockey Canada opposed to the way I was doing things. That solidarity with the players hung tough through a lot of NHL and international growth, rising salaries, bidding a fond farewell to the reserve clause, negotiating the first collective bargaining agreement, winning the first Canada Cup, making sure that when any of my clients signed with a WHA franchise that might look shaky the money should be guaranteed. All the same, I was feeling the pressure.

The NHLPA was only a baby when I found that my enjoyment of hockey games was lessened *because I couldn't cheer any more* (except against the Russians, when I could still shout my lungs out like any fan). In league games and playoffs, players on both teams were friends and clients. So how could I cheer for one side or the other?

I took my son Allen to a game in Maple Leaf Gardens. Naturally he was on his feet yelling for the Leafs, as I *used* to do. One player on the visiting team saw him up cheering, assumed that I was cheering as well, and brought that up with me afterwards. I literally had to sit on my hands – and not only that, make my face look as if frozen into a permanently non-committal expression. That just ain't me!

I remember Red Berenson gave me an earful for being in the Boston dressing room on television during the celebration of Bobby Orr's first Stanley Cup win. That was in 1970, with Red's team, St. Louis, being the losers. "I pay your salary, too," Red said. "You shouldn't be cheering against me."

It was a good point. I was careful about even dressing-room visits from then on, but I know that at least once I expressed this frustration and the reasons behind it to someone who told someone else, leading to a news report in 1971 that I was going to leave the players' association. The story was that a new assistant I'd hired, Mike Cannon, was being groomed to succeed me.

But I never did *seriously* consider stepping down at that stage. There was still so much to do – getting the pensions up, getting rid of the reserve clause that since 1940 had tied a player to one club for life or until he was traded. In those days a manager could shuffle a player back and forth to the minors for disciplinary reasons or no visible reason at all. There was no rule that a player had to be put on waivers before he could be sent down, so that another club might pick him up and keep him in the NHL. We achieved all those objectives in time. The formation of the World Hockey Association helped a lot by providing an alternative for any player not satisfied where he was.

To jump ahead a bit, the improvements we did make in owner-player rules eventually, in fact, shifted the balance of power slowly but surely to the players.

Through the 1970s, the players and I naturally had disagreements over issues from time to time, all being solved usually without publicity. However, those years led eventually, maybe inevitably – such relationships rarely stay peaceful forever – to my problems of 1979 and 1980.

Until 1979 there was never an open challenge to my role; or, as some called it, my rule. The challenge in 1979 came from Mike Milbury, a Boston-born former Colgate student who had spent a couple of seasons in the minors with Rochester before becoming a mainstay on Boston's defence. Mike decided flatly that the next change the players needed was to get me the hell out of the boss's job. He had his

say, and it was a furore throughout the league. He collected
a few supporters. But his charges and criticisms angered
the overwhelming majority of the players, including some
of his teammates at Boston who supported me and thought
Milbury was full of it. And when it came to the crunch – zero.

At that time, much more so than now, some of the older
players were still around to stress how far we'd come, even
if I was an obnoxious bastard sometimes. Still, I remember
about that time, with troubles mounting, wondering why
I worked that hard. I've often tried to put a name to whatever
it is that drives me. None of it was primarily to make money
for me. I don't think, either, that I was on a power trip.
I just felt that when something about the players came up
that needed doing, and I could do it, I would do it. And
if I was going to do it, sure, I stepped on people's toes.
Maybe even with hobnailed boots.

I paid close attention to the Milbury movement even after
it disappeared into the woodwork. I saw it as a symptom.
Even at that time, and later, he and I were not really enemies.
I used to tease him, "Hey, Mike, your heart is in the right
place but your head is screwed up." He came right back
with, "I could say the same thing about you." Either way,
that isn't exactly shooting to kill. He never really abandoned
his original objections, for which I respected him. A couple
of years ago when he was asked by a reporter about his
1979 stint as leader of the opposition, he said, "At that time
I thought I was right . . . " then quickly came to his senses,
adding, "Hell! I *was* right!"

Meantime, peace between us long since had been
declared – which was demonstrated in a rather striking way.
In the early 1980s he came to me about his contract and
said, "Could you help me?" I said, "Mike, I could help
you but the public's perception is that we're enemies. If
it ever came out that I'm negotiating for you, it would look
ridiculous for you." It's the old matter of the public and
press putting people into pigeonholes and saying, "Stay

there." I told him exactly that. People always get nervous tics when a one-time rebel shows up arm in arm with the guy he once rebelled against. "But now that you're here," I said, "I'll tell you what to do and how to do it. Forget your ex-agent. Do it on your own, save yourself the fees. You don't have to pay me."

I told him the type of things I thought he should do and he did do it himself.

A few weeks after the Milbury challenge, when it was still more or less alive, Orr left me. Then in December that year, 1979, I fell playing tennis and badly injured a disc in my back. For six months I could hardly make a move that wasn't excruciatingly painful, the most painful physical experience I've ever had in a sometimes rough and tumble life.

I've sometimes wondered at the way some bad news comes in bunches. Whether there's a connection between one hard punch and another is impossible to fathom. At any rate, when I was in agony, hardly able to walk, stand, lean, or sit, Bill Watters and Rick Curran quit my organization – I think partly because of the Orr situation. They took a couple of other staff members and several younger clients in the more-or-less low-fee category along with them. It's better to have fifteen players that you are charging $20,000 to $30,000 each than have 150 players paying you an average of $3,000 each. I found later, amusingly enough, that their bailing out saved me more in overhead than I lost in fees, which was certainly not their intention. Maybe they were convinced that I was down and out because I was physically incapacitated. If so, they learned in the next six or eight months that I had amazing recuperative capacity.

I hate to even think about that six months or so in agony because of my back. I tried everything. Many others tried to help, as well. Ken Thomson, Lord Thomson of Fleet, I knew as a friend. He suggested I go and see a doctor he knew of in England. "If you want to stay in a flat over there, I'll arrange everything." I went over, saw the doctor, was treated. For two days the treatment seemed to work, then it came back with a vengeance. Home again, I read every book on backs, became an expert on spinal fusion, chymopapain injections, micro-surgery, macro-surgery, the works. I think I could have become a medical doctor that winter and spring. Then one night Paul Godfrey, the Metro Toronto chairman who later became publisher of the *Toronto Sun*, called me. He'd been at a dinner. George Gross had mentioned me and my back. "My wife just went through the same thing," Paul said. "A doctor named Peter Welsh looked after her, did an injection. It's done and it's over. It's miraculous, go try it."

So I decided to try. I saw Peter Welsh. He told me how the procedure worked. As I understood it, if you can imagine in the old days when you had a bicycle and developed a bulge in the tire you'd just tape it and hope for the best. My trouble was that a bulge had developed in my disc and was pressing on a nerve. The operation would be to inject the specific bulge area with chymopapain enzyme, from papaya. What it does is work like a meat tenderizer to disintegrate protein in the bulge area just enough to take the pressure off the nerve. I'm not sure how much of that I understood at the time, but he told me that before anything could happen a test had to be done, a myelogram, much more difficult than the operation itself but necessary to determine whether the actual injection would work. So he did the test, then reported, "You're a good candidate. There's about a 90 per cent chance that it'll work. We'll do it tomorrow."

I said, "Hey, let's not wait until tomorrow."

He looked at me. "All right, we'll do it today."

The operation was done that afternoon. In the recovery room he came in and reached as if to grab my leg. I flinched. He said, "I haven't touched it yet," and then he did touch it. It really was miraculous: no pain. That was on a Tuesday. Peter told me I'd have to stay in hospital for a week. But my son was graduating as a grade 13 honours student at

Upper Canada College on Friday morning. That day I got up and Nancy and I went to the graduation.

But it wasn't *quite* that easy. Halfway through the ceremony I had just heard Allen's name called when I leaned over and told Nancy, "I've got to go." I was sweating. She said she'd go and get the car, parked out on the lawn at Upper Canada, but I said, "No, I'll get it." I got in the car, very faint, got home, lay down, and never looked back. I was back to normal very fast. Three months later my partner Norm Donaldson and I won the doubles championship at our tennis club, Toronto Lawn.

Meanwhile, my other main problem, Orr, was going to be with me a while. The Milbury problem appeared to have faded. But what he said was in some ways a wave of the future. A challenge once mounted in a group as volatile as the NHLPA does not just go away. Our meetings became more argumentative. Also, any dissidents were supported by a fairly steady campaign over the years in which Mark Mulvoy of *Sports Illustrated* seemed to be constantly on the watch for anything that might help them pin my hide to the wall. The way *SI* hovered over the case Vaclav Nedomansky brought against me, and lost, was typical of such initiatives. Anyway, one thing was sure by the mid-1980s – if I'd ever had a honeymoon in my job with the NHLPA, it was long gone. I had to beat off quite a few challenges through the 1980s, and did so successfully enough until I found myself nearly on the ropes in 1989, which we'll come to later.

It was only in the later years of what some call my "reign" that I discovered the impression I had been making for years when I thought I was doing all right. Bobby Orr said in 1980 or so that I was rude. So? I won't cop out. The way I act usually has a lot to do with the company I'm in – with the sometimes (not always) rough-talking hockey players one way, with royalty or prime ministers another. All I can say in answer to Bobby is that I never changed from the moment he met me, and he didn't seem to mind my rudeness when he was signing his big playing contracts.

In a 1984 *Sports Illustrated* article more or less profiling me by talking to people, including Orr, who didn't like me or my methods much, if at all, Lou Lefaive of Hockey Canada said, with regard to the rudeness side, that I was the only person he knew who would use the f-word under any circumstances that seemed fitting, to me.

Maybe he's right, but I've never considered the way I talk to be an act of defiance. Nor, for that matter, an act of compliance.

In the same piece, Phil Esposito remarked on the way I sometimes responded to matters raised by him and other players. He said that he might ask a question and I would respond with something like, "Are you an idiot or something?" He implied that this kind of abrasiveness actually scared other players into not saying what was on their minds.

"They'd think," he said, "hell, if Eagleson will talk that way to Esposito or Bobby Clarke or other greats, who am I to question him?"

I can't deny that I talked tough sometimes. I still do. I did it to Orr, too. I just didn't feel I ever had time, or they had time, to go pussyfooting around. All I can say about Esposito's criticism is that no player should have kept quiet on a legitimate question just because he thought he'd get a scathing reply. That isn't the way they play hockey.

In a game, if they don't like something going on, they'll do something about it. I can't really defend myself against questions that were never asked.

Anyway, *Sports Illustrated*'s sometimes justified niggling on various issues aside, NHLPA meetings in the 1980s were sometimes hot and heavy. One example was in 1986 when Jim Peplinski of the Calgary Flames came to the meetings loaded for bear. The terms of our new collective bargaining agreement were among policy initiatives that we discussed. Jim and his Calgary teammate, Jamie Macoun, sat in a corner

and dumped on everything that came on the table. Free
agency, one of our long-term aims, was one of the topics
debated. From Peplinski and Macoun on that and everything
else it was, "I don't like that . . . we are not going to do
that . . . you are doing it the wrong way, Al."

I remember a discussion in that meeting about something
we were working toward creating, a $250,000 nest egg at
the age fifty-five for every man who played 400 games in
the NHL. That kind of plan would sound okay to most
people – maybe Peplinski won't mind it when he's fifty-five,
for that matter – but that day Peplinski just kept saying, "Al,
what is the present value?"

Mike Liut chimed in, "The present value is $30,000."

Peplinski: "What's $30,000?" Reminding me of a time
when Trade Minister C.D. Howe asked in the Commons,
"What's a million?" and thereby helped the Tories beat the
Liberals in the next general election.

Liut: "I will tell you what $30,000 is – $30,000 at age
twenty-five or thirty is $250,000 at age fifty-five. My dad
is fifty-three. I wish in two years he had $250,000 sitting
waiting for him.

That year, too, there were rumbles again that I was going
to quit as executive director and replace John Ziegler as
NHL president.

Some owners had talked to me about that, a private
sounding-out that I appreciated, but my answer was firmly
no. Still, some players, feeling that I might be preparing
to join the other side, were never happy with my friendship
with Ziegler. He and I talked on the phone a lot. To me
it was a constructive relationship, enabling us to get many
things done either peacefully or at least without the constant
strike-threat confrontations common in some pro sports.

Probably what antagonized me about Peplinski originally
was that he is tough. I soon got over that. And he changed
some, as well. It's all right to be as tough as you like in
the meeting room, have every player agree to go on strike,
agree – for instance, that time – that if total free agency isn't

included we won't go along with any new collective bargaining agreement. That's what some of the debate was about
that year. Peplinski's position was that he knew it all. But
when the owners came in for their part of those meetings
and started talking about their problems – seven teams on
the verge of bankruptcy, seven breaking even, and seven
making dough, Peplinski's reaction was more or less, "Oh,
shit, I didn't know that." Because he's a smart and very
balanced young man, as I've come to know, he eventually
came to see that it takes two to make a contract; the other
guy has to sign it, too.

One other point is worth mentioning about collective
bargaining agreements. I worked it out one time: there's
a 20 per cent annual turnover in player personnel between
one CBA and the next. So, say in 1989 you get a player
looking at the agreement and saying, "Hey, I didn't agree
to that. I didn't sign that." And he's right, because he simply
wasn't in the league when it was done. I can make somewhat
the same point with a much longer time span: in the 1980s
there was nobody at the meetings, apart from me, who
personally remembered how far we'd come in twenty years
from the old Springfield Indians days.

I'm not saying that any outfit, including ours, should rest
on its laurels. But sometimes in the heat of an argument
I could have used a Normie Ullman or Lou Angotti or
Bill White to provide some perspective on how far we'd
already climbed up the mountain in pensions, owner-player
relationships, and everything else. On pensions, I don't think
I ever said it, it would be like trying to explain World War
Two to a kid born yesterday, but for years all any former
player had when he was down on his luck, broke, sick,
or in trouble was a form of league or club charity, a benefit
game, passing the hat among people who remembered the
guy when he was whizzing up and down the ice. Clarence
Campbell's early and unflagging support for the NHL
players' pension plan, meagre as the plan was at its start

in 1948, came because he knew how essential it was. For years he had at his disposal a small and carefully guarded special fund that he alone could use if it could be proved that such and such a player from pre-pension plan days was in real need and that a few hundred dollars would help him. Campbell never would divulge details such as the names, some well known, of those he helped, part of the reason being to avoid letting the public know anything that would make the league look bad and detract from whatever dignity the recipient had left. I'm thankful that that kind of reminiscing about the bad old days is totally irrelevant today. The players' association made it so. And many a hot argument in our meetings continued to help the process.

Which brings me to the first real dump-Eagleson movement, more or less secretly under way in the season of 1988-89, and which I first heard about, surprisingly enough, in a call from my one-time adversary, Mike Milbury. "Hey, Al," Milbury said, "there's something I think you should know . . ."

Up until then Rich Winter, an Edmonton lawyer and player agent, had done a lot for the dump-Eagleson orchestrating, along with two American agents and some dissident players, especially among their clients. As far back as in a letter written in December, 1988, Winter had been threatening to sue me for one thing or another.

One of his sidekicks was Ron Salcer of Los Angeles, a jeweller and part-time hockey adviser (Dave Taylor his star attraction).

Another was Ed Garvey, a lawyer who had been a moving force in the National Football League Player Association's unsuccessful strike, which had been more damaging to the players than to the owners. I doubt if Garvey had seen five hockey games in his life. To him, philosophically, hockey players were just small football players. He had no understanding of the reality of being Canadian and playing hockey well. I had known Garvey for twenty years. When he was executive director of the NFLPA he was much too confrontational for me and my colleagues Marvin Miller (baseball) and Larry Fleisher (basketball).

Garvey, Winter, and Salcer had been charging for months that I had misused my position as NHLPA executive director to the organization's detriment. While assembling their assault force, I guess naturally they'd been reminded of Milbury's disturber role ten years earlier and knew where to find him. After retiring as a player he'd spent a couple of years coaching successfully in the minors and was about to succeed Terry O'Reilly as the Boston coach. No doubt looking for an ally, or at least unspent ammunition, they called Milbury and told him what they had in mind.

That call was followed quickly by another to Milbury from a New York reporter. Obviously this reporter was hot on the trail of a story going around Edmonton about the impending demise of Alan Eagleson as union leader – set to happen, he'd been told, at the NHLPA meetings scheduled for June at West Palm Beach, Florida.

After hearing from Winter and the reporter, Milbury called me. He'd told both Winter and the reporter, he said, that his problems with me had long since disappeared and were out in the open, on the table. He told me, "I also said that I did not agree with what I gathered they had in mind."

He wanted me to know what was happening. What bothered him, I think, was that from what he'd heard I would be blind-sided, given no information on what the charges were and therefore no chance to assemble a documented defence. This plan had given Winter an overwhelming feeling of confidence. Around the time I'm talking about, while stimulating what became a pitched battle at West Palm Beach and later at Toronto, Winter told a few people that if he lost this one and I was confirmed as executive director he would be the first person to shake my hand and then would disappear, go away. He was that sure he was going

to win. Well, what he was talking about came to a head
in meetings beginning on Saturday, June 3, 1989, in Florida.
He lost, then and later, but he didn't go away.

The last time I mentioned one of our NHLPA meetings
in much detail we were at the old Mount Royal, swiping
a pizza truck, dropping the heavy cover from a hot room
service tray out of an open window by mistake, all this for
$5-a-night rooms or $20 for a big suite. Time had passed.
So there is some updating to do.

The modern meeting takes a fair amount of planning.
The association still pays for rooms and meals, but when
we had tight budgets in the past we might just pay for the
player rep's room, maybe two single guys to a room, and
hand out meal money in cash, the way the clubs do on
the road during the season. Now we invite the player rep
and his wife. That way, the attendance is better.

Our meetings used to be two days, but well before 1989
they were taking up most of a week. Counting the players,
club owners, staff, counsel, insurance people, anybody connected officially with the meetings, probably close to 120
people in all, we require between seventy and 100 rooms
counting suites. That gives us some leverage on price; I can
always arrange a pretty good rate. The players fly in and
we work at our own meetings for two days, then meet jointly
with the owners for two or three days. The owners throw
a big dinner for everybody near the end of the meetings
and it's always a lovely evening except this once, the owners'
dinner in 1989. But then nothing about the June, 1989,
meetings was lovely at all. Having been warned, I was in
a heightened state of tension for those meetings but couldn't
have even guessed the details.

What my attackers did at West Palm was table a sixty-
page document that suggested I had been guilty of financial
misconduct, conflict of interest, charging excessive rent and
expenses, and that I had not consulted the executive on some
financial decisions, and so on. You can get a lot of charges

in sixty pages, even though I could go through them all and say, malarkey, malarkey, malarkey, good point, malarkey, malarkey, malarkey.

But one thing was very plain: Garvey and his pals wanted me out. If they could gather enough votes, that's where I'd be – out.

The frustrating part was that not knowing what kind of ammunition they had, I'd had no time at all to prepare how to fight back. In a court of law, the prosecution must make its case known to the defence, give the people on the other side of the courtroom a chance. I did not believe these prosecutors had.

One thing kept me hanging in. When I thought their whole document through during sleepless nights in Florida, I couldn't see any reason why I should put up my hands and say, "Don't shoot, I surrender." As the sixty pages of beefs against me averred, sure, I might have been arrogant, dictatorial, certainly heavy-handed and unwise in making moves where I'd taken the union's executive consent too much for granted. I knew I'd done nothing unethical. My sole motive, unchanged from the beginning, had always been to do what I thought was best for the union.

Basically, Garvey was looking for a powerful vote of censure that would lead to me being fired and maybe even – Garvey and Winter had suggested – taken to court over one thing or another. They wanted a full audit of NHLPA affairs, including my personal expense accounts. They wanted a special investigation of mortgages held by the union, how they'd been arranged, financed, fees paid and to whom, everything. They also wanted to look at my income tax returns for the last three years. As you can see, they didn't want much. Just my hide.

Starting on the Saturday morning and going all day, we threshed out the charges and I tried to defend myself. There were a lot of picayune things: some had seen me flying first class and didn't like that being charged to the union, not knowing that I always bought economy-class tickets and if

I could wangle being upgraded without cost to the union, as I often could, I took it. They knew I drove a leased Mercedes, but they didn't know the cost was way down because it was three years old, again my choice. Under my employment terms I could have changed cars every year, but I didn't because I liked the one I had.

Looking back from this distance at the overall trauma of that week's meetings, I can remember only one positive element. That was due to an idea Bryan Trottier had. About a week earlier, Bryan said, "You know, Al, who has a great deal of influence with the players?"

"Who?"

"Darryl Sittler."

"What are you getting at?"

"He's a former vice-president, and everybody respects him, why doesn't he come to the meetings?"

I said, "You're the president, call and invite him."

He called and Darryl said, "I'd love to come." Paul Henderson also called and said he'd come if needed, to speak up for me. Darryl dropped everything else and flew to Florida. He'd been a player rep for eight or ten years, a vice-president for six. Players respected him.

When the opposition was hammering away about three mortgages we'd arranged, how do we know they're legitimate and so on, Darryl spoke up.

"I know this, Al Eagleson has looked after my money all the way and I've never lost a cent. Now, if anyone is concerned about these mortgages and ability to repay . . . first there's Irv Ungerman: he's worth $50 million and owes us $300,000, so forget him. Second is Marv Teperman, with the biggest demolition company around. He's worth several million, the property mortgaged has been appraised at $4 million, and we have a mortgage of a million against it. Third is Dave Baker, I know him, introduced him to Al. He's the biggest Jeep dealer in Canada, my close friend, and he could pay off this $200,000 mortgage tomorrow.

Just what Darryl said, the respect in which he was held, dissipated any concern of impropriety – and it was Bryan's idea to get him in there.

The mistake I made in Florida was totally against my usual custom. In normal circumstances, I always speak to the press after every meeting. I used to do that diligently and purposely because that's the best way to get yourself heard. In Florida we had agreed that everything would be confidential until we had all the documentation on the mortgages, expenses audit, my tax returns, and so on. I had agreed to all those demands but the results could not be presented until our additional meetings in Toronto. In the desire to keep everything confidential for now, I kept the details of the meeting confidential, as we had all agreed. The other side ignored that agreement. I should have known better.

In Florida within two minutes of a meeting being over, some of these people were out in the corridors yelling scandal, and back in Toronto the headlines had me looking like a crook.

Apart from writers who'd known me long enough to take my word over that of my accusers, Garvey, Winter, and their mouthpieces had a field day. Once the tide gets running one way in the media, it's almost impossible to stop. Corrections are taken as excuses. It's one case where offence beats defence every time.

All day Saturday and again on Sunday morning I was on the grill. Eventually, on all the evidence then available, my leadership was put to a vote. If that had gone against me, I can only assume that I would have been gone right then and there. However, I won a reprieve. The vote was too close for me to cheer about – sixteen in favour of giving me a chance to defend myself, twelve saying "throw the bum out." After twenty-two years, 16–12 was sure as hell no standing ovation. But at least I'd have a chance to throw more light on the charges that I'd used my position, and union funds, unethically.

Who was for me and who against?

It was a secret vote, so I can't be totally sure, but I *am* certain that Bryan Trottier as president voted for me, along with vice-presidents Lanny McDonald, Bobby Smith, Doug Wilson, Mike Gartner, and Mike Liut. They had worked with me for years as the NHLPA executive committee.

Among player reps, those who were on my side included Dan Daoust, Toronto; Stu Gavin, Minnesota; Bob Murray, Chicago; Brian Benning, St. Louis; Kevin Lowe, Edmonton; Stan Smyl, Vancouver; Jim Peplinski, Calgary; Kevin Maguire, Buffalo; Kevin Dineen, Hartford; and Gerald Diduck, New York Islanders.

Marty McSorley of Los Angeles was my most outspoken critic. He was a Garvey disciple and not even a player rep, but had a lot to say. When I thought through the whole matter of who was with me and who against, it became obvious that by far the strongest group of those against me was American.

I will never believe that the preponderance of Americans among those who wanted a total upheaval in the players' association was in any way a coincidence. Neither was it a coincidence that *no* American-born player voted for me. Nor that two of the three people most involved in the planning were American, with Ed Garvey mainly in charge of strategy.

To put it simply, I saw the whole operation then, and still do, as an attempted U.S. takeover of a Canadian union. I blame Garvey and Salcer – two Americans. I also blame Winter and Herb Pinder, both of whom are Canadians. They all had an axe to grind for some reason.

One more really lamentable event occurred later in the week. I've mentioned the annual owners' dinner as a good affair, usually taking place after most of the outstanding beefs had been looked after and we could all be hockey people together, intent on the progress of the game and our sometimes debate-stimulating attitudes to detail.

This time, after three days of internal union warfare, I finally told the owners that we had such a mess in the union that we should cancel the meetings and meet the owners again in August, when things could be clarified and disposed of, one way or another. The owners said fine, but we have arranged the dinner so we'd better have it. We're all here anyway. So we had the dinner, and some of the players who had voted against me–nine out of twelve of them, and their wives–stayed away from the dinner. So now the owners are stuck with paying for people who didn't attend, $2,500 thrown away because of the hostility stimulated by Garvey at the meetings.

So at the dinner I got up and said, "I just want to apologize, this is the worse situation I have ever seen happen." I laid into the no-shows pretty hard but also said that because of what had happened the union seemed to be split down the middle. "I hope this is not the end of what has been a very good relationship for players and owners and hockey. I apologize to you, the owners, for this happening and I promise that it won't happen again."

Then the next day one of the no-shows, Jim Korn, said that on a point of order he'd like to complain about what I had said to the owners. I told him to shut up and go to hell, I'd see him in August.

I can at least understand Winter. He had been battling with me and the NHLPA for the past two or three years. He was doing his best to undermine me any way he could. Herb Pinder was a different case. He should have stayed out of it. I represented his brother Gerry in the NHL when he first turned pro with the Chicago Black Hawks. Their dad is a friend of mine. In Florida after the players had voted, but before the ballots were counted, there was a break for lunch. Herb Pinder asked if he could meet with me. He suggested I resign as executive director and he would get Winter and Garvey and Salcer to approve my continued involvement in international hockey. What an insult to my intelligence and my integrity! While he was talking to me as a "friend," he was simultaneously counselling his player rep clients to vote against me. When I told Bobby Smith the story ten minutes later, Bobby said, "Well, Al, there's no doubt in my mind that we have won the vote and it looks as if Herb knows we've won too!" And then, get this: in one of dozens of interviews when I'd be asked to explain what had happened, and how, I identified Pinder as being right there with the other three in the wrecking crew – and he came to me and objected!

I said, "Herb, let's face facts. You are in this up to your ears on their side. How can you even suggest differently?" There was a little more, and then I said, "From now on I'm only talking to my friends and you aren't one of them."

Hard guy to discourage. He still had the nerve to come along a month or so later on the telephone, trying to play the honest broker.

"Al," he said soulfully, "I want to help you. I've just talked to Garvey and they are going to sue you. Maybe I can still be the man in the middle and try to help." Remember, that is what he said to *me*.

An hour or so later a reporter called me from Alberta. He'd obviously been researching a story on the general line of poor old Eagleson whose end is near. He'd talked to Pinder, who'd told him, he said, that the writing was on the wall, "Eagleson is finished. If I were Alan Eagleson I'd find a nice soft spot to land."

I had to laugh. Almost. I told the reporter, "Well, I'll land but it won't be a soft spot. It will be on Herb Pinder."

By that time, back home, I found that the daily papers in my home town were treating me as if I were guilty as charged, family and friends were upset, and I had gone to work for the defence – my own. I wanted my defence to be total. I sure didn't lack motivation. Everything that had happened since West Palm, the sting of what had been said there and later about me, were all the gas-up I needed to be ready when our next meeting began on Monday, August 21, in the Toronto Hilton in downtown Toronto.

CHAPTER TWELVE

EXONERATION

"They came to bury Alan Eagleson yesterday but
wound up praising him. . . . (He) emerged from a
nine-hour union meeting last night with his job,
his authority and his dignity intact."

– Toronto Star, *after the August meeting's second day.*

It isn't exactly the public image of hockey players that they do a lot of advance planning. You watch six or eight guys piling into a corner after the puck and you have to know that none of the elbows, high sticks, butt-ends, boarding, punching, and so on was scripted. But put the same people in the situation the NHLPA faced in August of 1989, involving not only the NHLPA's future but also its past, and you get a different impression.

Both my supporters and the opposition were at work well before the meetings started, but from our standpoint the first preliminary skirmish didn't go smoothly. We had decided that the NHLPA side of this meeting should be restricted to player reps, plus executive members. Bryan Trottier, our president, sent letters to that effect, well in advance, to everyone involved. Ed Garvey wrote back aggressively, which is typical, telling Bryan, in effect, stuff it – he was coming and would address the player reps at the meeting.

Closer to the actual event, five days before the meeting, we arranged a conference call for Wednesday, the 16th of August. That call, lasting between two and three hours, involved everyone we figured would be helpful and supportive in forming our strategy.

In on the call besides Bryan and me were vice-presidents Bobby Smith, Doug Wilson, Mike Gartner, and Mike Liut. We couldn't get hold of Wayne Gretzky or Lanny McDonald, but did get Darryl Sittler, as an adviser to the association, to sit in. Players Kevin Maguire of Buffalo Sabres and Dan Daoust in Toronto lived close enough that they came to our Toronto office. We also had on the line our counsel from Washington, Larry Latto and Wendy White.

Our general aim then and later was to achieve as big an improvement as possible over the 16–12 Florida vote. I didn't want just a repeat. That meant we needed all our supporters from Florida, including Ryan Walter who'd switched to us after the vote. Further, we had to be sure they were solid, hard rock, unwavering. You always have to think about the opposition. They'd be working, too. Could Garvey, Winter,

or Salcer somehow get to some among our previous supporters and weaken our position? I told those in the conference call that, to consider it a successful meeting, we had
to get at least eighteen votes. Twenty or twenty-two would
be even better, but no upward movement from sixteen on
our side would make it seem that the union was indeed
fragmented at that level.

The media build-up in the few days before the meeting
showed in sports-page headlines and in some cases full-page
stories summarizing what was at stake. The Saturday *Sun*'s
August 19 full-pager was headed in big black capitals:
EAGLESON DIGS IN. The story ran through what had
happened in Florida and what was at stake for me this time.
Other newspaper stories on August 21 more or less repeated
that theme.

Our preparations were headquartered in Bryan Trottier's
suite in the Hilton. We had a meeting there on Friday night,
August 18, but our real break came a couple of days later.
By then all the player reps were in the hotel. Most of those
on our side were gathered at Bryan's suite on the Sunday
evening, about twelve of us or more, when about 9 p.m.
young Brian Benning from St. Louis came into the room.
I'd known him for about eight years, since he was fifteen,
when I was looking after his brother Jim with the Leafs.
He sat down and quite nonchalantly reached into his back
pocket and said, "Here, Al. Some stuff you might want
to look at."

What he passed over was a twelve-page statement by
Garvey.

"Where'd you get this?" I asked.

"Well, I was walking through the lobby," he said, "and
saw a door open and looked in to see some of the players
against us and they are handing out this material. They
gave one to me and I thought you might find it interesting."

I glanced at it quickly and realized that what we had
was a full statement of their ammunition. We found later
that they'd handed this out quite freely, even to NHL old-

timers for discussion at their golf tournament. There were a lot of specific charges, but the part that most infuriated me was a statement that I had loaned $100,000 of NHLPA money to my daughter Jill. In fact, one particular mortgage, partly held by the union, was so sound that I'd suggested Jill put $100,000 of her trust fund into it. Yet this statement made it categorically clear, falsely, that the union had loaned her that money. More than ever, I was dying to see Ed Garvey.

The next morning I walked into the meeting. The setup in the quite spacious Governor General's suite had the executive at one end of a long table, with player reps along each side and some room at the other end, three rows of seats, for players who were interested but weren't player reps.

In that section also were Garvey and his three lawyers plus Rich Winter and Ron Salcer.

At that end it looked like a sea of enemy faces.

Bryan Trottier spoke immediately to the array of lawyers and agents. "Gentlemen, we'd like you to leave, this meeting is just for the players."

Up gets Garvey. "I'm here and I should be here," he said. "I represent 210 players." (That was true – out of a total of 600.)

I didn't need to be cued. I held up the statement Benning had given us the night before and said, "Let's get something straight. This is twelve pages of bullshit after bullshit after bullshit, lie after lie after lie, but you have gone too far. You have got me loaning union money to my daughter, which is a damn lie. She is a lawyer just starting out in her career and you have suggested that she and her father have been unethical in a business that absolutely relies on ethics."

He obviously knew by then that he'd been wrong. But instead of apologizing he just fumbled around. "If Benning had stayed around he would have heard me re-explain that later."

"Explain!" I stormed. "How do you explain a blatant lie? Did all the other people who got that statement get a copy of your explanation?"

That stuck the needle into his bubble. Still, we're stuck with all those people who didn't properly belong in the room. We hadn't hit on a way to get the most offensive ones out without offending others, for instance, players who weren't reps but were dues-paying members. We certainly didn't want them offended. We chewed back and forth, Garvey talking, others talking, everybody on the union side obviously suffering at the prospect of a rerun of the hours of wrangling we'd had in Florida. After the meeting had been going for about an hour, from 9:45 to 10:45 or so, Doug Wilson saved the day.

He said, "Look, we've been debating back and forth who should be in here, and we're getting nowhere. Let's get everybody out of the room except player reps and any player who is interested as a dues-paying member, and we'll bring back in whoever we want."

Everybody out except player reps – that meant me, too! So now I'm as offended as anybody. Those of us targeted by the expulsion order all march out into a small anteroom, which had a phone. I called Ed Sexton of the Osler law firm, our lawyer. I told him a little about what had been going on. "I don't know what's likely to happen and the majority of our problems are U.S.-related. Would you hold yourself available in case we need Canadian legal advice?" He said he would.

It must have been around 11:30 or so when someone came out and said, "Al, we want you back in the room."

I decided right then it was time to attack. I had the audience that counted. I waved Garvey's memo with its run-through of the main issues: the $2.3 million in mortgages that he and his buddies were challenging and which would be subject of a non-partisan expert's report later that day; their claim that I had cost the union a lot of money by possibly actionable misuse and mismanagement, a matter that would be reported upon by the audit committee the following day; and their feeling that I had not lived up to promises made in Florida to give up all personal clients, quit Hockey Canada, and a few other odds and ends, including forcing the NHL to accept the principle of salary disclosure.

I started out reasonably enough. "Gentlemen, what have I not done that I was supposed to do? I was supposed to give up my clients. There was no deadline on that."

Someone called out that the deadline should be December 31.

"Fine," I said, "But – and there's a big but. Am I going to give up all my clients and then find that I don't have a job?"

I guess about then I got warmed up. The June meeting had cast doubts on my future as an agent just at a time when I should be negotiating future contracts for some of my clients. I'd told those clients that if things did *not* work out for me to stay with the NHLPA, I could still represent them. If I did stay but could have no personal clients, I'd help them find somebody else who suited them. "However, in the meantime your buddy Winter has been phoning my clients, urging them to switch agents from me to him. Ron Hextall (temporarily, as it turned out) has left me and gone to Winter. As my client, Ron's fees have been worth $100,000 to me. Also, Ray Ferraro scored forty goals for Hartford last season and I was all set to negotiate a big contract with him worth fees of $20,000 to me – but the June meeting scared him and now he's with someone else. . . . In short, I have already lost $120,000 in potential fees right now just for starters."

I looked around. I couldn't tell how much impression I was making. There still seemed to be a lot of closed, suspicious expressions. Right at that moment, I hardly cared.

Why was I making those particular points? Maybe I asked that question myself, or maybe it was asked of me. I do remember the reply, because I'd been tossing and turning a lot of nights over this one. "If, when this is all over," I said, "I do still have a job on your terms, I'm going to want to negotiate a hell of a lot more money for myself. Right now I'm paid much less than people in equivalent jobs in basketball, baseball, and football, and if I'm going to give up a lot of the income I have now but still work for you, you better start thinking about where the money is coming from. Maybe double what I'm getting now. Maybe triple. We can go into that later, but this is fair warning – the equalizing pay has to come from somewhere."

As I looked around the table at the reaction, I knew I'd made some progress but there was still rancour.

Every time I looked out at those faces I was counting. In my mind the division at that point was still somewhere around 19–9 or 18–10. To me that wasn't good enough. The opposition hadn't really moved much and wouldn't until the integrity and honesty matters were out of the way.

"Ah-h-h," I said, "let's get the mortgage people in here, let's get the audit people in here. I know I've done nothing wrong but until you are convinced of that we're just spinning our wheels."

When we broke for lunch, Bryan and Sam Simpson and I went to Bryan's suite and had a beer. I was feeling really down. I must have been. I was thinking of just walking away, I know I wouldn't have done it, but the possibility was on my mind.

"After this afternoon," I told Bryan, "I'm not going to take this again. There is still that core of ill feeling and I don't think it is going to change. I can't handle, either physically or emotionally or mentally, another two days of maybe going through again the same shit we had in Florida repeated in the papers in my home town."

Amazing how things can change. When we met again in the afternoon, the first item of business was the mortgage report. William Dermody, a Hamilton lawyer, had been instructed by Garvey to prepare it. So now when somebody said, "Okay, mortgage report, let's hear it," Garvey jumped up and said that his group had commissioned the report and that therefore, "he's reporting to me. I asked for that report. It's my report."

A player rep: "I guess that means you're paying his bill?"

Garvey: "Uh-uh, no. It's for the benefit of the association . . . Alan, don't you think the union should pay?"

I just looked at him, glad that where Ed Garvey and some other people of his ilk are concerned, I am great at covering my ass.

In Florida, for some reason, no doubt named Garvey, I'd smelled possible jurisdictional trouble over this mortgage report and had taken defensive action.

I turned to Dermody, "Bill, what was the deal on your report?"

He replied that he'd given to me in writing, at my request, a paper stating clearly that Ed Garvey had retained him to do the mortgage return. In turn, he said, I had co-operated fully in providing him with all the documents and information. The only thing the union had engaged him to do was provide direction on some unrelated constitutional changes. "So my bill for the mortgage report will be referred to you, Ed."

A player rep: "Nice try, Ed."

So that ended the issue of who paid – whereupon I suddenly changed my mind about one thing. I had been planning all along to ensure that Garvey would not be in the meeting room when the report was read. Being purely union business, I'd felt it would be debilitating for the union to have him right there, the leader of the opposition. But having seen how ill-prepared he was, not only for the meeting but for the higher level of interested hockey players he had to deal with now, compared to Florida, I changed my mind.

I said, "Just a minute, guys, what's wrong with Ed Garvey staying in here for this report?"

I knew what had to be in the report, I knew it could not be anything damaging, so who cared if he was in the meeting when it was read? If he tried to make something damaging out of it we could deflate him as we went along. Also, I knew that if we'd tried to have him kept out, it would have meant a lengthy wrangle and a vote.

Copies of the report had been passed out. Everybody had one. As it was read, Garvey and I were only a few feet apart, close to Dermody.

Bobby Smith and Mike Liut were also up front, along with Mike Gartner, Bryan Trottier, Doug Wilson, Sam Simpson.

Dermody presented his report with everyone reading along, and any interjections mainly referred to specific criticisms of the mortgage loans made in Garvey's overall charges. For instance, Garvey's charges referred to one particular mortgage loan for $1 million to Marvin Teperman of Toronto as being really risky.

Mike Liut: "Just a minute, Ed. Let me answer that, Bill. Now" – he went on something like this – "have a look on page three, Ed, where there is, sure, something that might suggest that loan is risky. But let's go to another page in Bill's report that judges loans by five Cs – credit, collateral, capacity to pay, character of the borrower, and capital assets of the borrower. Here you have a guy, Teperman, who is a multi-millionaire, and the building mortgaged is worth $5 million. What do you think?"

Garvey: "Oh, yeah, yeah."

Liut: "So in other words that's not a risky loan."

Garvey: "Oh, no, I guess not."

As Dermody went on presenting his report, Bobby Smith and Mike Liut, both as bright off the ice as on it, knew what questions had to be asked. They didn't need my help. I wouldn't have intervened anyway. The mortgages were all well secured, good investments. They'd even been written at a higher interest rate than the bank would have offered because the principals wanted some variances in repayment that the bank wouldn't go for.

Garvey tried hard to indicate that I'd made money on the mortgages at the expense of the union. To get that matter absolutely straight Dermody was questioned closely by Smith and Liut about what Garvey had stated as fact.

Had Eagleson charged the union any legal fees? No.

Had the union paid a finder's fee to Eagleson for finding the mortgage opportunities for the union? No.

Was Eagleson paid anything at all in relationship to the mortgages? Only the normal legal fee, in keeping with rules of the Law Society of Upper Canada, as charged by any lawyer involved in legal aspects of a purchase (deed searches, etc.) that had no relationship to the mortgage.

Garvey had a few shots left, all blanks. All I wanted was the truth. He tried to get Dermody to say things other than as they really were. One of his final shots was to recommend that the union sell the mortgages right now, with any loss to be absorbed by me – this although we were able to show that by putting money into these loans over the four- or five-year period, the union had earned about $216,000 more than if they'd invested the money in the way Garvey argued we should have.

That pretty well looked after the union accepting the mortgage report. What a change. In the morning I'd felt oppressed, despondent. In a few hours I'd gone from very little support to a considerable victory. That was the basis of the story that ran in the *Globe and Mail* the next morning under the heading, EAGLESON FIGHTS OFF CHAL-LENGE, TO KEEP JOB.

The *Star* heading was a little more explicit: EAGLE WEATHERS UNION REVOLT BUT AGREES TO SOME CHANGES. The story read, in part: "They came to bury Alan Eagleson yesterday but wound up praising him. . . . (He) emerged from a nine-hour union meeting last night with his job, his authority and his dignity intact."

The story went on to say that the union would be handled much differently in the future. That suited me fine, because the changes would be in the areas that would let me take things a little easier. I didn't ever again want another battle like that one, caused partly by my lifelong habit of always trying to act like a one-man gang.

Just one more comment about the twelve-page Garvey document Brian Benning had brought to us. One of the dissident players, Larry Playfair of Buffalo, told a reporter that after listening to Garvey on Sunday night he had considered punching me out for all the things Garvey said I had done. Playfair listened to how the Monday meeting went, with charge after charge toppling. He came to me after, complimented me on the way I'd handled myself, and said he now was with me 100 per cent. I was rather glad to hear that. Larry is six feet four and weighs over 200.

That Monday night the audit committee, Kelly Miller and Bryan Trottier co-chairmen, met to go over the auditor's report from Bill Dovey of Price Waterhouse. Bryan phoned me once during the evening with a couple of questions. I referred him to Sam Simpson and our accountant, Marvin Goldblatt, so I knew on the Tuesday morning before the audit report was presented to the full membership that there were no problems. By eleven that morning it was pretty well over, the point having been made that any irregularities the auditor had uncovered were minor. Bill Dovey, in a straight-ahead manner, had made some recommendations about internal procedures, but, the membership was told, there was no sign of misappropriation of funds.

Then Kelly Miller did a great thing for me. He might not have intended it to be great, merely to ensure that every beef could be heard: he invited Bill Dovey, the auditor, to come in at one o'clock, address the meeting, and answer questions. As it turned out, this was a great favour to me.

Dovey came into the meeting and sat beside Mike Gartner. All the questions that Garvey and Co. had raised on the basis of suspicion, rumour, etc., came up. What about this? What about that? What about a lot of television sets being charged to the union, and so on?

Dovey said, "Gentlemen, there is nothing like the points you have raised. There are little things like chits missing, some expenses not properly substantiated . . . that's pretty well all."

His general message was very soothing to me and my supporters, but it still needed a sharp focus. This was provided by Gerald Diduck, the Islanders' defenceman, a solid twenty-four-year-old, born in Edmonton, who played junior in Lethbridge. I'll never forget his question. He was sitting down from the corner of the table, basically a middle-of-the-roader in union affairs but very demanding, a guy who had always made it plain that he was not ever going to stand for any bullshit from me. He voted for me . . . well, I'll amend that. I don't think he really voted for me as much as he voted against *them*. He had reasons to have reservations about Winter in particular.

He said to the auditor, "Okay, now, back up. These chits, and unsubstantiated charges, how much are we talking about here? Ten thousand dollars?

It was exactly the right question. The auditor's answer was that we were talking about hundreds of dollars in all, not even a thousand, a simple matter of improving some accounting procedures. The members asked questions for about twenty minutes. As in the mortgage report, there was nothing to support the charges of misuse or misappropriation of funds. I figured the tide had turned. I could go at things full steam ahead without having to keep looking over my shoulder, wondering if inadvertently something had been missed.

As the rest of the meetings went on that week, I settled some other matters with the players. For one, I brought up their demand that I resign from Hockey Canada.

"Are you guys crazy? You want me to resign from the organization that through my planning (meaning the various profitable series with the Soviets, the Canada Cup, and so on) has been directly responsible for bringing eighteen million bucks into this organization? Does that make sense, that I should step away from being an insider with control over our international play to becoming an outsider with no control?"

Kelly Miller, one of the dissidents, spoke up to ask about Hockey Canada and why I spent so much time on the Canadian team and didn't give the same help to the U.S. team. I explained that there was no way I, or anyone else, could get around the fact that for Team Canada in the Canada Cup we had such a wealth of Canadian players to pick among. In comparison, Team U.S.'s first ten players might be equal, or nearly so, to the first ten Canadians, but after that we had more quality players. I also argued that my efforts for Canada did help the Americans, too, from participating in pension fund money that benefited all NHL players, not just Canadians, right down to little things like negotiating good hotel deals for Team Canada because of my years of contacts and cutting the U.S. team in to save them money, too. I thought at that point that maybe I had Kelly Miller, who was also on the audit committee that had found nothing wrong, wavering a little as I went on to some of their lesser, and rather naive, demands.

One was with relation to what it cost the union to have its headquarters in my building. I mentioned, again, that I was the lowest paid executive director of any of the major sports organizations – football, baseball, basketball, hockey. I was getting $200,000 a year and out of that paying two secretaries who worked on union affairs. If the union wanted to say good-bye to my present operation, I'd want at least twice as much in my base pay and they could pick up the $75,000 a year for the two secretaries.

Regarding the rent I charged the association to have its headquarters in the building I own, I suggested that they had better look around and do some checking about what their own new offices would cost. They could move out tomorrow and I'd get a better rent from somebody else. In short, I laid it all on the line, including details that aren't really as significant as the matter of integrity and honesty that had been investigated in the mortgage and audit meetings.

As the rest of the meetings went on, it was rather pathetic to watch the ones still left from the dissident group. Garvey and Winter had left town right after they'd seen the way things were going in the first day or two. Those left to fight on were mainly Marty McSorley and Dean Kennedy from L.A., Dave Barr from Detroit, Peter Taglianetti from Winnipeg, Randy Moller from Quebec, and Larry Murphy from Washington. Larry was not really a rep but had been brought in to be a spokesman for Salcer, who was sitting outside in the anteroom. Every once in a while somebody would go out for a leak and come back with a question prompted by Salcer.

Once something came up about what kind of a majority vote it would take for the members to remove the executive (president and vice-presidents) from office.

McSorley, Gerald Diduck, Jim Peplinski, and others were among the main speakers. Finally Peplinski, a sane voice and strong for us, suggested a two-thirds vote would be reasonable, fourteen teams out of twenty-one. I said to McSorley, "Okay, Marty, how about that?"

He was hesitating. I said, "Don't be screwing around, going to talk to Salcer about it." I said that point blank in front of everybody else. Marty finally allowed that he could live with the Peplinski solution.

One of the last big arguments was about Garvey's demand that we should have full disclosure on player salaries, as was the case in other pro sports.

"Why have we not had salary disclosure?" I asked. "Because you guys did not want it. It's been on the table often enough. Two years ago 25 per cent were in favour, 75 per cent against. This year it's 45 per cent in favour, 55 per cent against. Running this union for you, I've had to respect the wishes of every single player. I can tell you that that 45 per cent in favour is probably now up to 55, maybe even 65, and I'm prepared to gamble on that. I've been for salary disclosure, gentlemen, for years and you guys have been against it and Garvey is pillorying me for not having obtained it. He argues that no sports association in history has been able to get this without going to court, and the reasons we don't have it is that I've refused to go to court. He's made that an issue of my lack of credibility. Now, I'm not going to talk to John Ziegler about it first, because you will think the fix is in. But when we meet the owners and the league tomorrow, I'm telling you what my first question to Ziegler will be tomorrow and you will all be here to hear it.

"I'm going to say, 'Mr. Ziegler, we want salary disclosure and I want it without a court fight. But if I have to go to court to get it, I'll do that.'

"And I'm betting my reputation that I'll get it without going to court. So we will see what happens."

Well, you never saw so many guys running for cover. You know who's *against* disclosure now – the dissidents. McSorley, oh, he didn't know if Wayne Gretzky would want it. Others were trying to protect their teams' stars the same way.

I said they couldn't have it half way, it was all or nothing. "You can't have salary disclosure for 90 per cent and no disclosure for 10 per cent. I'm satisfied that the majority is in favour, so let's jam it down the throats of the ones against it, they'll get over it."

Bobby Smith was against it, I knew. Bryan Trottier said he'd been against it, but that he would tell anybody his salary anyway, so now he was for it.

I said, "Hold it, let's go around the room."

Which we did. McSorley doesn't want Gretzky upset. Joey Johnson doesn't want Lemieux upset. Peter Taglianetti doesn't want Dale Hawerchuk upset. Dave Barr doesn't want Steve Yzerman upset. So here now are the core of the dissidents, whom Garvey has been using as his spokespersons for this major issue, and when push comes to shove they're all against it.

I knew in advance how they would react. Their position suddenly became basically, "Well, Mr. Eagleson, get the information from Mr. Ziegler but keep it under wraps until we get a majority vote of the membership. We'll go back to our teams and they may vote against it."

I said, "Do whatever the hell you want. I'm going to get it tomorrow and then we will decide what to do with it."

I had told them that we were not going to leave that room until we were unanimous on *something*, to re-establish our credibility with the owners. I figured right then that a vote on just simply me keeping my job, with changes, would have wound up well in my favour with maybe three or four votes against. I demanded unanimity, and I got it. Every vote was 29–0: (a) to demand salary information from Ziegler; (b) to confirm me as executive director; (c) to set up a search committee to find a deputy executive director.

The NHLPA was back on the right track. As soon as I had the 29–0 vote I told the executive that I had had enough and would retire with my reputation intact.

Bryan Trottier said, "No, sir, Alan! You are staying. If you leave now Garvey will be back in a flash."

Full salary disclosure didn't come for a few months, but the foregoing tells you how the machinery was set up to put hockey on a level with major league baseball and football – without even a hint of resorting to the Garvey-Winter-Salcer solution, fighting it out in court.

Regarding my staying on and giving them 100 per cent of my time, I pointed out that my present contract called for 60 per cent of my time. I was giving them a lot more than 60 per cent in return for about 30 per cent of my annual earnings from all sources, which were about $750,000 a year. Could they afford to pay me that? I didn't think so. What we agreed on was 60 per cent of my time until the end of 1991, when my replacement would take over, except that I would handle all international hockey until 1993.

Even as this is being written, Winter, Garvey, and some of the others are still criticizing me, Bob Goodenow, and the NHLPA. Heading into a serious round of contract negotiations between the NHL and NHLPA, we are being attacked yet again.

Garvey and Winter have persuaded some NHL retired players to sue the NHL concerning a surplus in the NHL Pension Society. Thank goodness that cooler heads prevailed and the retired players, in Canada at least, have distanced themselves from Garvey and Winter and have taken a court application in Ontario to have the pension surplus situation reviewed. The pension surplus is a very technical and involved matter. The NHL retired players say the surplus belongs to them. The NHL owners say the surplus belongs to the league.

The sad part of this issue is that there has been a lot of name-calling. Some retired players made statements that suggested the NHL had "stolen" pension funds that belonged to the players. The NHL announced its intention to sue Bobby Orr, Gordie Howe, and others for libel and slander in the courts of Ontario. None of this is good for the game.

I do know this. The NHLPA sought actuarial and legal advice in 1985 and 1986 with respect to the surplus. We were advised that it was not a black or white issue, that court decisions varied depending on the specific issues involved. The NHLPA did nothing that would adversely affect the rights of the retired players. I hope the courts make a speedy decision in the matter so that the problem is resolved once and for all.

CHAPTER THIRTEEN

THE BREAK WITH ORR – PART II

"I know where the rest of the Bobby Orr
files are."
"Why weren't they thrown out with the rest?"
"I just thought we might need them some day."

– conversation in my office, August, 1990.

After Orr and I split our business relationships in April, 1980, Orr selling some of his holdings to me, mainly I kept my own counsel. Despite some evidence that Bobby still had it in for me – he'd helped *Sports Illustrated* dig up some negative stuff for a 1984 article, and had something to do with Garvey and Winter when they tried to sink me without a trace, and threatened me with court action in 1989 – I kept pretty well quiet until it became plain in the summer of 1990 that the war was still on. This event is still uppermost in many minds, so I'll go into it in some detail.

I'd heard pretty well all along that Bobby's rancour had not subsided – reports that through a lawyer friend of his in Windsor, Harvey Strosberg, he had let it be known that he still had a lot of unsettled business with me.

I know and work with a lot of media people so have a pretty good entrée to anything going on behind the scenes. I'd heard that quiet offers were bandied about among media people that Bobby Orr wanted to fire a final broadside, get it all off his chest. Finally he and Strosberg found some-one – not even a sports reporter. This resulted in a story carried by the *Toronto Star* early in August, 1990, by a writer named Ellie Tesher. It is my understanding that she knew Strosberg before this matter was brought to her attention. My first knowledge that she was on the case came when I was at a five-day meeting with players and club owners in Cape Cod during the last week of July, 1990. In my hotel I received a message: "This is urgent – call Ellie Tesher at the *Toronto Star*."

I was busy with other things and didn't know Ellie Tesher so I didn't rush right out to call her back, but when I did she was very obnoxious – that is the least offensive word I can use. She said rather in a demanding tone, I thought, that I *had* to talk to her, that the story she was working on would wreck my reputation.

What story? I asked. Maybe not in exactly those words.

Her reply was to the effect that Bobby Orr wants to make public some things about you, that's what story. She went on to throw at me some of what she was intending to publish.

I said, "Miss, it is obvious to me from your attitude that you have made up your mind, and I want to tell you something: I don't have to talk to anybody. I don't know you and from the sound of you I don't like you. So, it's simple, I am not going to talk to you. You can write whatever you like on one condition. Just make sure it is the truth."

That was the last I heard from Ellie Tesher until the article appeared a few days later.

Meanwhile, I did receive a call from someone in the *Star* sports department who said that the article had been flashed past them and that they were not excited by it, that it was not sports news, that the events dwelled upon were twelve years old or more, and that the story would not be run in the *Star*'s sport section "if it is run at all."

I heard later that the story originally was planned as a two-parter, but apparently after legal advice it had been cut to one instalment. It was published as the main front-page story in the *Sunday Star* of August 5, 1990, under the heading:

BOBBY ORR SPEAKS OUT AT LAST

Strosberg was quoted as second-guessing what I had done to minimize Orr's income tax in the 1970s, saying clearly that he was not saying that I was negligent but that I should have been more conservative and in such a situation "you don't take tax risks." This quote was altered falsely in a headline that said I "took tax risks" – all part of the way some half-baked sensation-hungry media people grab at straws without checking with anybody who knows the truth.

I wasn't in the least surprised at the content of the story. I knew from my earlier conversation with Ms. Tesher that it was going to be detrimental to me. I knew what Orr had done in relation to the exposé-type 1984 *Sports Illustrated* article. Mark Mulvoy admitted to me (I have this on tape) that Orr had provided some information. Orr denied

it. Then there was what he had done in the Rich Winter-
Ed Garvey fiasco of 1989. In that one, some of the Winter-
Garvey ammunition had come from Orr, although, get this,
Orr indicated to me through an intermediary that he would
back off, not go to Florida to help Winter and Garvey, if
I would give him back a gold puck he'd given me in 1971!
I still have that puck.

My son Allen called me as soon as the Tesher article
appeared.

"Dad," he said, "it's a lot of crap, I wouldn't worry about
it, and as a lawyer I wonder where Bobby Orr was twelve
years ago if he had all these complaints. It's easy to complain
now; why didn't he complain twelve years ago? His people
went through all your files then and found you clean. Does
he think you've become dirty in the last ten years?"

So I read the story and could see the way Orr's old
resentments showed through. I came to terms with it in
this way: I could only figure that Bobby Orr was a very
unhappy young man. He thinks the world did him a bad
turn by cutting his career short because of his knee injuries
and operations. I'm convinced of that. Another thing is that
Bobby Orr actually has not changed much in all the years
I've known him. He left home to play hockey when he
was in his early teens. I think that was a major part of
his later problems. All along, he was not relaxed with most
people who came briefly into his orbit. With his cronies
he was relaxed. With people who were completely beholden
to him for one reason or another, he was not bad. As anyone
in the media would tell you, he was a pleasant interview
when we could get him in the right scenario, but don't try
to interview him after a game. He would run for cover in
the training room.

The difference is that all the time Orr and I were working
together, we kept his public persona in front of the media
at a much more positive level than his private person really
was. Maybe we made a mistake in that, and in keeping
quiet about some of the things I'm now mentioning.

Anyway, when the *Star* story came out and some people quoted in the story said they'd been misquoted and urged me to reply, I still planned to do nothing about it. If a reporter grabbed me after a press conference or meeting I might say something, but it wasn't any kind of a comprehensive response. All I did say, at first, was that for the things he'd said, Bobby Orr owed me an apology but I didn't expect an apology. I was right. His response was, "Yeah, when hell freezes over."

That was my attitude until I got a call from a lawyer I respect. He said, "Al, there are a couple of things in that article that I think you have to respond to. One is the suggestion that you didn't keep your client informed about contract negotiations, and the other is the tax issue. That's just my opinion."

So over the weeks of August the pressure was building for me to give an interview that would answer Orr point by point. George Gross, corporate sports editor of the *Sun* papers across the country, suggested I do something like that, with him.

I said, "George, that wouldn't carry any weight because you're known to be a friend of mine. No matter what you say it will be interpreted as coming from a friend."

Then he called me back and said he had talked about the situation to Wayne Parrish, head of the *Toronto Sun*'s day-by-day sports department. Parrish had a reputation for thoroughness, which no one could say about the *Star* story. When Parrish called he said that from his limited knowledge he thought the attack in the *Star* was unfair, especially in that I hadn't been given a proper opportunity to examine what the charges were and reply in what might then have become a more balanced story. "If I am going to talk to you," Parrish said, "I want the facts, a full look at the issues." That, I guess, was what I wanted to hear – that he would go for the facts, without promising me anything but a full hearing.

All the same, I had a problem. When the Tesher article had come out with a lot of things I thought were untrue, most of what I needed to protect myself was covered in files that by 1990 were ten or more years old. Usually after five years our files are destroyed. I assumed that they were gone. In the middle of wondering how I could find the documentation I needed to back up what I felt was the truth, Marvin Goldblatt, my accountant, came into my office with a couple of file folders and a Cheshire cat grin.

"Here are two files," he said, "and I know where the rest of the Bobby Orr files are."

"Where?" I asked.

"I've got them in my cabinet."

"Why weren't they thrown out with everything else?"

"I just thought we might need them some day."

That's an accountant for you.

The two newish files he brought me led to the other old files, six or eight of them. Without overstating it, I spent a hundred hours on those files. I read every letter, every document. Every time I turned over a page I found something to help me.

Part of the help was there on paper because when I read, or talk on the phone, I make notes. I date them. When I have a meeting with anybody I write down the date, time, and who was there. It's amazing how something like that can jog your memory. That had been a big help in a suit that Vaclav Nedomansky brought against me, and it proved to be of great help here again. By the time Parrish and I arranged to meet, I was well prepared.

He came in to see me at 5 p.m. one day. After exhaustively going through the Tesher story and my files, we finished at 2 a.m.

There were six main issues that we agreed had to be answered.

1. Orr claimed that his pledge of $90,000 to establish what originally was called the Bobby Orr Sports Injuries Clinic at York University had been made on his behalf by me without his knowledge or support.

2. He claimed foul over the Orr-Walton hockey camp property, because I bought it out for what eventually turned out to be $380,000 and sold it for $900,000 ten years later.

3. There was an attractive contract offer from Boston, made originally in 1975, that he claimed he had not been informed about.

4. The contract he'd signed in 1979 with Standard Brands was grossly downplayed in the Tesher article.

5. The contract he'd signed with Chicago in 1976 after becoming a free agent was misrepresented in the article.

6. They claimed the corporate contract concept that had resulted in formation of Bobby Orr Enterprises Limited was risky tax advice and should not have been pursued.

Parrish and I went through those points one by one to give him a lot more to work with than Tesher had looked for, or got, in her research. I felt that I had done all I could to correct the distortions and one-sidedness of what Orr had presented as his case.

I should now mention that through all this fighting-back phase, tackling Orr's version with chapter and verse, Nancy had hit my problem on the button with, "You can never successfully attack a legend." Maybe what happened with the Parrish article bore that out. He did good back-and-forth homework, seeking out information from all sides on the way to reaching his own conclusions. Then he would go from me to Orr and his lawyer, sharing my information with them. This created the opportunity for them to defend themselves in ways that again were suspect from my standpoint.

There were items in Parrish's final article where Orr either skated around the truth or shrugged off things he couldn't deny – in some cases because Parrish had evidence that proved Orr wrong. So what follows here embodies not only the documented material I gave to Parrish, but also, in some cases, Orr's reaction more or less in the line of "So what?"

Some of his responses were reported by Parrish unchallenged. I'll challenge them here even while recognizing Parrish's largely successful efforts to produce a balanced account.

1. Regarding the sports clinic arrangement made with York University in 1979, Parrish wrote: "Orr's displeasure at a recent article in the *Globe and Mail* in which Eagleson mentioned that Orr had backed off his (financial) commitment (of $90,000) to the clinic prompted Orr to end his silence." Orr claimed he had known nothing of any arrangement for him to fund the clinic.

Parrish replied that he'd seen a letter from Bobby's lawyer in Boston that refuted the claim of ignorance. In fact, I can't help thinking right here that if I were arguing this in a court of law, I would enter in evidence *all* the correspondence on the sports clinic matter from September 6, 1979, a week after Orr fired me, to January 12, 1988, when it had been settled with me pledging personally to pay what Orr had pledged originally.

All the correspondence? Considering the number of trees that would have to be destroyed to reproduce on paper such a wad of back-and-forthing, I will resist the temptation, but will give the highlights. On September 6, 1979, right after Orr left me, I wrote to his lawyer, Jack Herlihy in Boston, enclosing a photocopy of York University's draft announcement – not released at the time – concerning the establishment of the clinic in Orr's name. I added:

> In view of the fact that Bobby has changed his views about my involvement in his affairs, perhaps he would prefer to have his name withdrawn from the sports clinic rather than be committed to a $90,000 obligation over the next 5 year period.

At that point he could have bowed out. Until that date I had paid into the clinic fund, on Bobby's behalf, proceeds of speeches and TV appearances I had made, the fees assigned directly to the clinic in his name. A Bobby Orr sports day had been held in Oshawa with Bobby's active participation on the understanding that the proceeds would go to the clinic fund. About $7,500 was raised. In my September, 1979, letter to Herlihy I suggested that if Orr wanted out of the clinic we could arrange to have the amount raised at the sports day go, in his name, to the Oshawa General Hospital or some other Oshawa charity he could designate.

I said that I'd advised York to hold off their formal announcement until the matter was clarified.

In reply I received a letter from Herlihy dated October 22, 1979, which stated: "Bobby went to the Sports Clinic and was extremely impressed and glad that you had him become involved in it." Herlihy added that he was writing to York University "confirming that Bobby will honor the obligation to the extent of $90,000."

When Bobby was denying to Parrish that he'd known about his commitment, Parrish had said, "Hold it," and referred to Jack Herlihy's 1979 letter to the contrary. At that point Orr, according to Parrish, admitted that he had known about the letter. It was dated more than a month after he had left me, so if we wanted to clarify his attitude to the clinic situation in 1979 that letter did it in spades – much better than I expected because at first I'd thought it would just be my word against Orr's. To find that letter from his lawyer ended the matter of Orr not being informed. Maybe he'd forgotten, I don't know.

Having to acknowledge the letter's existence, Orr then told Parrish that when he heard nothing from York between 1979 and 1983 he presumed that I had paid off the balance for him. Once he began receiving correspondence from York asking for the balance owing on his commitment, he'd decided to wait. "I know how Al doesn't like to spend money," he told Parrish. "I wanted to see him squirm. I really didn't think they would take my name off the clinic."

That is it in a nutshell. He wanted his name on the clinic but didn't want to pay for it.

By 1985, there was a certain amount of hand-wringing going on at York. The amounts that I had mentioned above, including the sports day proceeds, came to about $26,000 and change. They'd laid out the rest of the $90,000 themselves, $63,531, and wanted to get off the hook somehow.

On February 20, 1986, York president Harry Arthurs wrote politely to Orr mentioning that balance of $63,531, which "has been outstanding for some time now and I can find few records of communication between the university and your organization." To resolve the matter, he proposed that he and Orr meet. This would be "at your convenience" and "Thank you in advance for your kind co-operation."

A week later Harry Arthurs sent a memo to Ian Lithgow, York's vice-president of external relations. "I had a call from Mr. Watters on behalf of Bobby Orr. He stated essentially that Orr had not made the pledge or approved it, but that Eagleson had made it on his own authority. Accordingly, he states that Orr is not prepared to honour the pledge."

So then they got in touch with me. I wrote to Harry Arthurs that I had press clippings publicly confirming Orr's pledge. I would prefer that he honour it. If he wouldn't, I would, on the condition that the clinic would be renamed. "It would not seem fair or reasonable that the clinic carry the name of Bobby Orr if Bobby Orr is not committed to it financially," I wrote, and suggested that he review the matter with Orr and Watters, who might want to reassess Orr's position.

Orr, Watters, and Arthurs met on May 20. I don't know what happened at the meeting but Orr wrote to Arthurs on May 28, 1986, saying it would be in his best interest to have "Eagleson honour the obligation he made without my consent."

He also suggested that if his name was to be removed from the clinic, I should be responsible for the entire $90,000. He wanted a refund of not just the $7,500 from the Orr sports day, but everything I had caused to be put in, too! "I will notify you of the charity or institution to whom I would like the monies forwarded."

Arthurs replied to that letter on June 27, to Orr, saying that, as he'd informed Orr and Watters in the May 20 meeting, the university "continues to regard you as responsible for the full amount of the pledge, given our understanding that Mr. Eagleson was acting as your agent (manager) at the time. In our view, the fact that your publicly announced contribution to the clinic was never denied in all the public utterances surrounding both the announcement and the opening only lends credence to the proposition that this pledge was made with your approval or acquiescence, either before or after the fact. In any event, Mr. Eagleson clearly had ostensible authority to make it."

Regarding the funds previously contributed that Orr wanted lodged elsewhere, that would be inappropriate "since the funds were not contributed by you."

Orr wrote to York repeating that it had never been his commitment, that at the time it was made he was being prosecuted by both the U.S. Internal Revenue Service and Revenue Canada, that I had been "painfully aware" of his obligations, and so on. "However, rest assured that I will not sit idly by and have my name besmirched . . . . I will divulge in a press release exactly why my name was removed from your fine establishment and who was responsible for it if this matter is not handled properly. . . . Please rest assured that Bobby Orr honors his commitments. I, however, refuse to honor Mr. Eagleson's."

We could go on all day, but won't. I agreed to pay the rest of the $90,000, arranging that such payment would be completed even if I died. At the same time I suggested maybe the name should be the Alan Eagleson/Bobby Orr clinic, or the Team Canada clinic.

York came back, bless them, and said that none of those other names were acceptable; the clinic would carry the name of the person who gave the money. "And as you are giving the money it is now the Alan Eagleson sports clinic."

One postscript won't hurt. In 1979, when Orr claims I didn't have the authority to commit him to the sports clinic – which I legally did have – I also executed an employment contract for him with Standard Brands that had made him more than $1 million U.S. in the subsequent seven and a half years.

He didn't argue about my authority to do that.

So if Orr, as he said at the start, was annoyed enough about the sports clinic matter to attribute to it his whole series of allegations about our financial arrangements over the years, he wasn't exactly starting from a solid base. The rest of his case wasn't much, if any, better.

2. In the matter of the Orr-Walton hockey camp property, Orr charged that I bought him out at fire-sale prices, then sold it at a big profit. Again, I have the letters between his Boston lawyer and me about his wish to put the camp up for sale. In these exchanges, I argued strongly that he should keep it, that values right then in the early 1980s were at their lowest, and that he should hold it until the real estate market would make it worth a lot more.

I even offered that if I put a deal together with eventual purchasers, or if I bought it and eventually sold to somebody else, I would make a commitment that if any subsequent sale was made within five years Bobby would get 20 per cent of any profit. They came back and said, "No, we want cash, we want to liquidate. Pay us cash in advance for it now and forget the 20 per cent."

Somewhere in there I suggested a trade-off. As part of our overall split I had agreed to pay Orr $10,000 a year for five years from Sports Management Limited, my company. It would be called a consultancy but would really be a good-bye kiss. In return for that $10,000 a year, I required him to promise that he would not get involved with Bill Watters in that period. Watters had left me by then.

However, I thought that if Orr joined Watters they might pose a threat to my own operation. Hence my provision. Orr agreed to that deal; he'd stay clear of Watters. Then he said that instead of the $10,000 a year, he'd rather have a lump sum of $50,000. The $10,000 a year would have been safer for me because I could have cancelled it if he abrogated the agreement about Watters, which he soon did. The real cash value of the five years at $10,000 a year, if paid in a lump sum, should have been more like $30,000, or even less, maybe as low as $20,000, because interest rates were very high then. I paid the $50,000 anyway, the condition still being that he would not deal with Watters in the next five years.

He admitted to Parrish that he breached that agreement on Watters within a year, but did so "because I knew that Al wouldn't sue me."

What is an agreement for? I paid him $50,000 for it. He should have honoured the agreement. He was right. I didn't sue him.

I took over the hockey camp, and thus was stuck with an investment, including interest, of about $380,000. I sold it within two years for $20,000 down, but the purchasers defaulted on the mortgage so I was still in for that investment of $380,000. I didn't get a nickel of my money back until the late 1980s, when it sold for $900,000 – which could have been Orr's profit if he'd taken my advice and held it himself. As for me, if I had put that original $380,000 in the bank or into other real estate I would have tripled or quadrupled my money. I have no apologies to make about the hockey camp deal. I tried to make it benefit him, and he wouldn't go along.

3. In the matter of the 1975-76 contract offer by Boston leading up to his becoming a free agent, Orr claimed that I didn't let him know the details. To my mind, that simply could not be true or he has blanked it out. It was such a great offer, but it did not come to pass.

That contract is a little complicated. The Jacobs brothers of Buffalo had bought the Boston franchise. I had meetings with Jerry Jacobs and Bill Wirtz of Chicago, who was representing the league. One of the topics was Bobby Orr's

future – important all around because he was not only a
Boston asset but an asset to the whole NHL. New owners
wouldn't necessarily have the same loyalty and appreciation
he'd earned from their predecessors. Out of that, I thought
I had an assurance from Bill Wirtz that the Jacobs brothers
would sign Bobby Orr, practically as one of their conditions
of their entry into the NHL. Accordingly, I had a series
of negotiations with Mr. Jacobs, beginning in 1975. Over
time, we reached what seemed to be a good deal. Bobby
would be paid $295,000 a year for five years, plus, at the
contract's end in 1980, either a lump sum of $925,000 or
an 18.5 per cent stake in the Bruin franchise.

I badly wanted to make that deal and keep Bobby in
Boston where he belonged. If we'd signed at that point,
great. A big hitch was that our tax counsel in Washington,
Robert Schulman, said that the tax risk was too high – that
the final $925,000 payment would be taxed as income
immediately.

To counter that possibility, I thought I had Boston's
agreement to spread the $925,000 over the length of the
contract as salary while, for half that amount, retaining
Bobby's option on the 18.5 per cent ownership. Jerry Jacobs
refused to accept the change.

Then came the worst of breaks, from the standpoint of
making what still might have been an excellent Boston deal.
By then we're into the 1975-76 season. After ten games in
the autumn of 1975, Bobby suffered a season-ending injury
to his knee. In my opinion, after the Jacobs brothers
determined that Bobby's knee was not sound, Boston had
a different attitude in negotiations. Their offers kept dropping.
They wanted Orr to pass a medical or no deal. They were
acting as if Orr's past was history and that basically they
didn't want him at any kind of reasonable terms.

I went to Bill Wirtz and put it to him that Bobby deserved
better than that. He agreed. When Bobby became a free
agent in June, 1976, he signed with Chicago – a contract,

and a set of circumstances, to which I've already alluded, totalling a maximum $3 million.

On the signing in Chicago, Bobby and I had our pictures taken, one of those smiling everything-is-great two-shots that had been done (it seemed) hundreds of times before. The difference was that this time Bobby was holding a Chicago sweater across his chest. He wrote across the white part of the photo, "To Al. Many thanks. Bob."

Meanwhile, with reference to Bobby's years-later contention that he knew nothing about the Boston ownership opportunity that hadn't worked out, I and others – including Bruins' president Paul Mooney – remember Bobby as being part of those negotiations. The deal was laid out in a Boston press conference. Details were published in Toronto nearly three weeks *before* Bobby signed with Chicago. Parrish called me late one night in August, 1990, to tell me he'd tracked down the old published story on the press conference, "and if you told the world, I'm sure you told Bobby."

4. The contract he'd signed in 1979 with Standard Brands was a financial coup. In the Tesher article he had studiously avoided mentioning that it was a multi-million-dollar deal on his behalf, arranged by me without charging him a fee. At the same time that he was telling Tesher how broke he was, he didn't mention that he eventually got more than a million dollars out of that contract, with more to come at a rate of well over $100,000 a year.

5. He told everyone through the Tesher article that out of the $3 million deal ($1.5 million guaranteed) that I'd negotiated for him from Chicago he'd only received $200,000 net after tax.

Well, what you get net after tax is what you get. Happens to everybody who hasn't managed to avoid it by some legal means. The frustrating part of that for me was that I had negotiated a contract that would have paid him $500,000 a year, with him paying the tax on that. We are talking now about the years from late 1976, when we did everything together, to late 1979 when he decided he'd be better off without me.

He played twenty games for Chicago in 1976-77, none in 1977-78. The exact chronology probably doesn't matter much anymore, but the changes do. Without consulting me, he decided, "Oh, I couldn't take all that money when I couldn't play."

Accordingly, in those first two years in Chicago he didn't accept any salary. In there somewhere he made a deal with Bob Pulford, Chicago's GM, and owner Bill Wirtz that he wouldn't take the $500,000 a year but would like $200,000 as an interest-free loan to buy a house. Then they could pay him $150,000 a year until the balance of $1.3 million on the original contract guarantee of $1.5 million had been paid.

This was all done without my advice or input. If he wants to blame people, he should start there with himself: that one cost him plenty at a time when he really didn't have as much money coming in as he needed. Parrish confirmed with Bob Pulford that I had no part in that revised contract arrangement.

After that Orr acted as Pulford's assistant coach and on the surface was looking at staying in Chicago. What happened, however, happened very quickly. It happens wherever Bobby goes: eventually, unless the only decision is his, he blows his cool. He called me one day (before our split) and said that I had to get Bob Pulford fired, that Pulford "doesn't know what the hell he's doing" and that he, Bobby Orr, should be general manager of the Black Hawks.

I said, "Listen, Bobby. I don't run the team. You go and tell Bill Wirtz what you just said to me. My guess is that he'll fire you."

Around the same time, Chicago players rebelled against him. I know the players. Tony Esposito was the Chicago goalie then. Even on the Team Canada trip in 1972 when Orr had been along but not fit to play, Esposito had called me over during the plane trip home and filled me in on what he thought Orr eventually would do to me.

Now, years later, he's saying to me, "Al, if you don't get Orr out of here the team is not going to play."

No doubt this message was getting to Pulford from other players as well. Within a few weeks of Orr becoming Pulford's on-ice assistant he was no longer Pulford's on-ice assistant. It only took Pulford that long to realize the effect that Orr, a very demanding young man, was having on the team.

He nearly destroyed Dale Tallon, who years earlier had been his successor as Oshawa's favourite junior defenceman. They wound up playing together in Chicago and he basically ran Dale Tallon out of town.

Dale would call me almost in tears saying, "I don't know what is wrong with Bobby but has he ever got it in for me." Eventually Dale was traded to Pittsburgh, where he played well until he broke his leg and had to retire. He went back to Chicago and a career in broadcasting with the Blackhawks*, where he's happy. It is sad, but Bobby left a lot of unhappy people in his wake.

Which reminds me again of Mike Walton. When he and Bobby first met through me, then became partners in their hockey camp, they were partners in everything, like brothers, absolutely inseparable.

As time went on and they went their separate ways in hockey, the friendship stayed the same. Mike worked a lot harder than Bobby at their hockey camp, drew the same pay, but never complained. Bobby was his buddy. Usually the camp made money. By the mid-1970s Bobby seemed to have lost a lot of his interest, which soon showed in his eagerness to sell the property. But the real crunch between the two came when Bobby split with me and figured Mike should, too, out of blind loyalty to Bobby, I can only guess – never mind loyalty to me.

---

*In 1985 the Chicago club changed its nickname from Black Hawks to Blackhawks.

He could have said, "Hey, Mike, I'm leaving Al and here is why. You make your own decision." That is not his way. What he told Mike was, "If you stay with Eagleson you are not with me." Orr hasn't said twenty words to Walton in the last twelve years.

One other thing that happened when Bobby was with Chicago might have contributed to his eventual decision to leave me. A defenceman named Dave Hutchison, one of my clients (as were both Pulford and Orr), had played tough inspirational hockey for Los Angeles when Pulford was coaching there, up to 1977. Before the 1978-79 season came up, Pulford had been a year in Chicago. He knew Hutchison was available and badly wanted to get him. Orr backed him up. They thought they had a deal for Hutchison with Bill Watters.

I intervened. The best deal for Hutchison was with Toronto, which is what I did. In return Orr roasted me, cussed me out, and was convinced – again, here's that jealousy showing – that Sittler, who years earlier had been a teammate of Hutchison's with the junior London Knights, had influenced my decision (as he saw it) to opt for the Leafs and against Chicago. He refused to understand that when I was making a deal, for him or anybody else, I dealt for the client – in this case not for Bobby Orr, Bob Pulford, or Bill Wirtz, but for Dave Hutchison.

6. I've wandered a bit from the list of Orr's complaints, but handling the last one, the matter of the tax arrangements built in to Bobby Orr Enterprises Limited, is almost a pleasure: I was right in what I did, but it turned out wrong. As simple as that.

My setting up of Bobby Orr Enterprises Limited was what many tax consultants to high-profile and high-income individuals were doing at the time. The aim of Bobby's company was strictly to minimize his taxes. Many other athletes, writers, actors, directors – people with a variety of income sources – were setting up companies that could deduct for pension plans, automobiles, rent, loan interest, or whatever, and qualify for tax rates about half of what an individual would pay on the same income.

This was considered legal under the laws that prevailed at the time. Among many other dozens of sports figures who took advantage of it were hockey's Punch Imlach and football's Ralph Sazio. Sazio was taken to court by Revenue Canada over having his football salary paid to his corporation, and Revenue Canada lost. Still, Lyman MacInnis, who was one of our tax consultants at the time, debated with me about the corporate plan I had in mind for Orr.

When MacInnis was interviewed for the Tesher article on this point and she chose to interpret, or extrapolate, his remarks into a criticism of me, he was furious. He told Parrish that despite his own reservations, which he had expressed to me, if all the tax experts in the country had been lined up in the early 1970s to debate the question the results would have been about 50-50 for and against. He recalled, accurately, that when he'd argued that I should be sure Orr understood all the ramifications, I said I felt that Orr was too young (twenty-three) and inexperienced to make that decision. So I had steered him as I did. Lyman MacInnis, speaking to the *Sun*'s Parrish, didn't sound at all the way he had been depicted earlier in the *Star*, whose treatment of me he termed tantamount to "character assassination," adding, "I have never known Al to rip anybody off, ever."

Other tax experts contacted by Parrish for his story were even more specific. Irving Rosen, senior partner of a major Toronto accounting firm, said that my decision to set up a corporation to handle Orr's income "was pretty well accepted then (in 1971)." Barry Weisman, a Boston tax expert who worked on Orr's taxes both before and after our split, went even further. He said that the benefits to be derived were "fantastic" and that "at the time, it is conceivable that one would have lost clients were one not to have taken a decision as creative as that."

As years went by, I defended that form of tax arrangement strenuously on behalf of Orr and dozens of other NHL clients, arguing that Revenue Canada's position required a change in law before it could be accepted. The law *was* changed, but not until 1978. Orr then, like others, was faced with tax reassessments in both Canada and the U.S. His case was never lost, it was settled (I was out of his life by that time) for a total of about $240,000 U.S. – about 20 per cent of what the feds in both countries were hassling him for. That meant, add it up, he wound up paying about *one-fifth* of the taxes that he would have had to pay years earlier if we had not come up with Bobby Orr Enterprises Limited. So he did quite well out of simply going along with a system that was accepted as legal at the time we did it.

The trouble was, when he did get the bill he had spent all the money that he should have been saving for such a contingency.

Of course, nobody likes being hit. He belly-ached in the *Star* about legal fees and accounting fees involved in the tax case, not mentioning that as long as he was with me I paid such charges from my Sports Management Limited company.

If he had stayed with me, I can say categorically that Sports Management would have paid any tax shortfall on the grounds that my company had given him the advice in the first place. Once he made the decision to go elsewhere, that was his problem. He paid more to the lawyer he hired on this matter than he had paid me in legal and accounting fees over twenty years. One lawyer charged him something like $48,000 on a settlement of about $200,000. My fee would have been zero.

From what I can gather, Bobby Orr is unhappy with the Parrish revelations in the *Toronto Sun*, and by now a series of articles on the subject may have appeared in a small Boston area paper. I wish Bobby would simply get on with his life and not continue to nurse any grudge against me.

He was an important part of my career, he helped catapult me into the hockey forefront, and he was part of our family for fourteen years, but our divorce is final. I have no time or desire for recriminations.

CHAPTER FOURTEEN

HOCKEY PEOPLE

I can still say that I don't miss Eddie Shack one
bit because when he was with me I nearly
went crazy.

I sometimes have the feeling that when anyone is thinking about where I stand in the world of pro hockey, what comes to mind is Bobby Orr, the '72 series, the Canada Cup, and the 1989-90 battles inside the players' association. When I think about the last twenty-five years or so, sure, all those people and events have been on the agenda. But there have been some comic turns on the program, too, along with tragedies or near tragedies, times of loyalty and friendship as well as back-stabbers, of players who had great talent and used it, some who had talent and didn't make the most of it. They're all part of the fabric of my life. I list them here in no particular order.

Punch Imlach. I've mentioned Punch Imlach a few times already. Once I went through his book *Heaven and Hell in the NHL* to check on what people he mentioned most. In alphabetical order they were Harold Ballard, King Clancy, Joe Crozier, Alan Eagleson, Dorothy Imlach, Gilbert Perreault, Darryl Sittler, and Floyd Smith. These were the people who seemed to mean the most to him – the most important on a personal level, of course, being his wife Dorothy. I was happy to be on the list.

Oddly enough, in light of our later public battles, in the early days before the players' association I had a friendly relationship with Punch – and not only as co-winners in the crap game at Pulford's stag that I mentioned in Chapter One. In the 1960s some Leaf road trips were treated as party time by club directors, led by president Stafford Smythe and vice-president Harold Ballard. Chairman John Bassett, principal owner at the time, was along rarely, if ever, but two or three times I was the guest of Imlach, Ballard, and Smythe on Leaf charters for hockey trips to New York or Chicago. In the fall of 1966 they asked me along on a four-day trip to New York for games on the Sunday and Wednesday nights. Leafs beat Rangers in the Sunday game, and to

celebrate Stafford and Harold threw a party at Mama Leone's.
Imlach, Ballard, and Smythe – what an outfit!

With the Spumante flowing like Spumante tends to do,
Punch handled the other two better than anyone I ever saw.
Stafford was a little unsteady, making his speech as host,
listing reasons why he and Punch were going to lift the
Leafs out of their last two less successful seasons and win
another Stanley Cup (which happened). After Stafford's
speech Harold leaned over to light a cigar for me, using
one of the big table candles. Punch yelled, "Look out!"
too late. Wax spilled onto my suit. Aghast, Ballard said
he'd get this one cleaned that night, which he did. And
back in Toronto he'd buy me a new one, which he also
did.

Imlach and Eagleson partying together – a few years later
no one would have believed it. So a few words about that.
Imlach's assessment of Mike Walton, with me in the middle,
was quite similar to his earlier treatment of Billy Harris.
He felt that both performed better when they were only
called on for spot duty. Neither enjoyed that role, and Mike
hated it. Maybe Punch was right when they were with the
Leafs, but later it's a saw-off.

Once Billy Harris had left the Leafs after playing his
spot role to perfection, he did nothing comparable with stints
in Detroit, Oakland, and Pittsburgh. Mike Walton had some
good years playing as a regular elsewhere. And Imlach did
make mistakes. One was to say that Jim McKenny, when
he was a junior with Marlboros, would be as good as Orr
when he made it to the NHL. McKenny is a wonderful
guy, good broadcaster, good friend, but that load Imlach
put on him with the Orr comparison didn't do him any
good at all.

I remember clearly where I was and what I was doing
when Stafford Smythe fired Imlach in April, 1969. I was
at the Metropole Hotel in Russia trying to talk the Russians
into what became the 1972 series and later the Canada Cup.

A telegram came to me through the Canadian embassy from one of my law partners. It read: "I'm loch fried." I wondered what it meant, then read on about Leafs getting beaten badly and deduced that it was meant to read: "Imlach fired." That day I thought about a lot of things he and I had clashed on.

We were generally on opposite sides of the table but I do know that each enjoyed a healthy respect for the other. Even before I knew him personally, I studied him a lot because I was a Toronto fan and from 1959 he was building a great team. I thought about when Punch was building the team that won four Stanley Cups between 1959, his arrival, and 1969, his departure. His philosophy was very simple: reduce every player to the same level of importance no matter how great a superstar one might be. He had no room for players who "marched to a different drummer." Those players included the likes of Carl Brewer, Frank Mahovlich, and Mike Walton. The perfect player for Punch Imlach was the Bob Pulford, Tim Horton, Allan Stanley type. They gave examples of leadership by their deeds, without any lengthy speeches or shenanigans.

There wasn't much fun between us in those years. A lot of the fun came in the years when he surfaced again with Buffalo Sabres. He stunned everybody by getting into the playoffs in Sabres' third season, stunned them again by finishing first and losing only in the Stanley Cup final in their fifth season. Getting Gilbert Perreault in his first draft was the luck of the draw, but later the people he drafted for and traded for had no luck attached – just Imlach's shrewd knowledge of the game.

I remember one fun story, the fun part being something involving Bill Watters. In 1974 Sabres drafted Lee Fogolin as their first-round pick. I acted for Fogolin. The NHL meetings were still on in Montreal when I got a call from Punch suggesting we meet for dinner at the Ritz Carlton. He brought along his assistant since Toronto days, John Andersen, and I brought Bill Watters. Before dinner was over I had Fogolin signed to a three-year contract for $410,000 – $200,000 to sign, then $60,000, $70,000, and $80,000. These were unheard of figures for a first-round pick. They set the tone for all the others signing and I had seven or eight players in the first round that year–with the WHA lurking in the wings.

For dinner I had steak tartare. Imlach and Watters had steaks, I'm not sure about Andersen. After we started Watters said to me, "Hey, Al, how's that taste?"

I said, "Well, you take half of mine and I'll take half of yours and you can taste it yourself."

He agreed. After one bite of steak tartare he put down his fork and said, "Gee whiz, Al. This food is hardly even cooked."

So much for Bill Watters the gourmet. Imlach and I couldn't stop laughing.

Some people often mention an incident a few years later in Buffalo, at the all-star dinner there in January, 1978. There were a lot of speeches from the head table. I kept expecting that some speaker would say right out loud that if Imlach had not gone to Buffalo in 1970, built that franchise, the Sabres would not have enjoyed their first eight years of remarkable success. Whatever beefs he and I had, I was always ready to acknowledge his success and pay respect to what he had achieved. I found it hard to believe that no one at that head table had thought to give the man his due. So when it came my turn to speak, I felt that if no one else was going to say a few glowing words about his contribution, I would. It was from the heart. I know a lot of people were startled, having been conditioned in the media to believe that we were mortal enemies.

One of the first people I heard from after the speech was right there at the head table, Imlach himself, in typical Imlach fashion. "Eagleson," he said, "who the hell put you up to that?"

So did that buy me future breaks from Old Ironsides? Like hell. Less than a year later Buffalo fired Punch, and in the summer of 1979 Harold Ballard hired him to replace Jim Gregory as Leaf's GM. It wasn't long before Punch decided to flex his muscles with the NHLPA. A show called *Showdown* was being marketed widely on TV intermissions, including *Hockey Night in Canada*, and had been approved originally by everybody that counted – a majority of NHL owners (although Ballard had voted against it), the league itself, and the NHLPA. Punch had been opposed to it in Buffalo and at various times had talked Danny Gare and Gilbert Perreault into declining invitations to participate. For the 1979-80 series of the show Darryl Sittler and Mike Palmateer had been designated to represent the Leafs.

Then Imlach arrived. He said no to both of them, but offered in exchange Paul Gardner and goalie Gord McRae. With all due respect they were not on the same star level as the other two – not to mention the many stars, one of them Phil Esposito, appearing on the show for other teams. We argued. Leafs hired a lawyer to seek an injunction to prevent Sittler and Palmateer from participating. I acted for the NHLPA and *Showdown*. We appeared, not in open court, but in chambers, before Mr. Justice John O'Driscoll of the Ontario Supreme Court. He made quick work of the matter by advising Leafs that their injunction would not be allowed. So Sittler and Palmateer did participate, but Punch had at least part of the last laugh. Invoking the old agreement that a club owner had the right to decide who would appear in TV intermissions out of the club's home town, Ballard refused to allow *Showdown* to be televised out of Toronto. By taking away one of the prime markets for sponsors, this effectively ended *Showdown*'s future and made a mockery of the agreement reached earlier by the NHL and NHLPA.

So Eagleson v. Imlach was tough to handle sometimes. Still, I think in some ways we both enjoyed the adversarial reputation we had built up over the years. At another all-star game, I think in California, Punch and I were sitting around a pool exchanging stories about our children when we noticed a couple of reporters looking in our direction.

With the same kind of mischief that I often found in him, Imlach said, "Let's shout at each other for a while and I'll bet we'll soon have a press conference." Within thirty seconds four or five of the media people rushed over to find out what we were arguing about. We told them it was a private matter and would remain just between us. Which it has, until you read this.

Marcel Dionne. I first heard of Marcel Dionne from a friend of mine in St. Catharines, Archie Katzman. He was also a good friend of Punch Imlach's, which tells you something to remember about hockey's tribal closeness – the prejudices of one friendship do not necessarily infect another. In the late 1960s, when Imlach and I were cutting each other up regularly in the media, it didn't matter a damn to Archie Katzman. If one of us could help him out, or if he could help either of us out with a room, a beer, or a meal at his multi-purpose Parkway Hotel just off the Queen Elizabeth highway, so be it; it was all the same to him.

I didn't have anything to do with junior hockey at the time, around 1970, but Archie asked if I would come over. Marcel Dionne was eighteen or nineteen then, working part-time in the bowling alley part of Archie's hotel. I hadn't met him, but Marcel had come into my life in absentia, as it were, a year or two before. This happened because the owner of the St. Catharines junior Black Hawks, Fred Muller, summered at Parry Sound and approached me figuring I might be able to figure a way out of a problem he had. At that time, he badly wanted to get Marcel sprung loose to play hockey for St. Catharines. Marcel's home was in Victoriaville, Quebec. Under Ontario Hockey Association rules, that meant he couldn't play in Ontario.

It wasn't an easy case to solve, but I found a way by having Muller arrange to have a St. Catharines resident appointed Marcel's guardian. Hence Archie's call a year later. Marcel had been picked by Detroit in the 1971 amateur draft (second pick, only Guy Lafleur ahead of him) and was ready to turn pro. Archie thought I should represent him. I got to know Marcel personally then and have acted for him since. I negotiated his first one-year contract with Detroit, getting him $50,000 to sign and another $50,000 to play, a good start for his spectacular career.

There was a rather funny incident when he came to my law office at Blaney Pasternak in Toronto to sign his first contract with Detroit. The *Toronto Star* wanted to take a picture of him signing. I always insisted that any player I represented look his best in the media. Marcel, barely twenty at the time, had come to Toronto without a dress shirt, jacket, or tie. I loaned him mine, for the picture. We've often laughed that I gave him the shirt off my back. Meanwhile, Marcel and his wife Carol became good friends with Nancy, me, and the rest of the Eagleson family. Once or twice a year after that we'd get together as families, in Florida or St. Catharines or somewhere else.

In the 1972 series with the Soviets, Marcel was on the team but didn't get to play. He was a rookie, just turned twenty-one that summer, but he never complained about not being able to make the playing lineup. It seemed to be enough, for him, that he had made the team while Guy Lafleur, chosen before him in the previous summer's draft, did not. In Moscow later, when the Quebec trio of Rick Martin, Gilbert Perreault, and Jocelyn Guevremont left Team Canada and went home, they tried to persuade Marcel to join them. No dice. He stayed.

After joining Detroit, in four years his goal production was 28, 40, 24, 47. In 1975 I did at least start to negotiate a new contract for him with the Detroit club's lawyer, at that time John Ziegler. Two things intervened. One was that Ziegler had assured me they would pay Marcel more than anyone else on the Detroit club. When they did offer a contract, Marcel checked his against Mickey Redmond's and thought Mickey's was better. That helped Marcel make up his mind to move. The other reason was that Marcel wasn't comfortable in Detroit anyway. He'd publicly used a common term for Detroit, Murder City. The Detroit press had jumped all over him because of that and his other outspoken opinions about the Detroit club. He told me that he definitely would not be going back to Detroit.

That summer of 1975 I worked hard for him, sounding out several NHL clubs and several WHA clubs. Once Marcel and I flew to Edmonton, where the WHA Oilers' Bill Hunter offered him $300,000 a year for five years. We thought we might take that, and word got around. Then I got a call from Jack Kent Cooke, owner of the Los Angeles Kings.

"Alan, Jack Kent Cooke. What's the price for Dionne?"

"Five times three," I said. "Five years at $300,000 a year."

"Okay, well, you've got a deal. I'll pay Marcel $1.5 million over five years to play for my team."

That was actually the same total as Edmonton's offer, but it was the NHL, the better league. However, staying in the NHL meant L.A. would have to make a deal with Detroit for his rights.

"Leave the rest to me, Alan," Cooke said. "I'll find out how we can settle the matter."

Which he did. He sent Dan Maloney and Terry Harper to Detroit for Marcel and Bart Crashley (which I always figured was a great name for a hockey player). Bob Pulford, coaching Los Angeles then, was absolutely apoplectic. He couldn't believe that Cooke would trade Maloney, a player Pulford had converted into a good tough NHL forward after getting him from Chicago in a trade for Ralph Backstrom. But Pully soon adjusted to Marcel, who became precisely the spectacular leader that Cooke had been looking for. His scoring tells you that: 40, 53, 36, 59, 53, 58. Over the years, Marcel played with many linemates in L.A. The so-called triple crown line with Dave Taylor and Charlie Simmer during the late seventies and into 1980 was the most famous, high among the best and most productive lines in the NHL.

Marcel won the NHL scoring championship in 1979-80 and was a free agent again, having played out his original five-year contract. Cooke then sold the Kings to Jerry Buss,

who was also excellent to deal with. I was having my crippling
back trouble that year, making travel hell. Buss suggested
he fly to Toronto to see me, instead of the other way around.
His message was simple: Marcel was the best player in the
NHL and should be paid accordingly. That was an easy
starting point for negotiations. We signed a contract that
would pay Marcel $600,000 a year for five years. We later
extended that contract by two years, so for seven years Marcel
was the highest-paid player in the league.

In 1987 when I suggested to Rogie Vachon, the L.A.
general manager, that the contract be extended again, he
said no. I said that in that case Marcel would prefer to be
traded immediately, which landed him with the New York
Rangers. That summer Phil Esposito, the New York GM,
worked out with me a contract guaranteed for three more
years. To help Phil manage that in terms of his budget,
we reduced Marcel's base contract but increased his per-
formance bonuses, a good deal. In his first year with the
Rangers he made more than $200,000 in bonuses alone.

In the summer of 1989 Phil was fired. The new management did not consider Marcel, then thirty-eight, to be
in their plans. It was bad planning, from our standpoint,
that they postponed that decision until training camp. When
it came, their word was blunt; they'd be sending him to
the minors for the rest of the season. Marcel didn't like
that kind of comedown. I supported him. Such an illustrious
career deserved better than ending it in the minors. Accordingly, I negotiated a settlement that would pay Marcel in
full for the time left on his contract, the payments to be
spread over three years.

That honourable retirement was no less than he deserved.
He'd been one of the outstanding players in the NHL, had
been on Team Canada for the '72 series with the Soviets,
was a member of the 1976 Team Canada that won the Canada
Cup, had an assist on Darryl Sittler's winning goal, played
on the 1979 Challenge series against the Soviets, and represented Canada several times in world championships. Twice

he'd been named best player in the world tournament. Every time he played he was named the best Canadian player. In international play he never held back, never complained. He always was the first one to agree to represent his country even though each time it meant leaving his family for three or four weeks at the end of a tough season in L.A. All this had been recognized in 1983 when Dr. Guenther Sabetzki presented him with a trophy for playing more international games than anyone else in the NHL.

When he was through, Marcel's career 1,748 total points, including 724 goals, were second in both categories only to Gordie Howe's 1,850 and 801. Financially secure, Marcel shopped around and then decided to take on a major dry-cleaning business in New York, which he worked at with the same energy that made him so great in hockey.

Mike Walton. Let me give Mike to you from my perspective. The first time I saw him in 1966 he was twenty-one, a bubbly effervescent kid wearing white bucks and a short haircut, just up with the Leafs after playing in their minor system. I liked him from the start. His dad's nickname was Shaky, and that became Mike's nickname as well. He was somewhat eccentric, but he had guts.

In subsequent years I got to know him well. As I've related, he and Bobby Orr became close friends, literally lived together in our cottage. Then Mike rented a cottage next door with a big backyard where we put a trailer, which Bobby used. So for a time we had a sort of hockey enclave, or compound, with other players often visiting. The noise on summer nights sometimes severely strained Nancy's patience.

After Mike's stormy times with Punch Imlach ended in 1969 when Imlach was fired, his running battle with management carried right on with Imlach's successors, Jim Gregory as general manager and Johnny McLellan as coach. In November, 1970, having watched most Leaf games that season from the sidelines, he became terribly depressed and quit the team. Later he was traded to Philadelphia on what turned out to be just a whistle stop on his way to Boston, where it was thought that by joining his friend Bobby Orr he would find himself. Mike had a couple of good years in Boston and won his second Stanley Cup ring in 1972.

In 1973 Minnesota Fighting Saints of the WHA signed him to a three-year contract. There, Harry Neale found something in Mike, and so did Glen Sonmor, that pushed him toward the expectations he had for himself. He was spectacular, partly because the WHA level of ability was a little lower than the NHL. I'd see him after three- or four-goal games when he'd looked as dominating as Bobby Orr ever did. He was an all-star, scoring champion, really sailing. As with the Leafs and everywhere else he could make spectacular plays, but keeping that up wasn't his style. He would get three goals in the first period and then spend the rest of the game hanging around the blueline.

I would talk to him after, protesting. "Mike! Knuckle down!"

And he'd say, "I was the best checker on the team, I was plus three." Meaning, on for three goals for and none against.

That might have been more good luck than anything else, but Mike was a player you couldn't criticize, constructively or destructively. He figured he always knew what was best for the team and best for him, which meant that for every coach he had, including Neale, he could be a headache. The personal record was just about as spotty. His eccentricity off the ice about matched what he did in games. He was the greatest hail-fellow-well-met you'd ever find anywhere. He was the kind of guy who would have $1,000 at noon and by 1:15 would have bought lunches and beers for his teammates and still would be looking to spend more money.

But Mike was a travelling man. By his last season with Minnesota, the team was on its last legs. Meanwhile, Boston had traded Mike's NHL rights to Vancouver. When he moved there, back to the NHL from the WHA, the competition was up a notch. He played two seasons and most of a third in Vancouver before finishing his career in St. Louis, Boston again, and finally as a regular with Chicago in 1979. That's a skim through part of his hockey record. He probably should have stayed in the WHA. He should have gone to Hartford, as Dave Keon did. As it was, when Mike packed it in, he'd had fifteen years of pro hockey. I remember talking to him some years later, trying once again at that late date to get him to settle down. As I said to him, "Mike, for twenty years you did everything in your power to screw up your marriage. Thanks to your wife, who Nancy considers eligible for sainthood, it stuck together and you have three great kids . . . "

However, after all those years of forbearance, Candy, his wife, decided things had to change. They sold their house and separated legally. I talked to both of them but sometimes you can't glue something together. Eventually they divorced, and that's about that.

The Walton kids stayed with Mike after the split, and he worked hard, both financially and otherwise, to keep them in school. Since, there's been a certain amount of the kids moving back and forth between Mike and Candy.

After hockey, Mike got into real estate. He's good at it. Late in 1987 I was looking for a big old house in downtown Toronto that could be converted to house both my law practice and NHLPA headquarters. On the day after Christmas I went with Mike looking at houses in a large area of downtown, bounded by main thoroughfares King, Spadina, Davenport, and Jarvis. I took more than fifty Polaroid shots. Nancy helped me reduce the list to ten. The one we liked best was at 37 Maitland Street, where we found that the tenants had an option to buy. I bought the building on their option. They wanted $1.8 million. I offered $1.2 and said I wasn't going to leave the room until we made a deal. Eventually we did, at $1.525 million, with Mike Walton handling the details. That's where the NHLPA headquarters have been since. He found houses for Allen and Jill, too. And he still always has another business deal in mind. If you ever run across a place in Bloor West Village called Shaky's Bar and Grill, that's his latest.

I don't want to leave Mike's story in any way negative. He has a lot of time left. I had to touch on any failings he has because they are well known, but he was an important part of my career and I owe him a lot. He stuck by me in 1967 and 1968 when a lot of guys, maybe higher on hockey quality than Mike, ran for cover. As soon as the owners looked sideways at me, they headed for the hills. But Mike, he never cared what others thought of me. He was my friend and he still is. Ask Bobby Orr.

Normie Ullman. My favourite off-ice Normie Ullman story dates back to 1970 or 1971. We were living on The Kingsway. There'd been a meeting of the players' association and we had them all over to our house, maybe about twenty of us in all.

Normie was the president then, I believe. He came in very quiet. I said, "What would you like to drink?"

"Beer, please." Okay.

At maybe 11 p.m. he said, "Al, there's no more beer."

"Okay, what'll you have?"

"Scotch."

At midnight we were out of Scotch. What would he have? Rye.

It must have been about 4 a.m. when he said, "Say, Al, could I have another rum or whatever you've got?"

I said, "Normie, I have to tell you we're out of everything."

He looked at me with a little grin. "Well, good night, Al!"

"Good night," I said.

So okay, that's one side of Normie Ullman, a warm memory. The other side is of a wonderfully hard-working and steady man both on and off the ice. He had a good presence, commanded respect as a player and as president of the NHLPA, in character and personality a lot like Bryan Trottier. There was no oratory in his speaking style, but when he spoke the owners paid attention. When it was business to be done, he did it.

Bobby Baun. I've talked about Bobby from the early days of the association and his problems at Oakland. For years before that we'd been friends.

I had no connection of any kind with hockey except that Bob Pulford and I had been lacrosse teammates and had kept in touch, so I'd met some other players, including Baun. One day some of us started talking about investments, and one thing led to another.

Hockey players in those days weren't the financial wizards some have had to become since – that is, the ones who take care not to get robbed blind by unscrupulous lawyers, agents, or people they'd met in a bar. I thought it would be a good idea to start a little investment club. It included several Toronto players – Baun, Brewer, Harris, and Pulford – as well as the late Herb Kearney, who was a car dealer, head of Hearn Pontiac, where players could always get a car; George Graham and Pat Savage from Ostrander Jewelers; Jack McFarlane, a friend of mine from university; and myself and my law partners, Irv Pasternak and Bob Watson.

We originally put up about $1,000 each, the ante, and then added $50 each month. We were very conservative, strictly in first mortgages. It worked out well for everyone as an investment, and through all the different places he played, Baun was always a friend.

And a character.

When he was an NHLPA vice-president, at meetings most everybody would be in a T-shirt except me. I'd be wearing a jacket and tie. But Boomer, as we called him, like as not would come in evening dress! For no real reason, usually. Wonderful man, a clean but punishing hitter on the ice

and with the kind of personal openness that maybe dated
back to his birthplace in Lanigan, Sask. His duels with Bobby
Hull, both clean players, were legendary. Anyway, every time
I saw him off the ice he'd be dressed better than anybody.

If he did happen to own a T-shirt, and he did wear one
occasionally, he would have bought it for $100 or more,
a Ralph Lauren or whatever, even if it was identical to what
the other players bought for $20 or $30.

Around Maple Leaf Gardens, now, Boomer sits in one
of the best corner seats a few feet back from the ice. When
he sees someone he knows from the old days he comes along
between periods booming out his hellos.

Jim Korn. I met him in 1979 in Moscow when he played
for the U.S. team in the world championships. He played
for Detroit. Then he was with Toronto for a few years,
Buffalo, and then on to New Jersey.

I remember particularly one time in 1989, the first serious
meetings in the players' association dump-Eagleson movement. Korn was a senior player in the league and was often
a player rep or alternate. I'd caught him off base in a couple
of things, medical claims and insurance claims. He was often
a pain in other ways. We'd arrange our meetings on the
basis of group fares and hotel rates for six days, and he'd
be saying he had to leave because someone was sick, his
uncle, his grandfather, whoever. In the stressful days of our
early 1989 meetings in Florida, me defending myself against
challenges to my stewardship of the NHLPA, he'd talked
a lot against me.

He was still on my case all through June and July. After
we finally threshed things out in our summer meeting it
was back to business as usual, including my annual meetings
with each team. One of the first of those, early in the 1989-
90 season, was at Maple Leaf Gardens. New Jersey Devils
were in for a game. That afternoon I met with the whole
team. The players were all sitting, except Korn. He was

sprawled on the floor with his head turned away, while we
went through our review of NHLPA business.

Finally he said, "Al, I have to ask you a few questions
on behalf of my teammates."

He always tried to establish somehow that his special right
to speak was because as a university man he was better
educated than the others were.

"I don't think they understand some of the things you
are talking about," he said. "That's why I have these
questions."

And he started on me. Obviously he was trying to be
a tough guy in front of his teammates.

I wasn't having any.

I said, "I will answer any questions you have if you sit
up and pay attention instead of lolling on the floor. Then
if you have a question, ask it."

When the meeting was over, with about five players left
in the room, he said he wanted to talk to me. I said we
could talk right there. He said, "Oh, no. In private."

Okay, I said, I will wait. So I wait, the others leave, and
we are alone. He suggested we should go and have a beer.
I said no, we'd go into the seats and watch the Leafs in
their practice.

So we sit in the front row of the golds, the Leafs out
on the ice in front of us, and he said, "Al, I think you've
got something wrong here. I just want you to know that
I'm 100 per cent with you. I don't know how my player
rep, Pat Verbeek, voted in Florida but I was 100 per cent
with you even then."

The thing is, he wanted this talk to be private, with no
teammates listening to him backtrack. I would have felt better
toward him if he had stood up that day in front of his
teammates and said, "Hey, guys, I was against Eagleson
in June. He has proved that he is right and I'm with him
now." If he had done that, fair ball. But he wanted to be
anti-Eagleson in front of his teammates, real tough guy, and
then be my friend a half hour later.

I said, "Jim, I want to tell you something. I think you are full of baloney. Now that it is over you think it is going to be in your best interests to be on my side. It isn't. I forgive everybody but I'm not going to forget. You used the word 'unethical' fifty times at that Florida meeting. You suggested that I misappropriated funds. You said you knew somebody that knew somebody that knew the value of real estate and you thought I was ripping off the players' association on mortgages or the rent for our headquarters in the building that I own. Those were all lies. You said those things in front of those players to make me look bad.

"I'm not going to forget that. And I'll tell you what else I think. I think your career is over. I think this is your last kick at the cat and you are probably going to apply for a job some day and you are probably hoping I'll say a few words about you. And I will, I will. Count on that. My recommendation is, don't give my name as a reference."

In his role as TV colour commentator, Harry Neale had the right line on Jim Korn on *Hockey Night in Canada* one night not long after that. Korn got into a fight. He sucker-punched a player. When it had cooled down and Korn was heading for the penalty box, Harry remarked that Korn belonged in the *Guinness Book of Records* as the guy who had thrown more sucker punches than anybody else in the NHL.

Marty McSorley. Another player I remember in the same general vein as Korn during that 1989 Florida meeting is Marty McSorley of the L.A. Kings. When I had scraped through 16–12 on the censure vote, he came up to me and said, "Hey, Al, you won the vote and we are with you. We have to keep the union together. I'm with you all the way."

Then he went out of the room. I stayed in. When I come out, he is in the corridor and doesn't see me. He's talking to the press. I came up behind him and he's saying, "We'll get Eagleson, the battle is over but we haven't lost the war. We will get him, that's for sure."

I patted him on the shoulder. You should have seen his face. I said, "Atta boy, Marty, all the way together."

Ken Dryden. I kept in touch with Ken after the 1972 series with the Soviets, and I'll never forget his words of support for me in his book about the series. When Dryden says anything you can believe it's exactly what he means. In 1973 when he was having contract trouble with the Montreal Canadiens and quit Canadiens to go back to law school, there were rumours that Ken would keep on at law school but sign for part-time goalkeeping with Toronto. There was never any suggestion by Ken that he was interested in that kind of a deal. I don't think it ever entered his mind. All he wanted to do was get his law commitments behind him, and eventually get what he thought he was worth for playing hockey.

I was guest speaker, at Ken's request, at their graduation banquet at McGill Law School. After that, the rumour mill worked overtime again. Johnny Bassett badly wanted him for the WHA Toronto Toros, offered him a five-year $1 million contract. Ken had shown earlier that whatever interested him most, it wasn't money. He signed with Canadiens instead at well over $100,000 a year, finishing there after the 1978-79 season.

Eddie Shack. Clear the track, here comes Shack! I see Eddie these days in the company of my friend Irv Ungerman, well known as a fight manager and a lot of other things that make more money than managing fighters or promoting fights.

Irv and Eddie are a good combination because they're each always trying to beat the other out of a nickel.

I looked after Eddie in 1967 and 1968, after he'd been traded to Boston by the Leafs. After Boston he played with L.A., then Buffalo. By then, I hasten to say, he was not represented by me. When he was with me he almost drove me crazy. He was absolutely unpredictable off the ice as well as on. He didn't know himself from one day to the next what he was going to do. I'd make arrangements and he'd mess them up.

At the time, Bob Watson was one of my law partners at Blaney Pasternak. One day in frustration I said, "Bob, will you look after Eddie?"

Bob has looked after him for the last twenty years and I can still say that I don't miss Eddie one bit because when he was with me he nearly drove me crazy. I can't even say that I love Eddie from a distance, but I do appreciate how he parlayed that Shack persona into probably more bucks than he made in most of his years in hockey.

Vaclav Nedomansky. The only time a player sued me, it was Nedomansky. He came to North America in 1974 from captaining the Czech national team. He was partly under the wing of George Gross, the *Toronto Sun* sports editor. George was from Czechoslovakia and could act as Nedomansky's interpreter and guiding spirit. One of Gross's friends was Johnny Bassett, who owned the Toronto Toros that later became the Birmingham Bulls in the WHA. Nedomansky was a high scorer and won the WHA's most gentlemanly player award in 1976. After twelve games in the 1977-78 season he switched to the Detroit Red Wings for the rest of the season, and that's where I came in, to make a deal for Nedomansky with Ted Lindsay, Detroit general manager. Bill Watters, who'd been helping me handle the 150 or so player-clients we had at the time, also had some input.

Negotiations dragged on because, for tax reasons, Nedomansky's was a very complicated corporate contract. By the time we got to the final stages of executing the contract, Lindsay had been fired. I knew what it was that Lindsay and I had agreed on but Detroit's new general manager, Jimmy Skinner, and the club lawyer, Bob Cavalieri, said, "That's not what we intended, that's not what Ted meant."

So it was up in the air for a while. We debated back and forth. Eventually I worked out a deal as good as, maybe better than, the original. But there was still trouble about getting Detroit to sign. In such cases, either the player or the club can refer the matter to arbitration.

I thought that if we went to arbitration, we could win it all. There is always the risk of losing. In some cases, maybe most cases, a settlement before arbitration is the best way out. Then there's no winner-loser situation, with a potential for lasting rancour.

Detroit decidedly did not want to go to arbitration, but they did have some changes they wanted to suggest in what Lindsay and I earlier had negotiated. Cavalieri, lawyer for the Red Wings, brought owner Bruce Norris into it about two days before the date for an arbitration hearing. To try to make sure that everybody knew exactly what was happening, I said that Nedomansky's financial adviser in Detroit, Charles Cattullo, who looked after Nedomansky's investments, should be there. I also called George Gross. I didn't want any accusations later that Nedomansky didn't understand English. He speaks English perfectly, but in my head I'm playing safety first. I'm saying, "George, you got us into this by helping bring Nedomansky to Canada in the first place, so you participate and make sure Nedomansky understands everything perfectly."

We threshed it out for maybe eight hours before reaching a middle ground that both sides accepted so that we could avoid the risk of arbitration. The idea was maybe a little bit off what Lindsay and I had originally worked out, but it was reasonable. Remember, this is 1979. Nedomansky was thirty-five years old. He made $1,525,000 for three years. It's hard to figure bonuses in such an equation, but that made him one of the highest-paid players in the NHL. Great. The only problem was that by 1981 Nedomansky and his wife had blown a lot of their money. There was a player who made a lot of money and spent most of it.

They had four cars, three houses, you name it, the same spending habits as Bobby Orr, except when Nedomansky found he was in trouble financially he didn't cry – he went to court. He owed me $100,000 in legal fees. I sent him a bill and he didn't want to pay, deciding to claim, "You gave me bad advice, I should have had a different kind of contract."

I had the writ served on me on or about the 30th of June in 1981, just before the long July 1st weekend. He sued me for $20 million. I'd love to know how they arrived at $20 million, but I guess I never will. Facing that, I can't tell you how happy I was that I'd taken the precaution of inviting his financial adviser to that meeting, along with George Gross, a friend of both of us, to verify that everything had been on the up and up. Eventually I entered a counter-claim for the $100,000 he owed me, but the main question was what to do about this big lawsuit.

When I was a child, John J. Robinette was my idol because of a case long gone from a lot of memories, but not mine – the Evelyn Dick murder trial in Hamilton in the late 1940s. It was a gruesome case, with a dismembered body, and Evelyn could have been hanged under the laws of the time. John J. Robinette saved her from the gallows. Every day in the papers I read that great name, John J. Robinette, and what he'd said and done in court. I was still in high school. That's when I decided to become a lawyer when I grew up (if I ever did). After I had my own practice I'd met him many times, without my original feeling of awe changing one iota. I had often sought his advice. On a murder case in 1960 he had told me exactly what to do. I followed his instructions and won the case. When I asked him how much I owed him he said, "Nothing at all. Just do the same for young lawyers when they seek your counsel."

Now I called him. "Mr. Robinette," I said, "I've got a problem." I told him what it was.

His response was, "Come and see me."

I went, handing him everything I had that was pertinent to the case. I think that was on a Thursday. "I'll take this with me on the weekend," he said.

He called me on Tuesday and said, "Alan, if you have some time today . . . " and I'm thinking, *John J. Robinette* is asking *me* if I have time . . . When we met he said, "Alan, I wouldn't be unduly worried."

Those were the nicest words I ever heard. I'm being sued for $20 million and he's saying he doesn't think there's too much to worry about.

However, it's rare in law that any case like that gets into court quickly. That one took three years. Roy Stephenson, a young lawyer sharing space with me who earlier had worked with John Robinette, carried the ball on the day-by-day material in the case. Every two or three months we would meet with Mr. Robinette to review the progress.

Then, not long before the case was scheduled to be heard, he wasn't feeling well. He called me and said, "Can I see you?"

I went to his office. "I think this is going to be a two- to three-week trial," he said. "I'm not doing trial cases any more but I told you I would do yours. And I will unless you will let me give it to one of my juniors."

I said I'd like to think about it. This is part of what I have learned along the way – it isn't always necessary to decide something on the spur of the moment. Sometimes, furious, I'll write a letter, put it aside, and the next morning tear it up. I recommend the system. I knew Mr. Robinette's juniors, both personal friends, George Finlayson and Doug Laidlaw. I knew that with John Robinette quarterbacking, either would be well above average. (George is now a Supreme Court justice. Doug was killed in a traffic accident.) Still, I didn't give Mr. Robinette a final answer right away. When I got home I called Bud Estey. He was a member of the Supreme Court of Canada and was chairman of Hockey Canada, a good friend so we met often. I know a lot of nice men and I know a lot of smart men. Bud Estey is the smartest, nicest man I have ever met.

I told him what was happening. "What should I do?"

He said, "There is only one lawyer to call – the best lawyer in Canada other than John Robinette – John Sopinka. Call him for two reasons. First, because he is the best lawyer, and second, because he is a great friend of yours."

John Sopinka and I had gone through law school together, both working hard and going in different directions. He had been my peer. It isn't quite that simple, though. Am I alone in sometimes being reluctant to acknowledge that a one-time equal, in this case John Sopinka, in some eyes stood a little taller than myself? Did I really want to share all this with him? This, remember, was years before he was named a justice of the Supreme Court of Canada.

I did call and he said, "Come on down." I took along all my Nedomansky files, which practically needed a moving van. A week or so later he asked me to come and see him at three on Saturday afternoon and we'd go over some of the files.

I got there and he looked at me and said, "Al, I like your case."

From John Robinette's "I wouldn't be unduly worried," to John Sopinka's "I like your case."

It was in the spring of 1984 when we went to court. I thought it was a terrible indictment on the legal profession to see poor Vaclav Nedomansky pushed into a court case by his financial adviser and then his lawyer. I'll bet his legal fees were $200,000 or $300,000. As I've mentioned, my counterclaim against his $20 million suit was just to get my legal fees for work I'd done for him.

He didn't have a chance from day one. On the first day of the trial Nedomansky's lawyer got up and said, "My Lord, we would like to amend our pleading – to reduce our claim from $20 million to $960,000."

Sopinka and I were sitting together. In a soft aside that everybody in the courtroom heard, he said to me, "Well, Al, I just saved you nineteen million dollars."

One other part of that trial leaves me with a good feeling. Ted Lindsay was a fiery s.o.b. and a great hockey player.

He'd been tramped on by owners when he tried to put the first players' union together in the late 1950s and for a while seemed to feel that whatever I did was wrong.

When he became general manager of Detroit in March of 1977 he decided he was going to take on the union the way Punch Imlach did, but he lost a couple of decisions and from then on adapted. Now he was approached to be a witness of behalf of Nedomansky. He made it clear, as only Lindsay could, that if he testified he was going to tell the truth and that the truth was not going to help Nedomansky. If he had decided to be a witness on behalf of Nedomansky and interpret the material the way Nedomansky's lawyer tried to interpret it, it could have made the case very difficult for me. I am forever indebted to Lindsay for his refusal to go along with that line.

I remember an afternoon a few weeks later in June of 1984 on the day when the trial ended, with the judgement reserved. It was a Friday. I was leaving at 6 p.m. to fly to Europe to meet Guenther Sabetzki on business to do with the Canada Cup due that September. Jimmy Lipa, the Team Canada photographer, was going to drive me to the airport. I had taken carry-on flight bags to court with me. At 5:15 p.m. Jimmy pulled up in front of the courthouse on University Avenue to pick me up. Late Friday on a summer weekend is the worst possible time on the worst possible day to get anywhere in downtown Toronto traffic.

I said, "Jimmy, I'd better drive."

I go south, turn west to get on Front Street. From where I was I could see away ahead that there was a big pileup all the way to Spadina.

There were train tracks along there.

I drove on the train tracks alongside the line of waiting cars. I must have passed 150 of them on the tracks, the curb, the grass, wherever there was an opening, until I pulled into a gas station near the corner of Spadina and Front, did a double U-turn, and just started to pull out somewhat ahead of the game when I looked up and there in front of me was a policeman on a horse. I nearly fainted.

He looked down at me and said, "Eagleson, what the hell do you think you're doing?"

"I have to be honest," I said. "I've got a flight at 6 p.m. I just came out of court being sued for $20 million."

"I don't want to hear any more," he said. "Away you go."

I finish the U-turn and shoot across the Spadina bridge and take the inside lane on the Gardiner and get to the airport at eleven minutes to six. But it wasn't over yet – Wayne Parrish, then with the *Star*, had called and found out where I'd be. He was at the airport waiting. He wanted to show me the latest copy of *Sports Illustrated*.

"You owe these guys money for public relations," Parrish said. The headline read, "The Man Who Runs Hockey." Many months of research, close to a year and a half in all, had gone into their effort to come up with a piece that would destroy my credibility. Orr and Watters and other people disenchanted with me lined up to complain. The magazine dutifully sent its writers to get it all down. Their reporters had been asssuring anyone who would listen that they really and truly had Eagleson in the bag this time. When this "exposé" was finally published and Parrish gave me the copy that day at the airport, it was obvious that the whole effort had been a flop. Page after page of articles filled with backbiting comments by the usual complainers added up to nothing new or startling. I'd heard that Mark Mulvoy, a senior *SI* guy who thinks I don't jump high enough, if at all, when he tells me to jump, had been telling other press people that the magazine had me cold, had copies of this and that document, had me in the bag and just had to tighten the string. Of course, when something like that doesn't work out as planned, such writers and editors don't lose any sleep at all – they just look for another pigeon. I caught the plane for Europe.

It was mid-September, back in Canada about ten weeks after the wild ride to the airport and the day after we beat the Soviets 3–2 in overtime in the Canada Cup semifinal, that I got a call from John Sopinka. The judgement on the case had just come in. "You won, won, and won, Al," he said.

Poor Nedomansky had lost his suit against me, and had to pay my outstanding legal fee. He lost everything and I won everything. The judge had believed me.

Darryl Sittler. I remember clearly the first time I met Darryl. Toronto Marlboros had just defeated London Knights at Maple Leaf Gardens in the seventh game of the 1970 Junior A championships. Dale Tallon had played outstandingly well for Marlboros. Three players had been great for London – Darryl Sittler, Dan Maloney, and goalie Dan Bouchard. Bep Guidolin was London's coach. I'd known him from the days he coached Bobby Orr. He invited me into the dressing room and told his players who I was and said, "if any of you need an agent the only one I can recommend is this man, Alan Eagleson." He took me over to Sittler, Maloney, and Bouchard and I wound up representing all of them that summer.

My first impression of Sittler was of a shy, gangly young man, a lean, raw, hungry, smalltown Canadian, typical of many in the NHL. He came to my office and after Leafs picked him in the first round of the draft that summer I negotiated his first contract. I think his signing bonus was about $25,000 and his first two years were less than $20,000 (this was before the WHA). He had a frustrating first year because of injuries, but Leafs' GM Jim Gregory never lost confidence in him. He really came through as a hockey player in his third season, with twenty-nine goals, and Johnny Bassett really wanted him for the Toros, which influenced the bidding on his new contract.

Jim Gregory had assigned King Clancy to do Leafs' negotiating. King started at $35,000, $45,000 and $55,000.

We said no, but that we might look at $50,000, $60,000, $70,000. By the time Clancy got back to say okay to that, we again said no because Bassett had gone higher, and we were now looking for $50,000, $75,000, $100,000. By the time Leafs agreed to those figures, we again said no – Bassett was higher. If Leafs had acted quickly that summer of 1973, they would have got him for a lot less than they did. Darryl finally signed a seven-year contact starting at about $150,000 and going up from there.

The most important clause in the contract, as it turned out years later, was a written agreement between Harold Ballard and Darryl Sittler that he could not be traded during the term of the contract. Jim Gregory and I had decided that rather than have Gregory sign it alone, as general manager, we should have Ballard's name on it, too, as owner. In retrospect, that was one of the smartest signatures Jim and I ever added to a contract – because when Imlach came back to the Leafs in 1979 and wanted to trade Sittler, he couldn't.

I really can't say enough good things about Darryl. In 1979 Bobby Orr decided to handle his own affairs. In March, 1980, Bill Watters left me, saying he wanted to be an NHL general manager and agreeing with me that he would not work as an agent. In April, however, he and Bobby Orr took Sittler out to dinner after a Leafs game. Into the early hours of Good Friday, 1980, they tried to persuade Sittler to leave me and go with Bill Watters. Darryl came out of that session very confused by the untruths that had been said about me. He went home, woke Wendy, his wife, and told her what had been happening.

She said, "Darryl, you phone Al and tell him you want to meet him. I want to have his side of the story."

I thank Wendy for that intervention. The next morning Darryl came to my house in Rosedale before the practice. We talked for about an hour and at the end he shook my hand, put his arm around me, and said, "Al, I'm with you and I'll stay with you."

Mike Palmateer. Mike was one of the most surprising players I've ever represented. We held a big luncheon at Lambton Golf Club for players eligible for the 1974 draft, along with their parents, about fifty or sixty of us in all. Everything was rolling along smoothly, giving out news of the draft taking place by conference call involving the sixteen NHL teams. Suddenly, Mike Palmateer's name was called as a fifth-round pick. He looked around the room as cockily as anyone could and said, vintage Palmateer, "Hey, guys! I might be a fifth-round pick, but I'll be playing in the NHL a hell of a lot sooner than some of you."

He spent the next three years in Saginaw of the International League and Oklahoma City of the Central League and had played three games with Dallas in the Central League in the fall of 1976 when Leafs called him up. He walked into the dressing room. Everybody looked up. "Relax, guys," he said. "I'm here to save the franchise." Well, maybe the franchise did not exactly need saving, but in the next three years he contributed greatly to Leafs' success.

Off the ice, he always seemed to have some problem or other – a flat tire, lost his car keys, you name it – that drove everybody in the organization half-crazy. But he could stop the puck, and often did so in such an unusual manner that he earned the admiration of his teammates as well as his opponents, and the fans loved him. The worst time he had, I guess, was one night when Jim Gregory couldn't get me, but did get Marvin Goldblatt, to go down to a hotel on Church Street where Mike was in a room with a very messed-up arm. The stories on how this accident happened vary wildly, but he'd cut his arm and didn't want to bother anybody about it so was trying to give himself first aid, and when that didn't work he called Jim Gregory. Jim and Marvin got Mike into hospital. He was in a cast for several weeks but was back playing hockey before the end of the season.

We were regularly in touch after he was traded by the Leafs to Washington. He finished his career in Toronto, opened a profitable restaurant in Aurora, sold real estate around Toronto, did well. He's still the bright, energetic, bubbly young man he's always been, and he and his wife are welcome in our home anytime. We love him.

Harold Ballard, in a nutshell. At one o'clock on a Friday afternoon in July, 1989, when I was in the middle of my Garvey-Winter-Salcer battles, I received a call from Harold Ballard, who always used to call me Big Bird. Leaf's most recent coach, George Armstrong, had quit. So had Gord Stellick, general manager. The hockey world was full of rumours about who would replace them.

Harold said, "Big Bird, will you take the job?"

I was astonished, "What job?"

"Whatever goddamn job you want – Leafs' general manager, coach, president, trainer – take all of them."

I won't deny that it made me think. How many people would give their eye teeth to get that offer? But I couldn't breathe easily until I cleaned up my NHLPA problems, and said so. I also offered to say nothing to the media. I should have known better. He'd already told Jim McKenny, a former Leaf who had become CITY-TV's sports commentator. Hours later the papers and other media had it as well.

Harold and I agreed to meet at the Gardens the following Monday at 10 a.m. I asked if son Allen could come along. We got there and sat down for coffee. Yolanda, widely known as Harold's woman friend, was there for a while. When she left, Harold pressed me again to be Leafs' president, general manager, whatever I wanted.

I told him I appreciated it, but . . .

"What would make you take the job?"

"Nothing," I said.

There was silence for a moment, then Allen said, "Mr. Ballard, I'll bet my dad would take it if you gave him an option on all your Gardens stock at $1 a share."

Harold erupted, but with a smile and then a laugh: "What the hell are you, your old man's agent?"

It was the right note to leave on.

CHAPTER FIFTEEN

ONE MAN'S
TROUBLE WITH DRUGS

We knew it would be a suspension – the question
was, how long?

– regarding the NHL's hearing on Grant Fuhr.

Before the Grant Fuhr case became public in the late summer of 1990, for years we in the NHLPA had been chewing over related examples of bad judgement, even tragedy. If we have a problem of abuse in the National Hockey League it is alcohol abuse, and even that is not as bad as it was. I think the young people of today, including hockey players, are much more aware than they used to be. They know all about the safety of having a designated driver who hasn't touched the stuff and who after a party might drive others home without any danger of getting in trouble with the law.

One thing that it's hard to guard against, however, is taking a chance – especially on or near your home turf, where players tend to feel protected and secure. If you take a look at the NHL's problems with impaired driving, 99 per cent of them happen in the player's home base. Pelle Lindbergh in Philadelphia drank too much and went out and smashed up his car and killed himself. Bob Probert's troubles mainly happened in Detroit, where he played; Dave Hunter's in Edmonton, where for years he was as much at home as Gretzky or, for that matter, Fuhr. What happens to some people is they go out after a game and have a few beers, think they're invulnerable, drive home – and may or may not get into trouble. The percentage of drivers of any trade or profession who get away with it must be fairly high, I'd say higher than it is with high-profile athletes. When a player lifts a glass in public, someone notices. They and their cars get attention that Joe Blow wouldn't get unless he smashed into something or somebody.

Twenty years ago I think police were generally disposed to be as fair with public figures – including hockey players, coaches, or managers – as they would be to anyone. Maybe more so. If a Toronto Maple Leaf was stopped and obviously had been drinking, shouldn't be on the road, I've known policemen to say, "Hey, take a cab home, we'll straighten this out. Away you go."

They might even drive the player home in his own car, or make sure his car got there later.

As I've been telling the players for years now, times have changed. If there ever was a widespread tendency to give athletes a break, that has gone into fast reverse – any time a well-known person in sports or other pursuits is involved with the law, it's front page, the person getting the book thrown at him. I've had something like that happen to me, not because of drink, or an accident, but what's less life-threatening than a local by-law? I wanted to make a couple of structural changes in a house we owned. To do so, I had to apply to the Toronto Committee for Adjustment for permission. If my name had been Smith or Jones it would have been through in a minute. It's Eagleson and suddenly it's a big public deal: "Eagleson demands this! Eagleson wants that!" All I wanted was what others on my street had been granted, but because it's Eagleson the press says I'm using my political clout with the mayor and all that.

I tell the players, that is the price you pay, the price of admission.

In August, 1990, when Grant Fuhr admitted publicly that he'd been using cocaine, he did so under heavy pressure from *Edmonton Journal* people that if he didn't say so, they would. I said earlier that everything that happens around the NHL hits my desk, or my phone. The Fuhr confession was the exception, a bolt out of the blue.

Then I had an uneasy feeling, remembering a furore a few years earlier. During the playoffs of 1986 *Sports Illustrated* used an article initiated by a former hockey writer and Winnipeg Jets front office employee, Don Ramsay, saying that the Edmonton Oilers had drug problems. Even though Ramsay was not considered to be the world's most reliable reporter, John Ziegler and I reacted with deep concern. We talked about it at length with Edmonton coach-general manager-president Glen Sather and with several senior Edmonton players including Kevin Lowe, Mark Messier, and Grant Fuhr. They had a team meeting and assured Ziegler, me, and the whole hockey world, "That's not true of our players."

No one had been named in the article, probably because Ramsay's information was not specific enough, but on the basis of the Edmonton club's inquiries and angry denials, Ziegler and I issued a statement. We said that if *Sports Illustrated* had players in mind they should be named and let those people take their chances in a subsequent inquiry. Once we challenged the magazine to provide names, and they didn't, or couldn't, or weren't allowed by their lawyers to do so, that killed the issue. Killed it except, of course, for the lingering aftermath of suspicion among people who would rather believe anything bad than anything good. When Fuhr made his admission four years later, that made Ziegler and me hark back to the *Sports Illustrated* article.

Another element, not in Fuhr's favour, was the fact that he did not make his admission in a freely given confession. From what we understand, his name had first come to light in a court document on another case when a drug dealer claimed he had sold cocaine to Fuhr.

That started a month-long investigation by David Staples of the *Edmonton Journal*, during which teammate Esa Tikkanen confirmed seeing and being shocked by a drug transaction by Fuhr that took place when the two players were having a beer in a bar. Other details were confirmed by Fuhr's ex-wife, Corrine, who said she'd decided to speak out because she hoped the whole thing would help Grant take the necessary steps to recovery. When Staples had all the material he needed, he phoned Fuhr and said, "Here's what we've got, and we're printing it this way. You'd better get down here."

At first he denied the allegations, but later the same evening he went to the *Journal* office with Sather and acknowledged the truth. At a press conference, Fuhr made the admissions that then became public just in time for the weekend papers.

The first I heard from Fuhr and his lawyer was a day or two later, on a Monday morning. His lawyer asked, "What do we do?" I told him to wait and see. Ziegler immediately suspended him and wanted a September 2 hearing with

everybody involved. I asked him to delay it: the Oilers and
the St. Louis Blues were just about to go to Europe for
a tournament in Dusseldorf; I was leaving for IIHF meetings
in Sardinia. I didn't want to leave with the Fuhr uproar
in the background. It wasn't going to go away. Could we
postpone the hearing until we got back? He assented, so
the meeting eventually was called for 1:30 p.m. on Wednesday, September 26, in the Royal York Hotel in Toronto.

People have asked me since if Ziegler and I discussed
the matter at all before that meeting. The answer is that
a day or two in advance, Ziegler and I were both at a meeting
of league governors about international hockey. When we
met I said to him casually, "What about Wednesday?"

All I'd been going to ask was, would he adjust the time
a little, make it earlier, so the Edmonton group could catch
flights home.

He refused to talk even about the day, let alone the
issue – which I'd had no intention of bringing up. He just
went rigid and said, "Al, we're not talking about Wednesday
until Wednesday."

In that meeting were Ziegler, the only person from the
NHL; Eagleson, Bob Goodenow, and Sam Simpson from
the players' association; Richard Rand, Fuhr's lawyer; Grant
and his new bride, Jill; Bill Tuele, Edmonton's director of
public relations; and Glen Sather. Such league hearings for
disciplinary reasons are confidential, so can only be reported
here in general terms.

John Ziegler started with a general statement, asking Grant
and his lawyer if they knew why we were here, went through
the situation as he knew it, and asked for their position.

Fuhr's lawyer, Richard Rand, then spoke at length. He
is from Edmonton, a competent lawyer who had got to know
Grant through his earlier divorce and his decision to fire
Rich Winter as his agent a year earlier. I was very comfortable
with Rand and how he handled the issue. He went through
the history of other suspensions for drug use: Don Murdoch,
Ric Nattress, and Bob Probert, all of whom who had been

suspended after being found in possession of drugs, and Borje Salming, who had been told that the whistle was about to be blown on him and had confessed to having used cocaine experimentally. Salming got a light suspension, eight games. Rand argued that Fuhr was in the same position as Salming in that neither had been charged or convicted of any offence but had publicly owned up.

Ziegler said yes, but both confessions had been made only when details were about to be revealed anyway. "So I'm not sure you can call either of them a simple admission, as you say." From then on, everyone present had a chance to speak, and when it was over John Ziegler left to ponder his decision. We knew it would be a suspension – the question was, how long?

As all this went on, I was thinking that Grant's history included a lot of problems beyond his control As a child he was adopted. After the adoption the parents separated and divorced. The father died. Grant married his first wife, Corrine, who already had a small daughter, had taken the child as his own, had another daughter with her, and then they divorced.

Then there were his agents. In junior he had Frank Milne from St. Catharines. Before he turned pro he switched to Bill Watters, but later left Watters and went to Rich Winter. Fuhr was sometimes used by Winter in attacking me and the union. I had the feeling he didn't really realize how much he was being used. In 1989 he'd been involved in a bizarre series of events. In 1988-89 he'd been on the NHL's first all-star team and had won the Vezina Trophy as the league's top goalie. Then, in June of 1989, Winter announced Fuhr's retirement from hockey, saying Fuhr didn't want to play any more because he was not getting the respect he deserved, and he was going to sell cars.

I couldn't believe that at the time, but some details were given in a *Canadian Press* news service story published on September 27, 1989, three and a half months after the announced retirement.

The main news in that story was that Fuhr had fired
his agent, Winter, saying he was convinced that Winter had
not always acted in his best interests. "I got more stress
out of the summer than I did playing hockey," Fuhr told
a news conference.

The rest of the CP news report read in part:

At the time [of Fuhr's June retirement], few believed that
the move was anything more than a publicity ploy engineered by Winter. Fuhr abandoned the retirement after
sitting down with Oilers coach-GM-president Glen Sather
in August.

His decision [to fire Winter] centres around letters sent
to the Oilers that Fuhr says he knew nothing about until
after the August meeting with Sather.

One of the letters, dated May 10, said Fuhr would retire
on June 10 unless the Oilers and the NHL provided written
permission for him to conclude an agreement with Pepsi-
Cola that included wearing the company name on his
goal pads.

When Fuhr retired, he said the Pepsi dispute had
nothing to do with his decision. Tuesday [announcing that
he was firing Winter], he said, "As for my retirement,
whose idea was it? That [letter] will explain it."

Fuhr, considered by many to be the best goalie in the
world, has hired an independent lawyer who is challenging
the validity of the contract between Fuhr and Winter.

That independent lawyer was Rand, who told me that
by 1989 Fuhr's financial obligations, after tax, were between
$15,000 and $20,000 a month. What a load even for a well-
paid person to carry! I couldn't help wishing that Rand
had been with him all along. Of course, that opinion of
mine would be no surprise to anyone who knew what I
thought of Winter.

To sum up, to me Grant had always seemed likeable,
modest, quiet, susceptible, easy to delude, a sucker for bad

people. Once you get into the drug scene how do you get out? It was amazing to me that he'd kept this thing secret as long as he had.

On the more positive side, I could not help thinking that Edmonton has a good record in giving people a second chance. When their players had got into trouble, Sather and the club always showed compassion, and not only to their own team members, Mark Messier and Dave Hunter among them. I thought of what they'd done for Craig MacTavish of Boston Bruins after he missed the entire 1984-85 season of hockey, spending part of it in jail on being convicted of driving while drunk, leading to a fatal accident. When he was released he found that as a free agent nobody in hockey was really eager to give him another chance, except Edmonton, who'd signed him. He had played well there since. I hoped that the good instincts Sather and Peter Pocklington had shown in this and other cases would, in the end, be Grant's salvation as well.

When the hearing was over, I thought Ziegler had two options he might consider. One was to suspend Grant for a year but let him come back after forty games if his behaviour warranted. The other was to suspend him for two years with a chance to come back after a year, like Probert. What Ziegler chose was a one-year suspension, without a chance for reinstatement until after sixty games, a time during which Grant had to establish beyond any doubt – not any *reasonable* doubt, but *any* doubt – that he is off drugs.

He'd done that voluntarily for a year, as he'd told us at the hearing. My guess is that he will continue to do it, and take advantage of the fact that in the spring of 1991 he was reinstated into the game he plays so well.

After Ziegler announced his decision, I told Fuhr, Rand, and Sather that if they wanted to appeal, the NHLPA would appeal, do whatever they wanted; but they said they had decided to take their lumps and let it sit.

During the previous five years or more in the union we talked often about what we might do to change our policy on drugs, which is zero tolerance: if you're caught at it, you're out, without pay, for whatever length of time the league decides. Often suggestions are made in the press and elsewhere that we should consider what is done in basketball to meet the drug situation. The basketball system on substance abuse is that if you voluntarily confess to addiction, you get treatment and you get your pay. The second time you confess that you are doing it again, I'm sorry and all that, fine, you are suspended *without* pay. Or, if you *don't* confess but are found out because you are charged, the punishment is the same – suspension without pay. The third time, hey, sorry, bad news, I'm doing it again – you are out for life, with the right to appeal within one year.

At our August, 1989, summer meeting the union spent at least two hours discussing our zero tolerance policy, followed by another hour with both players and owners on the same subject. The net outcome was that what we had been going on, zero tolerance, suspensions without pay if caught, remained in place. The players told me specifically, "We like the system the way it is. It scares the hell out of players. If they get caught now they know they are out, and we think that keeps a lot of guys clean that might not be clean otherwise."

Regardless of what opinions I have, which are not necessarily those of the players, my job is to reflect their opinion. I'm executive director, not executive dictator, no matter what some people think. As a matter of course, from time to time I have done a bit of kite-flying. In 1986, I announced jointly with Ziegler that maybe it was time to have some type of random testing. I said I was sure the players would go for it. I was wrong. Bobby Smith, then a vice-president, spoke against it and called me to say so in person. "I'm not taking any test and you have no right to say that players should. If you want to bring it up at a meeting, fine, but I don't want you to bring it up without my participation, and I want no part of it."

We are still discussing various ways and means. Some feel that there should be some sort of amnesty, offer one free ride on a freely given confession – if only to head off surprises, like Fuhr's. If we'd had that amnesty policy in 1989 at the time he decided on his own to go off the stuff, he could have come forward and said so, saving himself and many other people a lot of damage.

I think maybe a voluntary confession system of some kind is what we seek. That doesn't necessarily suggest that we in hockey have a bigger problem than anyone else. The players' association is a microcosm of society. I'd say we have proportionately as many divorces, as many drinking problems, as many drug users as there are in society – with maybe one difference, a difference in upbringing. On a cross-sectional basis, in my opinion, hockey players still represent smalltown Canada or smalltown U.S.A. We don't have the disadvantage of growing up in a drug-sodden ghetto, as many basketball and football and baseball players have – not at all their fault, just their circumstance.

The bulk of our players still come from Canada, Sweden, Finland, where they don't face the same problems that exist in big American cities. Very few of our American players come from big city environments. They may come from the suburbs of Boston, Minneapolis, and even New York, but if you read a list of NHL players' birthplaces it's amazing – smalltown backgrounds everywhere, and smalltown backgrounds do not tend to produce as many drug problems as are common elsewhere.

Anyway, whatever we eventually do, I'm leaving to my successor as executive director, Bob Goodenow. I've said to him that he should take the lead role in this, for a lot of reasons: "First of all you're going to be here, in this job. More importantly, you are twenty years younger and much more aware of what goes on in this age group than I am."

At one time in my life I wouldn't have felt that way. I remember in the union's earliest days when people used to see me with the players and think we acted like brothers. That changed over a few years to me becoming more like an uncle, sometimes even a crazy uncle. Now I'm more a father figure, and fathers can be right out of it when it comes to solving modern problems even for their own children, let alone for hundreds of young men unrelated by any factor other than the game they play.

CHAPTER SIXTEEN

THE WAVE OF THE FUTURE

We won something like 51–10. The Soviets
couldn't believe it.

–the first time an IIHF *vote was by secret ballot, instead
of a show of hands.*

It's amazing how one man can put his mark on an organization. Don't jump to the conclusion that I'm talking about myself and the NHLPA. I'm talking about J.F. (Bunny) Ahearne, who ran the International Ice Hockey Federation almost forever. My mark on the NHLPA will have a good shelf life in a lot of ways, but while I had my detractors I also had overwhelming support in everything that mattered. I have never met anyone of importance in North American hockey who had anything good to say about Bunny Ahearne. Long-time sports columnist and author Jim Coleman probably knew Ahearne longer than anyone still on the hockey scene in Canada. In Coleman's book *Hockey Is Our Game*, he labels Ahearne as being "a wily little Irish conniver," a man who "even his European colleagues conceded readily . . . was a double-dealing, self-serving little rascal from the opening face-off to the final buzzer."

How's that for an accolade? Sounds like the Winter-Garvey-Salcer gang talking about me. Except that if Coleman wanted to put his view of Ahearne into the form of a motion, I could second it. The only thing Ahearne and I had in common was our Irish bloodlines, but he'd lived in England so long that most people whom he ruled with an iron hand in the IIHF thought he acted English. From our first meeting in Stockholm in 1969 he obviously saw me as a threat to his IIHF authority and worked against me when he could.

The IIHF was not his creation; it had been going for years before he came on the scene. But from his emergence in 1933 as head of the British Ice Hockey Federation, the IIHF tended to do his bidding – and after he had put together a "British" team of Canadians he'd imported to win the hockey gold at the 1936 Olympics against Canada, he seemed to take a delight in knocking Canada, Canadians, and Canadian dominance in hockey, which put us on a collision course from the start.

At that time the IIHF was structured much as it is now. Ahearne was president, his directorate made up of people he approved from other nations – many of which did not have significant hockey programs at all. Although Dr. Guenther Sabetzki as president has worked hard and effectively, as recently as the IIHF elections in 1986 the eleven-man directorate did not include anyone from Finland or the Soviet Union, but did include a lot of fringe people. That is ridiculous. In 1990, the Finns and Russians made it but Sweden didn't, while countries not really in the mainstream of hockey still had what I consider to be too much to say.

In both years it was good enough at the top, headed by Sabetzki, with (in 1986) Gordon Renwick from Canada and Miro Subrt from Czechoslovakia as vice-presidents and Curt Berglund of Sweden as treasurer. From there on the lineup of directors became somewhat hazier from a hockey standpoint, once you were past the knowledgeable Walter Bush of the U.S. The other directors that year included Shoichi Tomita (Japan), Marjan Luxa (Yugoslavia), Hans Dobida (Austria), Rene Fasel (Switzerland), Georgy Pasztor (Hungary), and Fred Schweers (Holland). Many countries were brought in originally by Ahearne, partly to contribute to the spread of hockey and partly because they would support him.

But in today's terms it's as stupid to have the Soviets and Finns not on the directorate as it would be to have no Canadian director, either. Substantial changes are due, as was obvious in the 1990 elections at Aosta in Italy when a Finn, Kai Hietarinta, and a Soviet, Yuri Korolov, won seats but Sweden didn't. It is clear, and not only to me, that the changes are well overdue.

First, I think it is essential to restructure the directorate so that the top teams in hockey have much more control. Some thirty-nine countries are members of the IIHF. If you have a team entered in the world championships, even in the B, C, or D pools (sometimes between twenty-five and thirty countries), you get two votes in elections or other major issues. The others, with no teams entered, still get one vote each. The whole voting setup thus becomes illogical, allowing, for instance, an anti-Soviet group of voters that resulted in Vladislav Tretiak, the great Soviet goalie, nominated by his country for the directorate in 1986, failing to get enough votes to be elected.

If one place each were reserved on the directorate for the major countries, the A pool in the championships, that would cover seven seats. Then you would allow one seat each for the B pool, C pool, and D pool, with one more seat for the non-participating countries, the ones without competing teams. That way, the directorate would be dominated by the countries that make the major contribution. There are other changes I would like to see – for instance, they should allocate one seat to the Soviet Union for at least the next four years, one spot to Canada, and maybe the same for Czechoslovakia and Sweden. If you take a look at the last twenty years of world championships, those four teams have always been there. The odds are that they always will be. I wouldn't be against adding Finland to that category.

In Bunny Ahearne's day, for most issues, including election of officers, it was almost always by a show of hands. As soon as I became involved and Guenther Sabetzki won the presidency in the IIHF congress at Gstaad, he asked me for my views on a few things. I said, "First thing you have to do is change to a secret ballot." It didn't happen right away, because the IIHF congresses only happen every three years. The year 1978 was Sabetzki's first after his election as president – but it was also the first time major decisions were decided by secret ballot. I remember that well because, since I was not running for any office, I was asked to be a scrutineer.

On other issues it was still by show of hands, which meant rigging a vote was too easy. When communism was the power it used to be, on some issues the Soviets had the muscle simply to tell some satellite countries how they should vote. The best example of that came about in 1982, when there was a challenge to the traditional carry-forward of points from the world championship round robin into the finals.

Maybe this is a little esoteric for anyone who is not a dyed-in-the-wool fan of hockey backrooms, but the Soviets just loved the carry-forward practice, for good reason. Usually they would win all or almost all of their seven games in the round robin. That meant they would go into the finals with so many points that nobody could ever catch them. The rest of us would be scrambling for second. Canada wanted a big change: to have the championship series start with no carryover points at all. This had some self-interest, too, of course – we almost always got better as the tournament went on and our players from different NHL teams got to know one another.

During the debate on that issue the Soviets were putting the heat on everybody. Under the old show-of-hands system, it probably would have worked. The rest of us, led by Canada, managed to introduce a secret ballot for that particular vote. We won something like 51–10. The Soviets couldn't believe it. Of course, some years – such as in 1990 – the old system of carryovers would have guaranteed Canada a medal. You win some and you lose some, but the no-carryovers principle is still right.

The IIHF is still a very flawed structure in some respects. As a minor example, the IIHF's head office is located in Vienna, not the easiest city in Europe to reach by air when sudden directors' meetings are called. The office there is headed by a technical director, Roman Neumayer from Germany, and a secretary, Jan Ake Edvinsson from Sweden. They run the day-by-day operations and are to the IIHF what Bob Goodenow, who is replacing me, and Sam Simpson are to the NHLPA. Sabetzki's office is in Dusseldorf. He is more like the chairman of the board, overseeing operations from a distance but making all the major decisions. That separation of functions might seem to be a bit of a problem, but it has, or has had, its rationale: mainly that Vienna, with the working office, is right on the border between East and West. With changing attitudes in Europe, that "iron curtain" reasoning has lost its former importance. It would be more convenient and efficient if the Vienna operation were moved to a central location. Zurich would be my choice. Everybody can get to Zurich non-stop from almost anywhere, while Vienna doesn't have non-stop service on a daily basis from a lot of the countries involved. I have recommended this to Sabetzki and the move to Zurich may have been made by the time you are reading this book.

Other perhaps more substantial changes must come. Bunny ran things by the seat of his pants largely on behalf of what was best for Bunny. Under Guenther Sabetzki the IIHF became much more organized and business oriented, with enhanced attention not only to the financial element but to where the IIHF stands in the hockey world. You only have to remember the level of importance, or lack of it, that international hockey had twenty years ago, compared to today.

In this line, Sabetzki's contribution has been tremendous, particularly where it applies to financing hockey programs in the small countries. This is a double-edged advantage for him. Not only does his work improve that level of hockey, but by him writing the cheques, handing out the money, he also probably gets a fairly strong lock on many votes.

At any rate, while contenders for his job *almost* surface from time to time, there hasn't been a real challenge to him in the years he's been in office. At the 1990 congress, in Bern, Curt Berglund of Sweden made some noises about running for president but got a real kick in the pants when he learned (not even firsthand, but from the Swedish press) that his own federation in Sweden wasn't going to nominate him for president, vice-president, or treasurer. They wanted him out and somebody else in, a tough insult for him to take. A week earlier, he'd thought he had a chance to be president. Suddenly he didn't even know if he'd hold any office at all.

I think what happened to Curt Berglund was caused by the real ill feeling that followed his announcement that he would challenge Sabetzki for president. Other voting delegates asked, "What is going on? Sabetzki has done a good job, why don't you let him finish what he's been doing and then you run for president next time?" That year, after testing the waters and finding he had no chance, Berglund left Bern a few days early.

Maybe you can get a sense, and it is accurate, that although I don't hold any IIHF office myself, I'm involved in who does and who doesn't get in. A couple of years earlier, in my presence, Berglund had said to Sabetzki, "Guenther, as long as you run I will support you. The minute you don't run I will seek the job." Two years later he'd changed his mind, for whatever reasons, and Guenther learned that not from Berglund, but from the press. If Curt had called him and said, "I have to tell you, Guenther, that I think you are getting too old and that I can do a better job, so I've changed my mind," there would have been a different aspect to the situation. To get that news from the press didn't endear Berglund to Sabetzki, or anyone else.

I should say something more about my close involvement with the IIHF from about 1977. That's when Guenther and I started working as partners. In 1978, through arrangements made with Guenther, I got Canada's Gordon Renwick appointed to the IIHF directorate without having to win a vote–just on the sensible idea that at least one director had to represent North America and Renwick's presence would ensure that. He was re-elected without a vote in 1982, and again in 1986, and 1990. Ordinarily this automatic seat was intended to change every four years between the U.S. and Canada. I have been able to help Renwick keep it since 1978. As you may imagine, there was resentment in some other countries on the line of, "What is going on? How come we have to run and Renwick gets on automatically because of Sabetzki's relationship with Eagleson?"

When I was challenged on that, I just pointed out that it was obviously in everybody's interest to have a Canadian council member. Enough agreed with me, or decided not to challenge Sabetzki and me, to carry the day. The point

I'm making is that even without holding office I have a close relationship with most of the people who do. Whether it is the congress representative from Romania, a former Davis Cup captain, because I play tennis with him, or anybody else, I make a point of talking to every possible national delegate at every meeting. They've all got a vote or votes and they usually listen to my view and many times ask my opinions about this candidate or that.

When Berglund was thinking of running for president he said, "Alan, will you support me?"

I said, "Curt, I can't support you because I don't have a vote."

He said, "I know, but you can control so many votes."

I told him maybe so, but I wouldn't get involved between him and Sabetzki. "If I were going to work for anyone it would be Sabetzki, but I'm not going to be working for anyone at that level. You are friends. What you do is up to you. Don't expect me to intercede."

Conversely, there may be a couple of members of the directorate whom I always help because they are strong in the committee room. There are a couple of others that I will do my best to get defeated.

I've mentioned that I feel the need for changes in the IIHF's overall structure. Foremost, it's time someone had a good look at the directorate and asked, "Where is the functional group that is going to lead this federation through the 1990s?" Right now five out of the eleven directors are simply not with it in terms of economics, hockey, or business. Some of those simply look on the IIHF as their own private old boys' club. That is no good. I've urged Sabetzki to make structural changes. As it is today, he's a one-man band. He might confide in three or four directors he can depend on, but if he does so he alienates four or five others. The directors simply don't have enough meetings. Nobody makes sure that everybody involved is right up to date on matters that need decisions.

That kind of involvement, either by meetings or by telephone conference calls, is necessary when you have a business getting bigger and bigger, as the IIHF is. I have told Sabetzki that he should appoint a working executive committee that meets once every two months.

Sabetzki has caught himself at least to some extent on the horns of a dilemma. He has a good business relationship for advertising revenues with a company called CWL (the initials stand for Cesar W. Lüthi), a Swiss company that creates for the IIHF through board advertising and television rights between two and four million Swiss francs every year, the variation depending on the success of the many IIHF tournaments.

Any time you have that type of success, jealousies arise – so now you have people who couldn't raise fifteen cents and don't know anybody who could, saying, "Oh, Sabetzki's too close to Lüthi and therefore it's not good." That reaction is the same as I ran into from some in the NHLPA: "Oh, Eagleson's too close to Ziegler, therefore it's bad." Bald statements like that always sound good and are very palatable to people who are uninformed.

Sabetzki and Lüthi have combined to make a great thing work because they both had faith in what they could bring about. Lüthi lost money for the first few years to get to the situation he has now. He put together a deal in the world championships of 1989 whereby a German insurance company, Allianz, had its name on every helmet and every shirtsleeve, an advertising advantage for the company. I don't have the exact figures, but let's say the deal was worth $2 million. The finder, Lüthi, would probably take 20 per cent as his commission, taking the pot down to $1.6 million. The IIHF would probably take $600,000 for its own purposes, leaving $1 million to be dealt out to the participating teams.

Since the major part of the revenue is generated from the world championships, the bulk of the $1 million would go to the eight teams that participated, with the top four finishers getting the most, emphasizing the importance of finishing in the top four. Canada, for instance, got about $100,000 out of that 1989 deal, other major teams more or less the same, depending on finish. The other twenty teams in the lesser pools would get about $10,000 each.

So now Lüthi is making money and so is the IIHF – that's the way those things go. You don't begrudge anyone making money when you know how hard he worked to get to that position.

CHAPTER SEVENTEEN

THE HOCKEY BUSINESS

Hockey is in some ways a sport, in some ways a business, but mostly it is a tribe with its own cruelties and allegiances.

Now I'm going to say things that maybe some people are going to wish I hadn't: how Bobby Clarke was treated the wrong way (fired) after doing more than any other player to take the Philadelphia Flyers from being a franchise worth $2 million in 1967 to $50 million and more today; what I advise coaches to do after they've been fired; what Bryan Trottier, president of the NHLPA, replied when Ed Garvey said Bryan and I might be subject to a million dollar fine and two years in jail for improper filing under U.S. laws.

I'll eliminate the suspense on that one. "Well," Bryan said, "Al and I'll be good company for each other."

Also, like Bobby Clarke, Bryan was treated the wrong way in the end.

In Bryan's case, it does not seem to rankle him – he's like that. Still, I don't care what the reasons were, what the financial aspects were, to me it is an indictment of the New York Islanders that they couldn't reach an accommodation that would let him ease into after-hockey life the way Montreal Canadiens permitted Jean Béliveau to do that – with lasting benefits to both club and player. The decision could have been made: "Hey, you have two years on your contract, we're not going to play you any more, but we'd like you to stay here."

In my opinion, if they owed Bryan $2 million they should have said, "We'll pay you that, $400,000 a year over five years. We'd like to hang your suit in the rafters right now, have a big farewell night for you, and have you stay involved in the management of this operation."

He had earned that with his unquestioned leadership ability, which he had also showed me during the Garvey-Salcer-Winter challenge of 1989. The Department of Labor later confirmed in writing that such filing was unnecessary because we were a Canadian union. You can't rattle Bryan. He's impossible to scare. Our opponents tried everything. In return, he proved that he was one of the great NHLPA presidents.

Through that whole mess, there were three of my hockey associates without whom I could not have survived. First was Bryan. Islanders hadn't made the playoffs in the spring, so he had time to do a lot in the first pitched battle, a big advantage to me because I had the world championships to handle that spring and was running back and forth to Europe. Second was Sam Simpson, NHLPA director of operations. Third was Marvin Goldblatt with his invaluable store of documentation for things we had done. During the worst of it, the four of us would talk around our boardroom table. Many times I said, "If all they want is my head let's give them the damn thing. Let me get on with my life. I don't need this after starting this association and handling it for twenty-five years."

Those three never flinched: "That's just what they want you to do. If you quit, they're winners, so don't quit."

As to Bryan today, signed by Pittsburgh after he'd settled his contract with the Islanders, I wish he'd been in Pittsburgh four years ago. If he had been, he and Mario Lemieux could have made that team a Stanley Cup contender much sooner. They needed a player like Bryan to go with Mario, because Mario can do everything on the ice but he's not interested in the leadership side any more than Guy Lafleur was in his prime – and any more than some other great stars, Stan Mikita, Paul Coffey, Brett Hull among them, who show no inclination to get into the trenches and work for their brothers of the NHLPA. Bryan, the Esposito brothers, Pit Martin, Bobby Clarke, Mike Liut, Normie Ullman, other stars of their time, were different. They felt that strong involvement with the union was a duty, even a privilege.

Pit Martin was excellent at a very important time in 1975 when we threshed out our first collective bargaining agreement.

Phil Esposito, very outspoken, did a great job a few years later although sometimes tending to change his mind from

one day to the next. Two years after doing something he'd
be saying, "Geez, I didn't do that," or "I should have done
that," or, "Eagleson didn't do what he should have."

On the other hand, Tony Esposito was absolutely rock
solid. If you're going anywhere you want to be there with
Tony Esposito. He is pragmatic, always concerned with
practical consequences and values.

I remember a conversation with Bobby Clarke I had on
that 1972 plane back from Moscow. Clarke, twenty-three,
a year younger than Orr, just glowed all the way home.
Walking up the aisle, he said, "Eagle, if you ever need me
for anything, anywhere, anyhow, just call." As he went on
through his great career as player, playing coach, coach,
general manager, I did call on him from time to time and
he never let me down. He also did a good job as NHLPA
president, which brings us to when, as general manager,
his situation in Philly was coming to the end. Mike Keenan
was fired as coach, and Bobby had to be the one to deliver
the bad news.

I called him and said, "Clarkie, what the hell?"

He said, "Well, a lot of the players have gone to Jay (that's
Jay Snider, who succeeded his father, Ed, as head man of
the Flyers) and they got his ear and pretty well persuaded
him that Mike can't coach them anymore."

In other words, the players had bypassed Clarke.

I said to him, "Can you imagine ten years ago if you
and Billy Barber and Reggie Leach had gone to Ed Snider
instead of going to Keith Allen (Clarke's predecessor as
general manager)? You never would have done that, but you
know what Ed Snider would have done? He would have
kicked your asses out of the room and Keith Allen would
have traded you."

That's the difference now. Players are going to the owners,
bypassing the managers, hanging them out to dry. That's
what they'd done here. Mike Keenan got more out of that
team than they deserved. Take a look at the Flyers' record
since Keenan left. Mike is a great coach. He's like Imlach.

You give your all or you don't play, I don't care what your reputation is, which was Imlach's philosophy and it worked. Imlach could do it with no talent. Same with Keenan. Whether it's a whip or a carrot that does the trick doesn't matter to Mike. He's a winner. He could coach Toronto Maple Leafs and make them a better hockey team. For one thing, Gary Leeman or Eddie Olczyk or some of the other guys of recent years – he'd have had them playing hockey or they'd be gone, as Denis Savard found out under Keenan in Chicago.

On Clarke's situation, having seen that happen to Keenan a year or two before, he should have been ready for it to happen to him. Jay Snider apparently just said, "Clarkie, it's not working and you're out" – totally the wrong way to do it. Clarke and I talked at length. As I had known, he didn't want the job in the first place. He didn't really like coaching and management at the time because doing either of those jobs meant he had to confront the players. When he was dumped in 1990 he couldn't believe it and I couldn't believe it. I was overseas when it happened and called Sandy, his wife, that morning. She couldn't believe it, either. It was the old story, they would find him some other job in the organization, but he wanted no part of that.

That was exactly the same sort of thoughtless mishandling that the Islanders laid on Trottier. Bobby Clarke should never have been practically forced, a man with such personal pride, to leave Philadelphia. Ed Snider should have interceded and told his son, "Jay, I don't care what it is, but don't fire Bob Clarke. Move him up to be your assistant, bring in another general manager, but don't fire him." As Ed Snider knew better than anyone, Clarke had built that franchise.

In fairness, Ed Snider is paying Bob Clarke for the rest of his life, all insured by annuity, so he should never have a financial worry. No matter how good that is, being fired still hurts. I saw the hurt part of it at a subsequent Hockey Hall of Fame dinner when Bill Barber, Clarke's longtime teammate, was inducted. A Philly photographer wanted a picture of Barber and Clarke and Ed Snider and me. So we get up on the stage and I noticed a Minnesota North Star badge on Clarke's lapel. By then Clarke had been signed as Minnesota's general manager.

In a little tease, I said, "Hold it. This is a Philadelphia picture. Clarkie, you have to get rid of that badge."

He went ice-cold, as if I'd hit him with a pitcher of cold water. "Al, I'm not a Flyer any more, I'm a North Star. The badge stays here."

At that same dinner I called him aside and pointed at Ed Snider and said, "That man's a friend of yours. Don't judge the father by decisions of his son." I also had breakfast with Ed Snider the next morning and told him, "You've got a young man there who's very hurt and you owe it to him to explain."

He said that Clarke should never have left, "we wanted him to stay," and I said, "Well, somebody told him the wrong way and you know it was Jay, and you also know that it is totally wrong to have Bobby Clarke of all people with a sour taste in his mouth about the Philadelphia Flyers."

I gave Clarke the same speech, but he said quietly and grimly, "Because of them I've got to uproot my family, change schools for my children. I shouldn't have had to do this."

I said, "In fairness, you didn't have to take the job with Minnesota, you could have stayed."

"Al, I wasn't wanted." The depth of his hurt was there. His success with his new team in Minnesota a year later might have lessened the hurt a little.

I run into this kind of situation too often, but I usually give the same advice, or a version of it, that I gave to Scotty Bowman, Cliff Fletcher, Dan Maloney, Doug Carpenter, anyone I value who gets fired. When Bryan Murray was bounced by Washington in 1989, I talked to him. He was deeply demoralized. He had the best winning record of any coach in the NHL but had been fired anyway and didn't know what to do next.

I suggested maybe his agent, Herb Pinder, could help.

"Well, Al, I was just wondering what your advice would be."

What I did was suggest that he could do some scouting for our next world championship team. "I can't pay you anything, but we'll take you to Europe as an assistant coach. It'll get you back in and keep reminding people that you are a coach, and available."

As luck would have it, who's on the world championship team that year but two good Detroit players, Steve Yzerman and Shawn Burr. Later when names started to come up in Detroit about who's good, and who's available, bingo, Bryan Murray got the job of general manager. He went from being fired as Washington's coach to being general manager at Detroit (later taking on coaching as well), up instead of down, a much better job, and all within eight months.

I look back at others I've known in that situation, fired and at loose ends, and how they were able to bounce back – occasionally with my advice being part of the solution. Or part of the problem, if they didn't take my advice, which is always to take the best job you can find, but to stay in hockey, even as an assistant.

The main thing is that when the right job comes up you should be right there in the showcase, up to date, remembered.

I'm thinking of the Stanley Cup playoffs in 1971, when Ken Dryden was a rookie in goal for Montreal. I was watching a game on TV when the phone rang. It was Scotty Bowman calling. He'd been coaching in St. Louis, winning the West division in each of the club's first three seasons. That was when the West winner went straight into the Stanley Cup final. In those finals, even though outmatched by the established clubs that had won the East, Scotty's teams always had played respectably.

But in 1971 when the playoff format was changed, they'd lost in the quarterfinal and now on the phone he was saying, "You're not going to believe this. I've just been fired."

We talked for a while on the general lines of that's hockey and then he said, "What should I do?"

The Stanley Cup playoffs were still on. There probably were lots of teams he could have started talking to right then, teams that were out of the playoffs, but I had a different idea. For years before Scotty took his first NHL coaching job with St. Louis he had been in the Montreal organization, doing very well with top Montreal farm teams like Peterborough.

I said, "For now, I wouldn't do a thing, but the first person you want to talk to is Sam Pollock."

He said he didn't think so, I'm not sure why – maybe something that had happened when he left the Montreal organization.

I insisted. "You asked my advice, that's the first person I'd call."

I might have had some inkling that the Montreal job would be open, even though Al MacNeil had taken over from Claude Ruel in mid-season and seemed to be on the road to winning the Stanley Cup, which would seem to make him hard to dislodge.

Anyway, Scotty did call Sam Pollock, signed a few weeks later as Montreal coach, won the Stanley Cup his second year there, and four more Cups out of the next six.

Before any of that happened, about a week after Scotty's call I had another caller from St. Louis.

"Cliff Fletcher, Al," he said. "I've been here with Scotty, and you don't know me, but . . . "

I think he'd been Scotty's assistant GM. Now he was looking elsewhere, too. What I'd heard about him was all positive.

"I know enough about you," I said. "Listen, there are two expansion franchises coming up. One's in Atlanta (which became the Flames) and the other in New York (the Islanders) and they're coming next year so your timing is right. My recommendation is to call Clarence Campbell. The new clubs will be consulting him a lot. Get your name in quickly because I know that on the new clubs nothing has been done about hiring."

Then I called Clarence Campbell and mentioned Fletcher's name. "If one of the new teams is looking for somebody, he'd be worth considering." Within two months Cliff had the job as general manager of the Atlanta Flames, was still with the team when it moved to Calgary in 1980, and was Calgary's president, general manager, and league governor when he resigned in May of 1991, of his own accord, to look for a new challenge, which he found in Toronto.

Hockey is in some ways a sport, in some ways a business, but mostly it is a tribe with its own cruelties and allegiances, its own written and unwritten laws. Many of hockey's customs fit the tribe analogy perfectly, especially if you think of a constantly changing scene in which, for every impatient young brave who shoulders his way in, someone already established has to make room. In hockey nothing is forever – ask any star. This goes for all of us, including me.

At the first round of NHLPA meetings in 1989, a number of points were made as conditions that I would have to accept under a new contract. The issue that dominated all the others was whether I should be replaced as executive director and, if so, by whom. I've referred to the number of times, right back into the 1960s, when I suggested stepping down. Once in the early 1980s, post-Milbury, a committee had even been formed to hunt for a replacement. It rarely, if ever, met.

Milbury used to ask once in a while, "Say, what about that committee?"

In the 1989 summer meetings there *had* been action. It was decided that a search committee would be set up to find my successor by the end of the year. Price Waterhouse was hired as a professional headhunter to conduct an executive search. Whoever was chosen would work as my deputy for two years, 1990 and 1991, and then either would be given the main job or the search would begin again.

I made it clear that I would have no input, would give no advice, to that committee. I felt that I had been burned badly by unknowing or uncaring players. When I got some unanimous votes that summer, that was enough vindication. I was getting out. I felt that if I had anything to do with the search committee, Garvey, Winter, and Salcer would suggest that my successor was an "Eagleson man."

The committee was chaired by Kevin Dineen and we asked people at the August meetings who would like to serve with him. Those who joined originally were Bryan Trottier, Bobby Smith, Dean Kennedy, and Gerald Diduck. That made five, counting Dineen. Someone in the Garvey group said we'd better have six, balance it out. Randy Moller then joined as the sixth member, meaning that four on the committee had voted for me in June and two against. I didn't care, one way or the other.

As the weeks went by, Price Waterhouse produced a list of about fifteen candidates for consideration. Bill Watters, incidentally, was not one of the fifteen. One newspaper report said that Watters had been on the list but had eliminated himself by insisting that, if chosen, he did not require a training period – the inference being, especially one that would include working with me. The fact is that any mention of Watters had been made only by him.

By the December deadline, when the fifteen candidates had been reduced to six, the committee decided it needed a little more time to determine, among other things, how interested each candidate would be in the job. The six finalists included my friend and former associate Lyman MacInnis of Touche Ross, and Steve Bartlett, who was Kevin Dineen's agent. Another was Bob Goodenow, a lawyer and agent from Detroit. He represented twenty players at the time, including Brett Hull, Kelly Miller, and Tom Kurvers.

The word came back to me in December that if Lyman MacInnis would agree to stand, the job was his. From what I heard, Gerry Meehan, general manager of the Buffalo Sabres, was running a close second. I'm not sure where the others stood at the time. MacInnis withdrew in January.

The decision point came just before the all-star game in Pittsburgh. All day on January 19, the committee interviewed the candidates. They went back at it the next day, starting about noon and running until 2 a.m. Halfway through that session, if Gerry Meehan had wanted it, he would have had the job. But the Knox brothers, the Buffalo owners, felt it would be too tough on their franchise if Gerry left. They also thought that Gerry knew too much from a management perspective to be thinking of a union job.

I felt differently. Gerry had everything that would have been perfect for the job. He had been a top player in the NHL, team captain, an NHLPA player rep and then vice-president, was a graduate lawyer, had been assistant general manager and then general manager. He had every base covered and would have made a great leader for the NHLPA. For basically the Buffalo reasons, he declined. At the past-midnight end of the meeting Bob Goodenow was all alone at the head of the pack. The next morning after tying up a few loose ends the committee announced that Goodenow was the unanimous choice, backed by player reps of the twenty-one NHL teams, to be my deputy and eventually my successor.

The NHLPA wanted the "deputy" provision as an out, just in case. The next big item on the agenda, Goodenow's first major test, would be the new collective bargaining agreement in 1991, when a better deal for free agency would be a main issue. They would want to see how Goodenow handled those negotiations. At the end of 1991 he would either be confirmed as executive director or his contract would be terminated with two years of severance pay. The players felt that the severance decision was fair, and so did

I, but to me also it was particularly a hockey decision: in line with the way we had fought to have NHL players treated. They knew the feeling, and that for Goodenow to take the position for 1990 and 1991 he would have to give up a great deal.

It was a good choice on all grounds, including Bob's experience as an agent and that he is twenty years younger than I am, that much more in tune with the younger players and modern demands of the job.

Goodenow worked with me part-time from March to September, 1990, and full-time from then on. A few weeks after he moved into NHLPA headquarters with me, he began to divest himself of his clients and, with my support, began assuming more and more of the role he would eventually fill.

The two-year break-in period was an excellent idea, leaving me increasingly free to concentrate on the international role that would be my main work at least until 1993.

Goodenow is thirty-eight now, an American, and his attitudes are quite different from mine. He seems to have a more confrontational approach on the labour side than I have had.

The one element that I am unable to pass on is the personal relationship I have had with John Ziegler. Some players, I am sure, will see that as a Goodenow plus. On the other hand, my way with Ziegler has always seemed to me to work to the union's advantage. Our relationship has been such that whenever there was a complaint involving any-one – owner, player, general manager – I could call Ziegler and he'd often be able to settle it in a minute with a phone call. Our relationship was unique in professional sport, where top league executives and top union people are usually on opposite sides of the table, opposite ends of the gun barrel. That has not been the case in hockey, for whatever reasons.

That relationship is going to be difficult for Goodenow to duplicate, even if he wished to, until he establishes his own level of credibility with John, or with John's successor.

In that case the new NHL president and the new NHLPA executive director will create their own relationship.

To be realistic, what Ziegler and I have been able to do for the NHL without strikes or threats or disruptions that might hurt the sport itself has been as much a reflection of changing attitudes among NHL owners as anything else. Back in the old six-team league the NHL had aspects of an old boys' club. I think now, with twenty-one teams and more coming soon, it is a businessmen's club, and that's the way it should be.

Whatever one says about them, the new breed of owners has a different attitude to the game, the spectacle, than some of their predecessors. I give a major share of credit for that change to such owners as Chicago's Bill Wirtz, the league chairman, John Pickett of the New York Islanders, and Ed Snider of Philadelphia, as well as to John Ziegler's presidency. My most frequent contacts were with Wirtz and Ziegler. There is no one I trust more than those two men. Their word is their bond. We have always been friends at the end of each day no matter how we'd argued across the bargaining table.

The NHLPA also had great leaders over the years of big changes. Through the 1980s, Phil and Tony Esposito and Bryan Trottier used their stature as top players for the benefit of the NHLPA. The negotiators for the collective bargaining agreements in 1982 and 1986 could not have succeeded without the commitment of other top players and NHLPA vice-presidents, such as Darryl Sittler, Lanny McDonald, Mike Gartner, Marcel Dionne, Bob Smith, Doug Wilson, and Mike Liut. What a lineup of all-stars, on and off the ice as well as in the boardrooms. I hope Bob Goodenow is as fortunate as I was.

So what does the future hold for me? I do know the essential part of the answer: I will not stop working as hard as I can. More times than I can remember interviewers have asked me, "What makes you tick? Why do you keep running so fast?"

I think the reasons lie in my background. I saw my parents living on the tightest of budgets when I was growing up. They would both work ten to sixteen hours a day to put bread on the table for themselves and their four children. I saw myself earning $2,000 in my first year in the practice of law, saw my wife Nancy work for the first four years of our marriage so that we could survive financially.

I think those memories make me concern myself, perhaps unduly, with working hard to make money and to save money. I have no chance whatsoever of spending what I have, yet I work as hard as I did when I had nothing. Money in itself is not a motivation. I simply have a desire to keep doing bigger and better things. I could have retired after the 1972 series, knowing that as a hockey spectacle it could never be improved upon. I kept at it, and the Canada Cup was the result. Once I have completed a job I look back to see how I could have done it better and then plan ways to improve the next time around. The development of the Canada Cup is an example. I have calculated, adjusted, recalculated, and now seem to have found a formula that is the best possible. The day the 1991 Canada Cup ended, planning for the 1995 Canada Cup began.

For the immediate future, I have been busy arranging for U.S. and Canadian Olympic teams to play NHL teams as part of season ticket packages in 1991-92, guaranteeing $500,000 for the Canadian Olympic team for seven games against Canadian NHL teams and $750,000 (U.S.) for their American counterparts for fifteen games against American NHL clubs. These funds will help both Olympic programs. I'm also hoping that I can create a series of competitions for NHLPA players and national teams in Europe and Asia.

There are still a couple of problems in hockey that concern me. For coaches, managers, and trainers in the NHL there should be a standard form of contract with standard rights and obligations. Most coaches are paid less than the worst